The College History Series

Centenary College of Louisiana

CENTENARY COLLEGE OF LOUISIANA

LABOR OMNIA VINCIT

The College History Series

CENTENARY COLLEGE OF LOUISIANA

ERIC J. BROCK

ARCADIA PUBLISHING

ISBN 978-0-7385-0558-9

Published by Arcadia Publishing
Charleston, South Carolina

Printed in the United States of America

Library of Congress Catalog Card Number: 00-100020

For all general information contact Arcadia Publishing at:
Telephone 843-853-2070
Fax 843-853-0044
E-Mail sales@arcadiapublishing.com
For customer service and orders:
Toll-Free 1-888-313-2665

Visit us on the Internet at www.arcadiapublishing.com

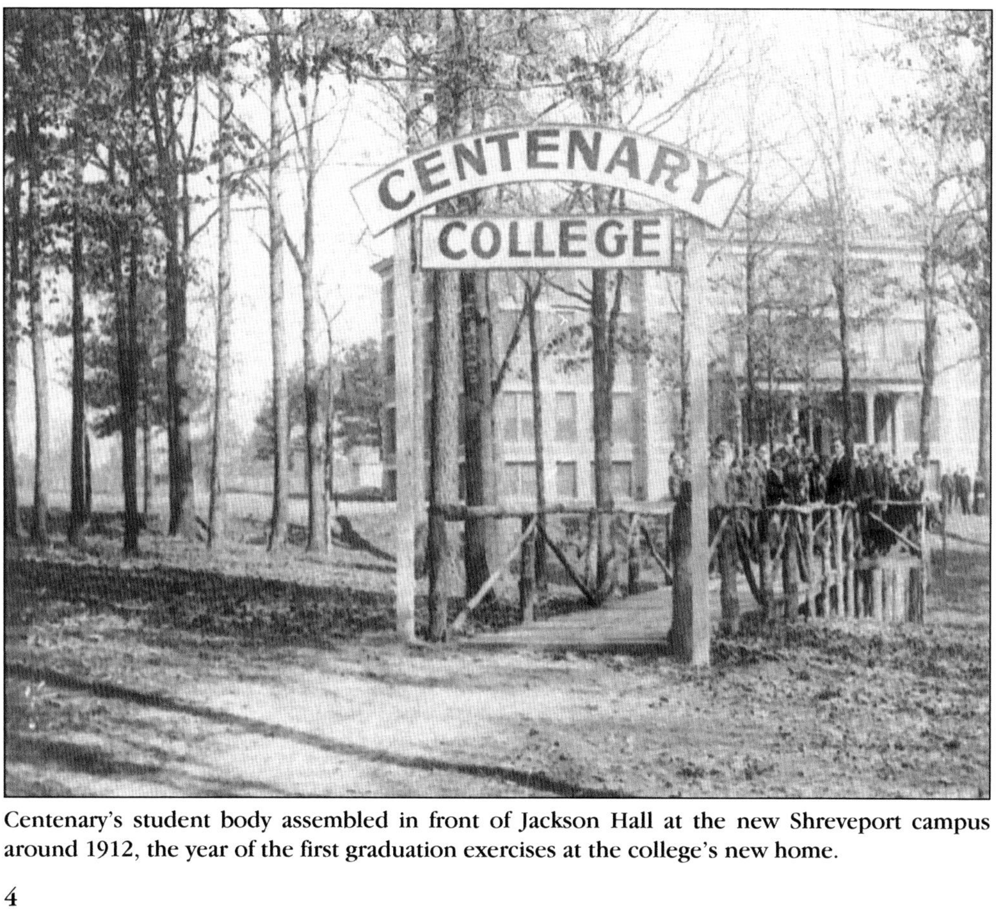

Centenary's student body assembled in front of Jackson Hall at the new Shreveport campus around 1912, the year of the first graduation exercises at the college's new home.

Contents

Alma Mater

By James Church Alvord

Where the sleepy silver bayou
Gleams among the pines,
Watching o'er the throbbing city,
Alma Mater shines.

Chorus

Like a wave the mighty city
Surges 'round thy feet.
Guide it, train it, teach it wisdom,
Alma Mater, sweet.

Chorus

Green the boughs that rustle 'round thee,
On thy stately crest;
Greener is our memory of thee,
Alma Mater, blest.

Chorus

Forward, forward, Centenary!
Time and tide may fail,
But our hearts shall love thee ever,
Centenary—Hail!

Introduction

Centenary College of Louisiana has a long, rich, and distinguished heritage. The oldest accredited and continuously operating private liberal arts college in the United States west of the Mississippi River, Centenary celebrates its 175th anniversary in the year 2000.

Centenary College of Louisiana started life on February 18, 1825, as a public institution known first as The College of Louisiana. The College of Louisiana was in many ways the direct successor of the older College of Orleans, the first institution of higher education established in the territory of the Louisiana Purchase. The College of Orleans was founded in 1811 at New Orleans, but ultimately failed due to financial problems and legislative hostility towards the strong French influences prevalent at the institution. In 1825 the state legislature, comprised primarily of members who were of English-speaking descent, authorized the creation of a new public college at Jackson, Louisiana. The money formerly allocated to the College of Orleans was then allocated to the new College of Louisiana, and the former institution closed.

The College of Louisiana started off small, but with lofty ambitions. It was authorized to confer the usual degrees granted by any university in the nation, and the curriculum was to include courses in English, French, Spanish, Latin, Greek, mathematics, natural philosophy, moral and political philosophy, chemistry, ancient and modern history, natural history, geography, logic, and rhetoric.

The original act of establishment provided for a board of trustees, the original members of which included such august personages of the day as Governor Henry Johnson; future governors Pierre Derbigny, Armand Beauvais, and A.B. Roman; and state supreme court justice and Louisiana historian Francois Xavier Martin, as well as several others.

During its 20 years as a public institution, the College of Louisiana averaged around 100 students at any given time. Though small by today's standards, this figure was actually substantial for the era. Many of the students became noteworthy citizens. The first two graduates were no exception. David L. Phares later became a professor of Natural Science at the Agricultural and Mechanical College of Mississippi, and Samuel W. Briggs later became the third mayor of Shreveport, Louisiana. These two men were the only members of the college's first graduating class in 1827. Later classes grew in size, but the majority of students in the early years did not ultimately become graduates, many attending for just a few classes at a time.

Meanwhile, in 1839, the Methodist Conference of Mississippi and Louisiana was busy establishing another school in Clinton, Mississippi. This new school was called Centenary College, in honor of the hundredth anniversary of the founding of the first Methodist Society by John Wesley. In 1840 the school was moved to Brandon Springs, Mississippi.

Centenary College was comprised of two departments: the collegiate department, which included schools of law and medicine as well as religious and standard collegiate courses, and a preparatory department. Although the college began under prosperous circumstances, financial problems soon became pressing and the location ultimately proved to be an inauspicious one.

In 1845 the trustees of Centenary College negotiated with the trustees of the College of Louisiana, itself foundering for want of support, to acquire the Jackson, Louisiana campus and merge the two schools, which would operate thereafter under the older college's charter. This done, the newly formed institution was first dubbed "Louisiana Centenary College," but within a short time came to be known by its present name, Centenary College of Louisiana.

Centenary College of Louisiana was at first prosperous, but again circumstances intervened to change its fortunes—in this case the onset of the Civil War. Contrary to popular myth, the entire class of 1861 did not perish in the war, though all did go to fight for the South and several did make the ultimate sacrifice. When Union troops entered Jackson, they occupied the college buildings and vandalized them badly. After the war, the college was forced to operate with minimal funds in buildings that were in a state of disrepair. Few students returned initially, owing to the generally poor economy that accompanied the end of the war and the onset of Reconstruction.

Time brought gradual improvement, but Centenary's Jackson campus never again returned to its pre-war prosperity. In 1900, the formerly all-male college went co-ed, and, in 1903, an offer was made by several Shreveport alumni to provide land for a new campus in that city. At first the trustees objected, but by 1906 they were won over. Two years later classes began at a new campus in Shreveport, and the Jackson campus was then sold.

At Shreveport, Centenary would grow again to its antebellum standards of prosperity and size, eventually surpassing and even eclipsing them. Under the often-dynamic leadership of its 20th-century presidents and boards, Centenary developed many innovative academic programs and an outstanding athletic department. During the first half of the century the school's football team was among the top-ranked college teams in the nation. Though football has left Centenary, other exceptional components of the college's reputation have only grown larger and better with time.

Since 1908, Centenary College has been a vital part of the city of Shreveport. Both city and college have prospered since the relocation, and today Centenary averages 1,000 students at any given time. Consistently ranked among the top small colleges and among the best private college values in the nation, Centenary offers outstanding programs in music and athletics as well as in undergraduate academics. Still operating under the auspices of the United Methodist Church, Centenary also excels in religious education and works to incorporate moral values into its curriculum, while maintaining an ecumenical environment which welcomes students of all religions, races, genders, and cultural origins.

The following pages constitute a tribute to Centenary College of Louisiana through 175 years of images, 175 years of history, and 175 years of academic excellence.

One

THE JACKSON YEARS

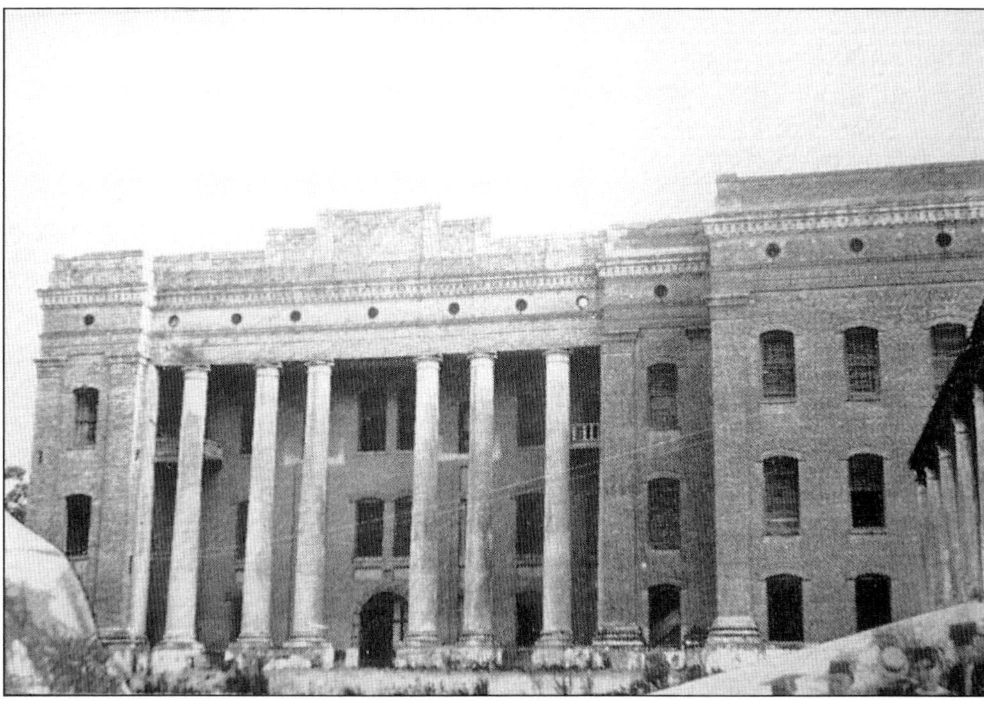

From 1825 to 1908, Centenary College held classes at Jackson, Louisiana—first as the College of Louisiana from 1825 to 1845, then as Centenary College of Louisiana, from 1845 through 1907. For much of this era, the focal point of the campus was the huge Center Building, completed in 1857, almost seven years after first being planned. To the left of the Center Building in this early-20th-century image is the East Building, better known as the East Wing. From 1858 until the move to Shreveport a half-century later, Centenary held its commencements in the Center Building's 2,000-seat auditorium.

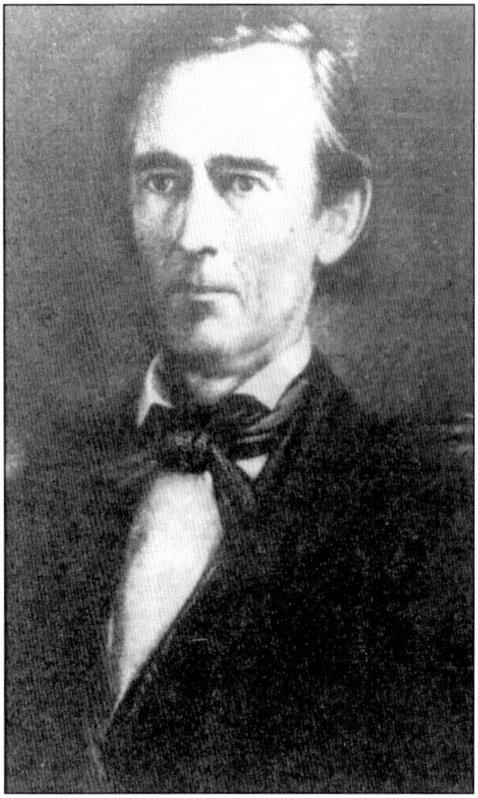

The Reverend Benjamin Michael Drake of Mississippi was a founding member of the board of Centenary College in Mississippi, prior to the merger with the College of Louisiana. Drake was a tireless and confident leader of the college, both in its Mississippi days and in its Jackson, Louisiana days. In fact, he was among those who worked to facilitate the merger and the move to Jackson. Additionally, he was a pastor and founder of churches in New Orleans and in Natchez and Washington, Mississippi. Drake served as Centenary's president in 1854.

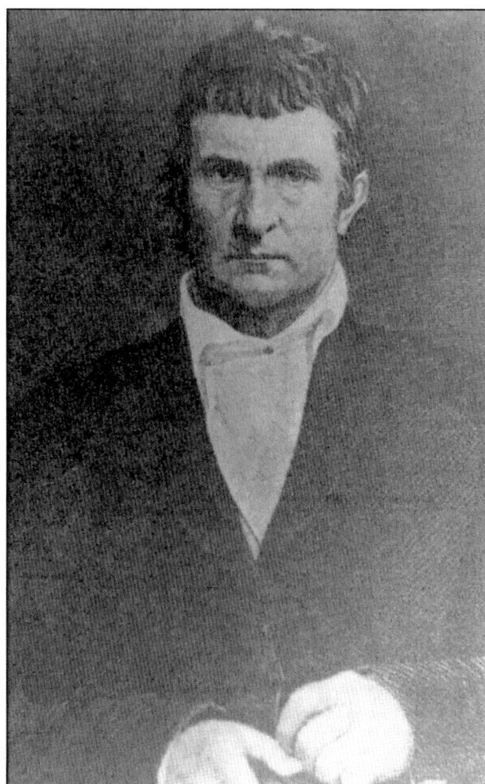

The Reverend William Winans was also influential in the college's establishment and served as Centenary's president in 1844–45, presiding over the first meeting of the board of trustees of the college following the 1845 merger. Winans was an influential figure in the history of American Methodism, establishing churches and schools throughout the South. He was succeeded as Centenary's president by Judge D.O. Shattuck in 1846. Judge Shattuck later moved to San Francisco and was involved in the creation of the University of California in 1868. A street is named for him in Berkeley.

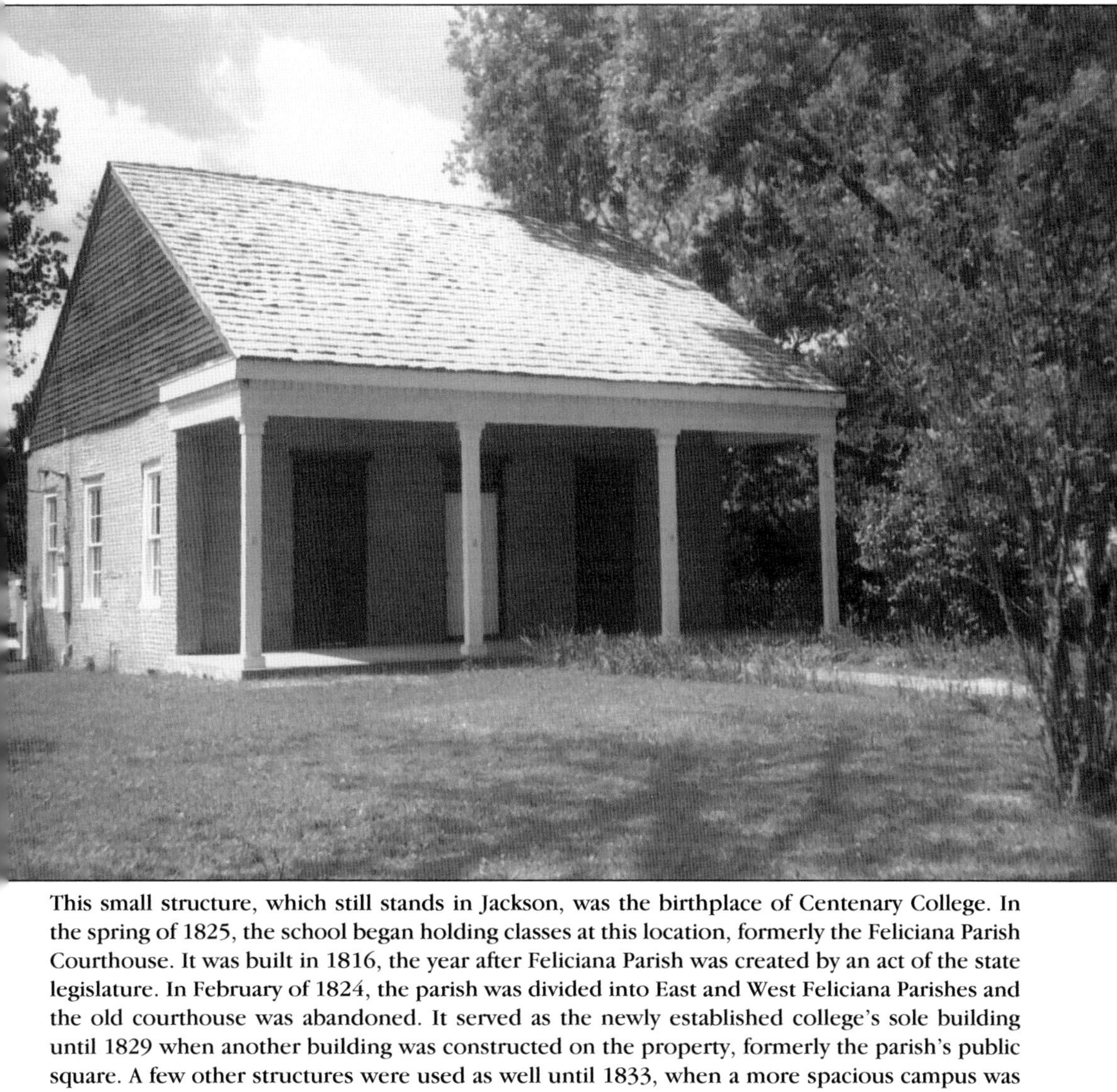

This small structure, which still stands in Jackson, was the birthplace of Centenary College. In the spring of 1825, the school began holding classes at this location, formerly the Feliciana Parish Courthouse. It was built in 1816, the year after Feliciana Parish was created by an act of the state legislature. In February of 1824, the parish was divided into East and West Feliciana Parishes and the old courthouse was abandoned. It served as the newly established college's sole building until 1829 when another building was constructed on the property, formerly the parish's public square. A few other structures were used as well until 1833, when a more spacious campus was laid out on land acquired in 1828 in the northeast part of town. The courthouse/college building is listed on the National Register of Historic Places as an element of the Jackson Historic District, first listed on the Register in 1980.

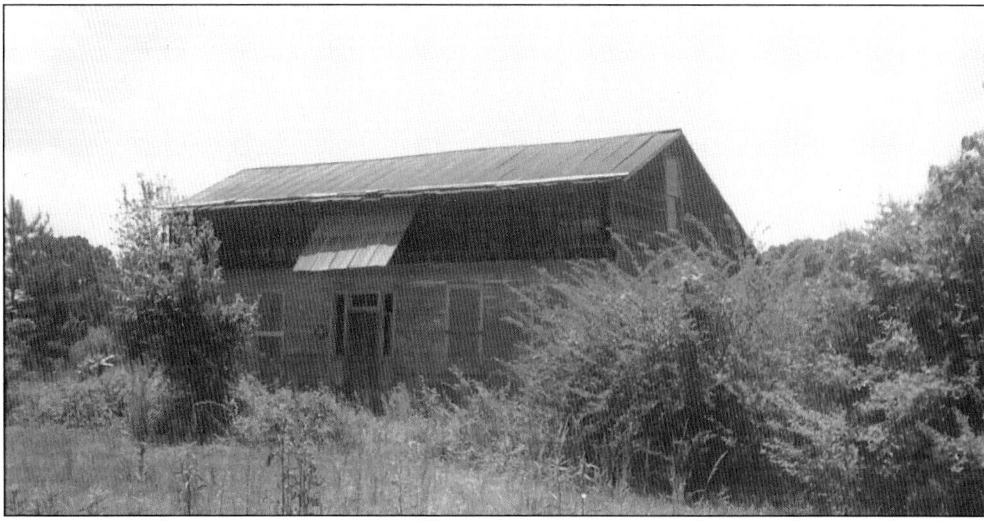

The Austin house, a Jackson landmark dating from around 1820, was used as the first president's residence of the college and later as a residence for professors. It still stands, though relocated to a property north of the former campus. When this photograph was taken in 1991 it was in a state of disrepair. The Austin house is believed to be among the oldest buildings in Jackson.

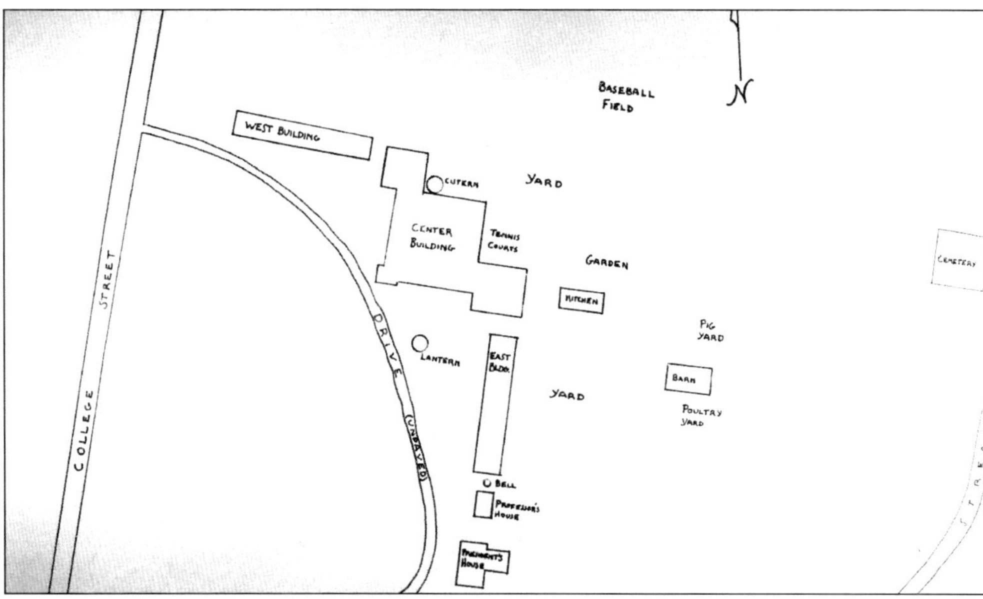

A diagram illustrates the Jackson campus in the late 19th century. Acquired in 1828, the campus was originally over 100 acres in size and the first buildings were erected in 1833. Parcels of the original campus were sold off following the Civil War to earn money for the college's operational expenses. Today, the remaining 50-plus acres of the campus mark the site of the Old Centenary State Commemorative area. Established in the late 1970s, it is one of the most visited state parks in Louisiana. Among the buildings shown on this map, only the West Wing and the Professor's House still stand. The cemetery was established at the time of the Civil War as a burial place for soldiers who died in the area during the nearby siege of Port Hudson.

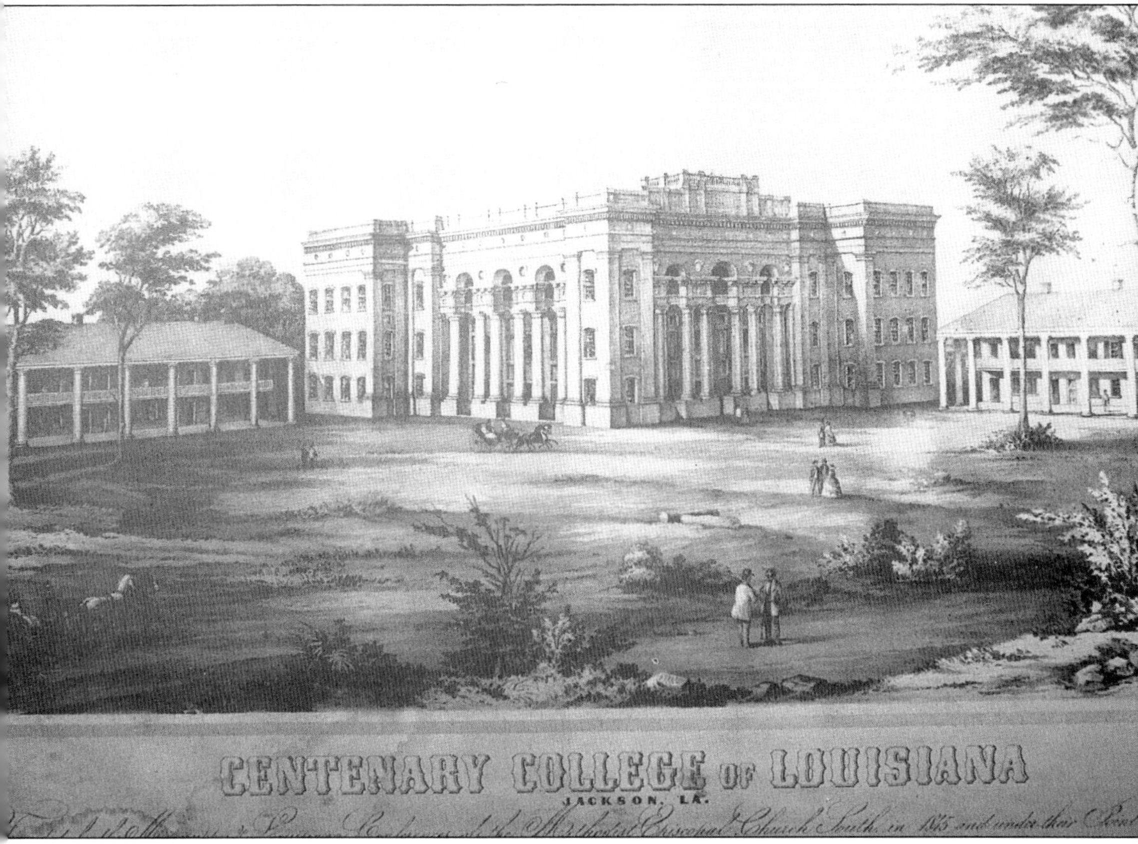

A famous engraving shows the campus as it appeared in the late 1850s and after. The massive Center Building is flanked by the West (left) and East Wings. The West Wing, built in 1833, was the first structure built on the Jackson campus. The East Wing, its twin, was erected in 1837. The Center Building was first planned in 1850, but fund-raising delayed construction until 1855 and it was not ready for occupancy until 1857. Designed by architect G.W.A. Simpson, the Center Building cost a staggering $60,000 to construct, and was the largest structure devoted to education in the entire state of Louisiana. The engraving is based on Simpson's own drawing of the building and was produced in 1857.

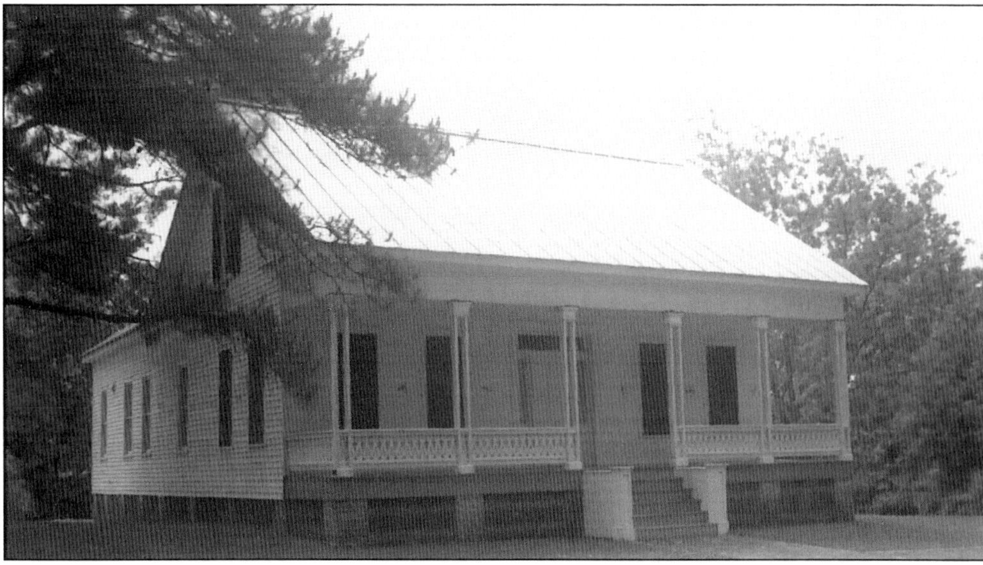

The restored professor's (or faculty) house, dating from the mid-19th century, is pictured on the Jackson campus. More than one professor would have resided in this structure, which was quite spacious. The faculty in those days was small but effective and the rules governing their lives every bit as stringent as those placed upon the students. The campus, together with its remaining buildings, cemetery, and archaeological sites, was listed on the National Register of Historic Places in 1979.

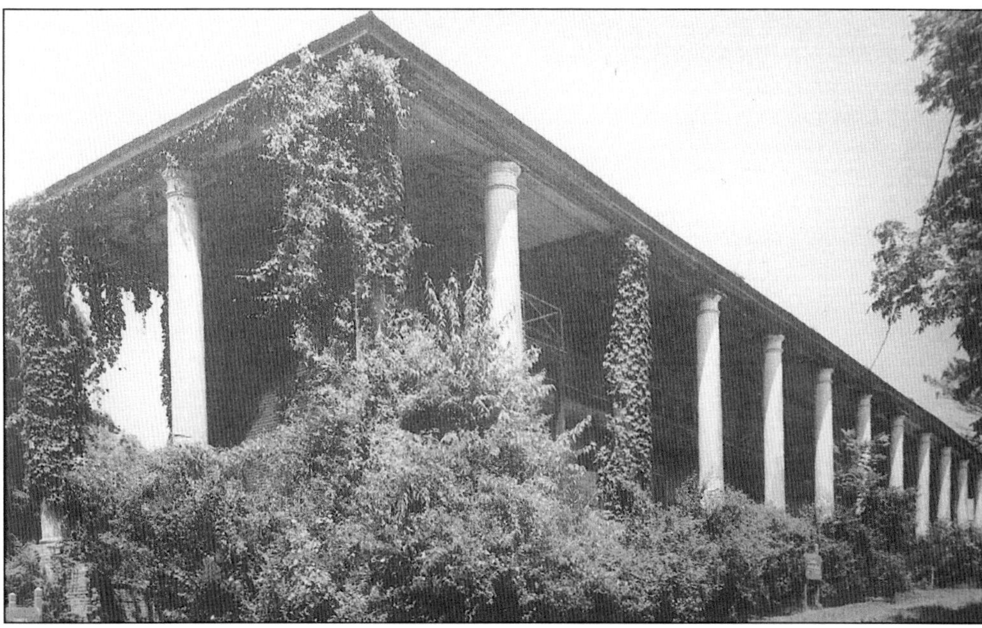

The West Wing is pictured as it appeared for many years following its abandonment in the 1940s. Built in 1833, it served as a dormitory throughout much of the history of the college's Jackson years. It was severely damaged by fire in 1850 and extensively remodeled in 1851. After the move to Shreveport, it was used as a hospital for a number of years, together with the other remaining college buildings. After 1935 it was converted into an apartment house, and later stood vacant for many years.

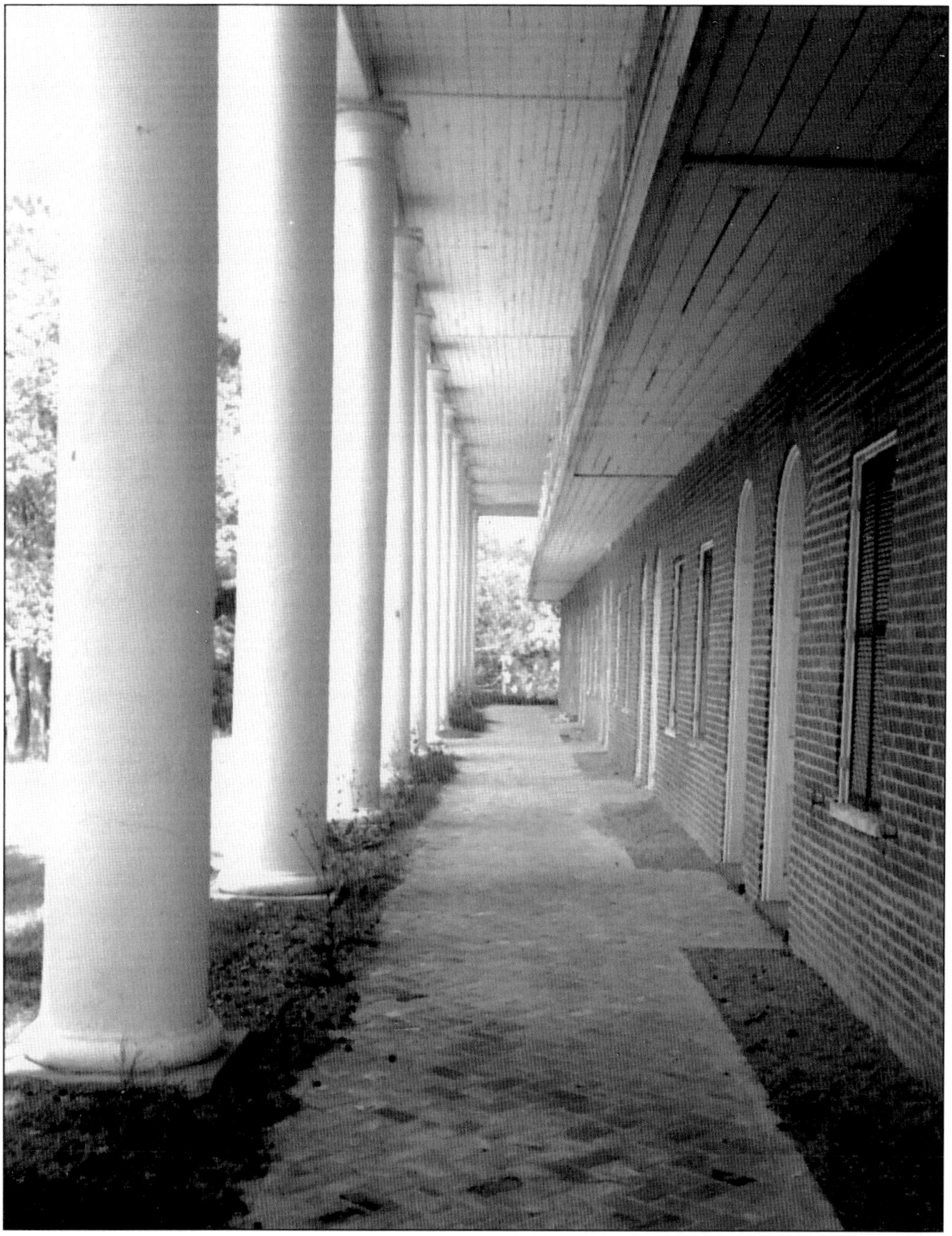

This view is looking west along the front gallery of the West Wing. Although it was dwarfed by the gargantuan Center Building, the West Wing is an enormous structure in its own right, containing 500,000 bricks. Fifteen columns, each some 25 feet high and a dozen feet apart, span its long colonnade. The building contains 24 dormitory rooms, each with a fireplace and windows on both front and back.

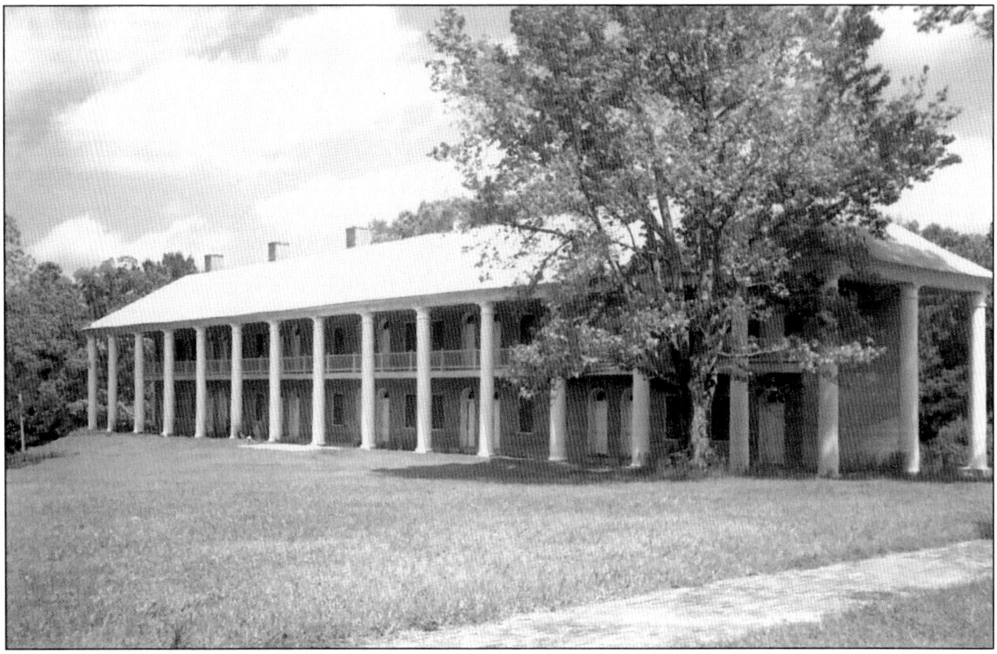

Two modern views illustrate the restored West Wing. The top view is from the site of the old East Wing, which was identical. The buildings were heated by burning wood and coal in the dorm room fireplaces. Wood and coal were stored in rooms on the ends of each building and were paid for by students as part of the cost of board. In the early days, the water used in the buildings was rainwater collected in wooden cisterns. Hot water was obtained by heating the water in a huge kettle located outside each structure. In later years, some of the rooms of the East Wing were used to house faculty members and their families.

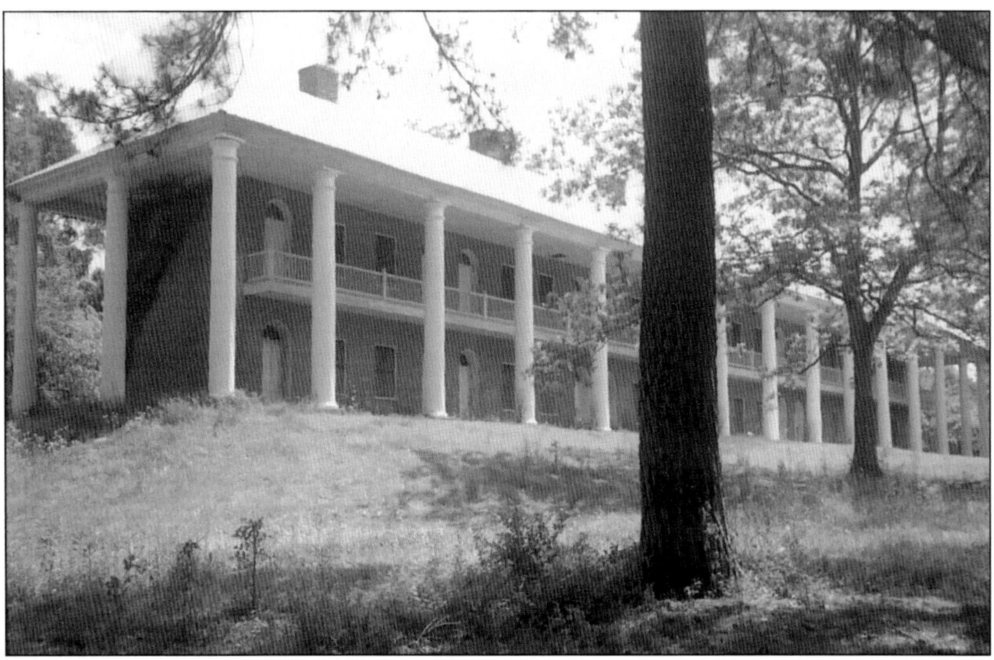

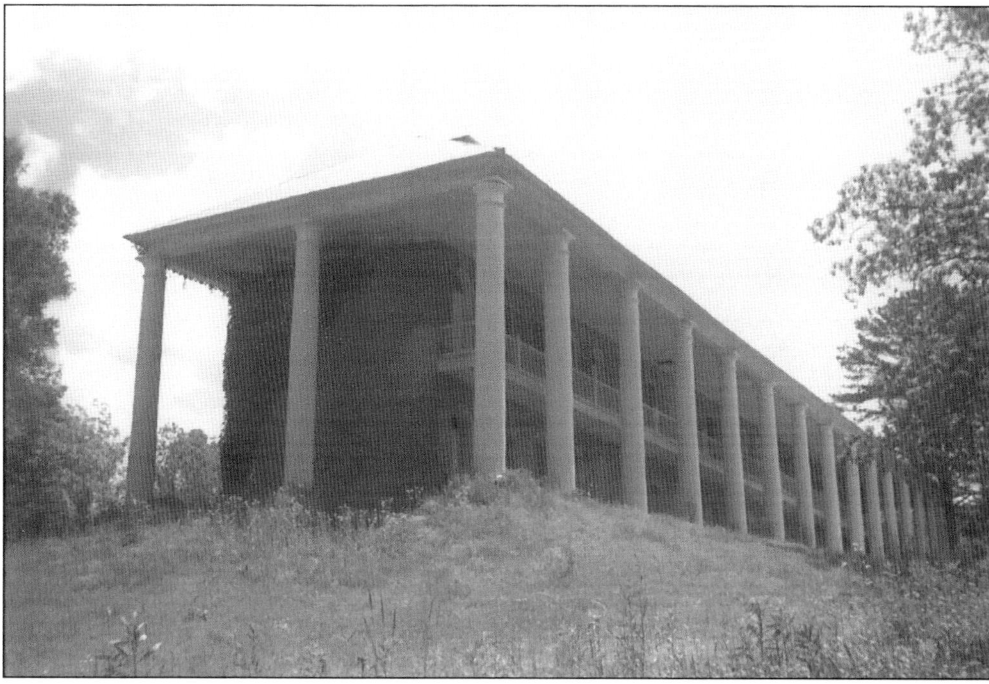

Two more views show the West Wing today. Student life in these buildings was spartan, and the rules of the college reflect the lifestyles of the students of the day: Not more than one dog per student (this cut down on time spent hunting) and not more than one servant or slave (most students were the sons of planters). There was also to be no alcohol and no card playing on or off campus. The day began at dawn and ran until 9 p.m., six days a week—a rigorous schedule indeed.

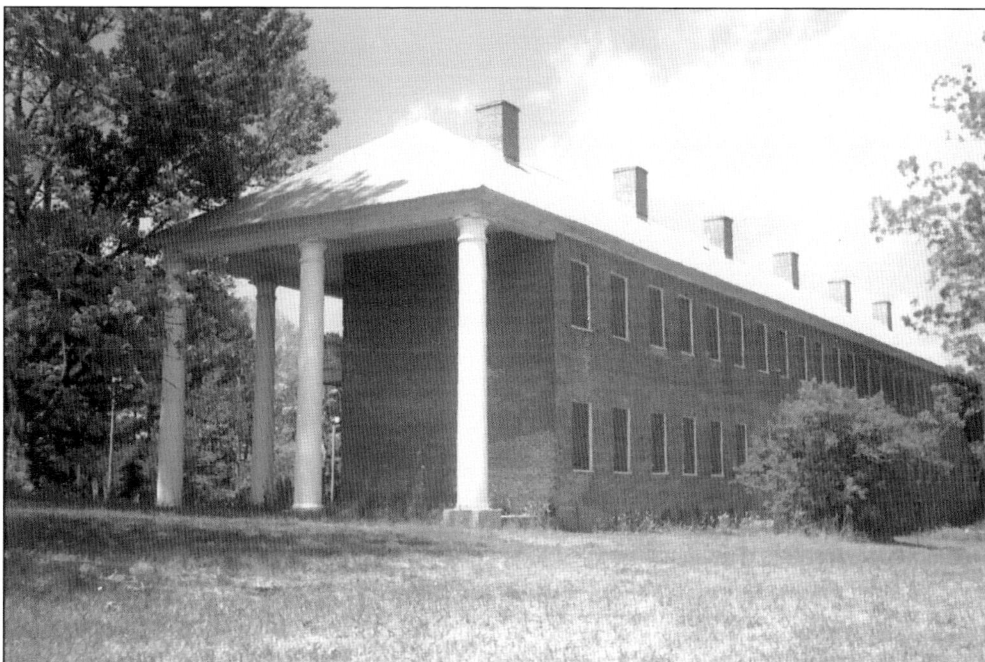

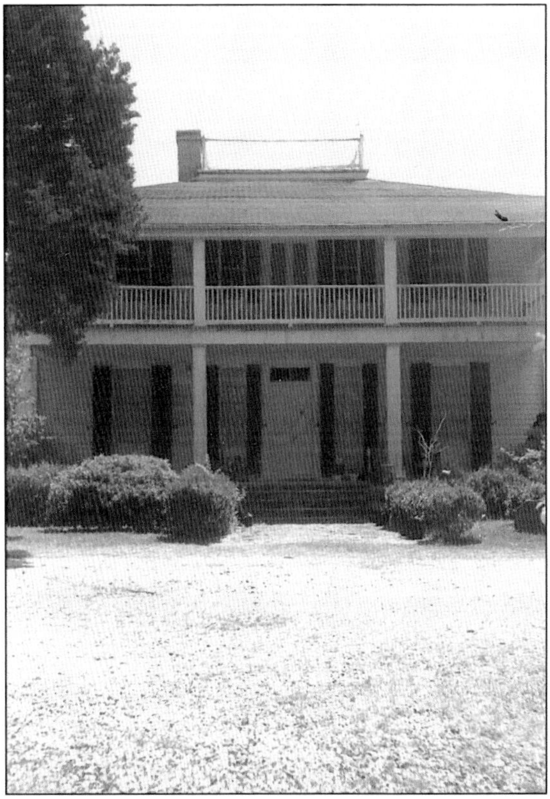

The antebellum president's house of the Jackson campus was sold by the college in 1870 and still stands on a large tract of land that also includes the Austin house, the first Centenary president's house. The second president's house, shown here, was built around the time the new campus was dedicated in 1833. It has been carefully restored and is known today as "Centenaria." For a time faculty members resided upstairs, with the president and his family below. After its sale, a third president's house was built just south of the East Wing. It was demolished in the 1920s.

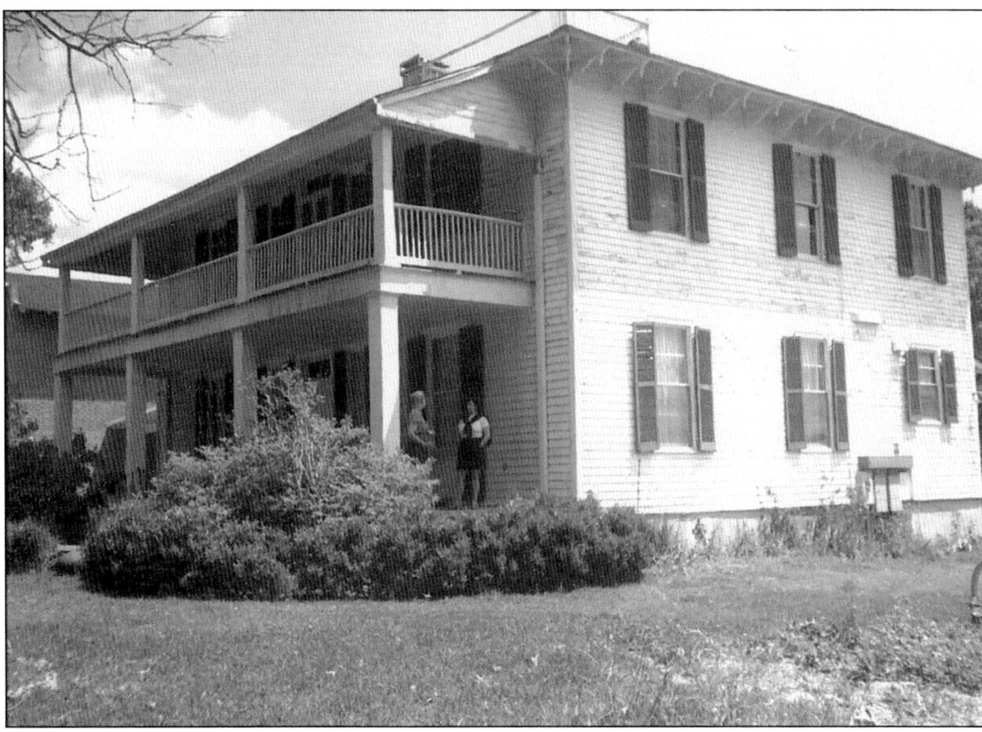

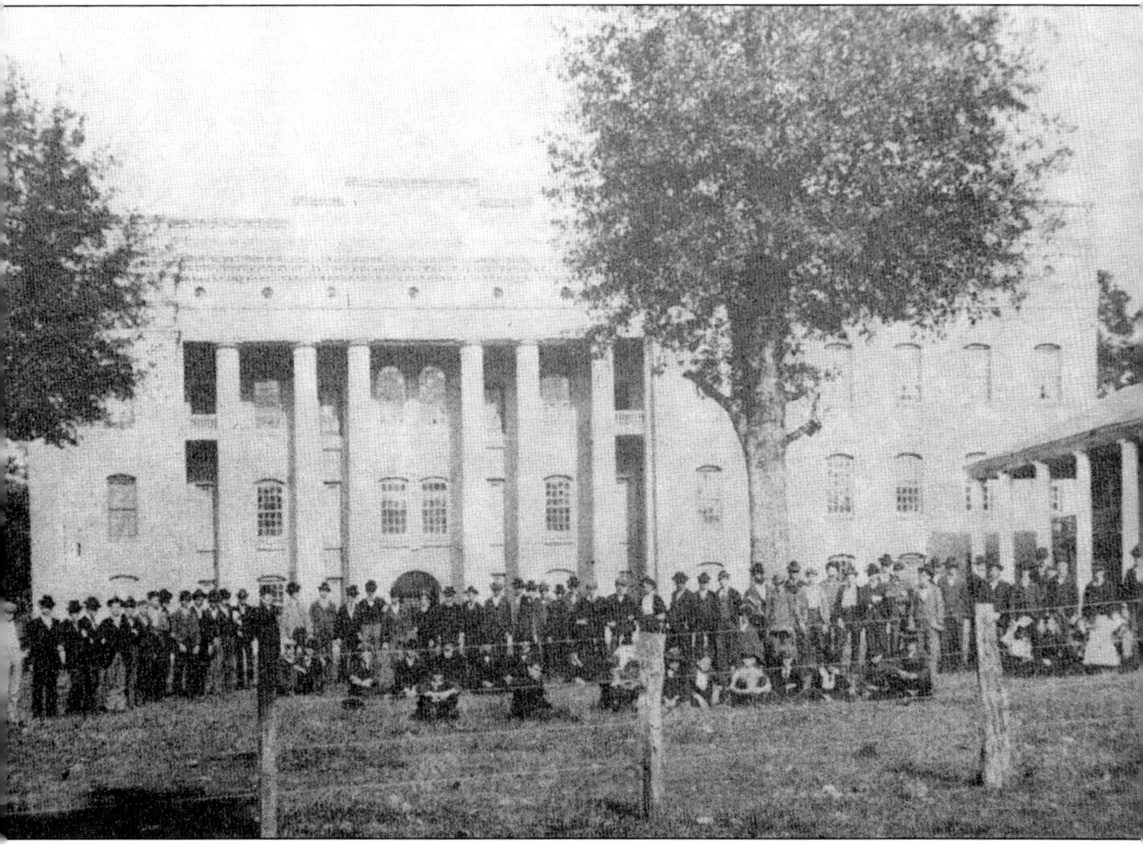

The Center Building and the East Wing are seen as they appeared in the 19th century. The 700-foot-wide Center Building contained a large recitation room, the dining hall, a gymnasium, and a museum. Its domed auditorium could seat over 2,000, but was notorious for poor acoustics. The building also housed the chapel, college library, virtually all classrooms, the prep school, science laboratory, fraternity and society rooms, and offices and meeting rooms for the president and board of trustees. The fence seen here was put up in order to keep roaming livestock out of the college's classrooms.

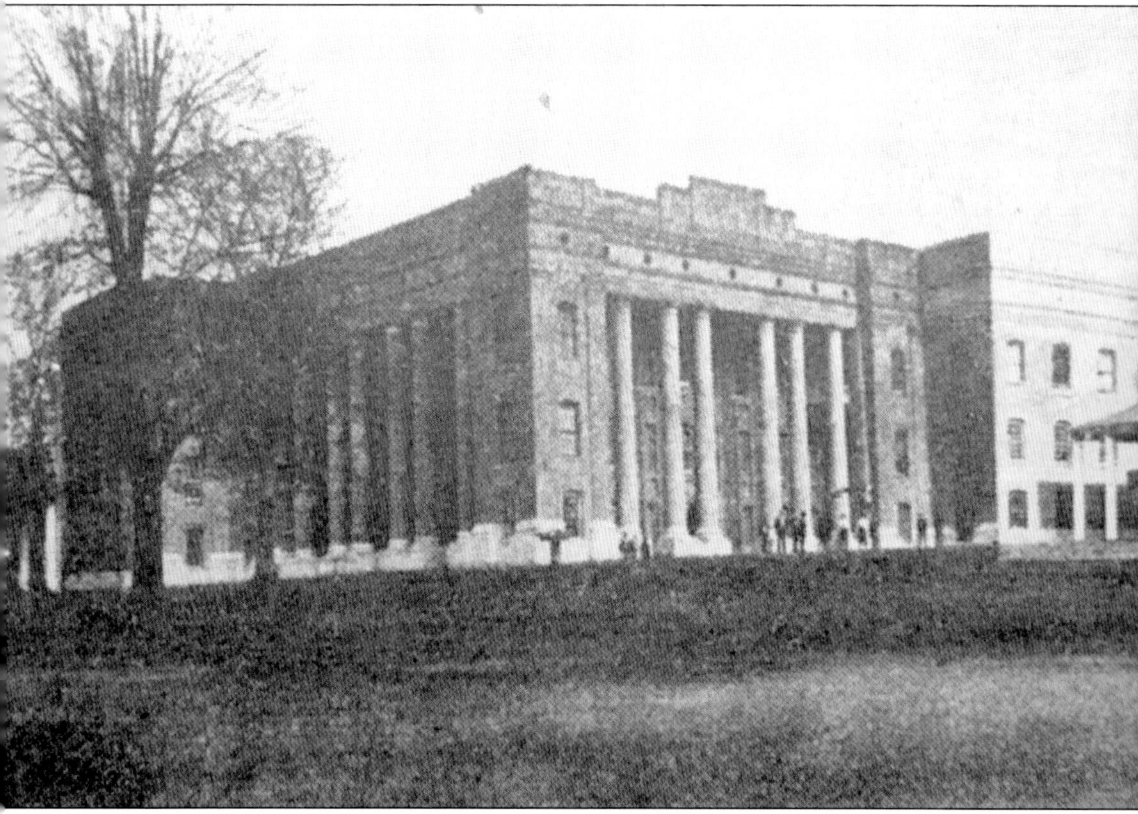

The Center Building is pictured in the late 19th century. Although it had been occupied for fewer than six years when seized by Federal troops in 1863, the damage they inflicted upon it caused it to look as though it were a half-century old by the time the Civil War ended. Afterward the building continued to be used, though there was little money available to make necessary repairs. The one part of the building not vandalized by Union troops was the Union Literary Society's apartments—evidently the soldiers believed that the club's name reflected a political allegiance which it did not. Much of the library having been looted, the books of the Union Literary Society made up the bulk of the college's library well into the 1870s. After the move to Shreveport, the Center Building and East and West Wings became a tuberculosis sanitarium. In the summer of 1935 the Center Building and East Wing were demolished.

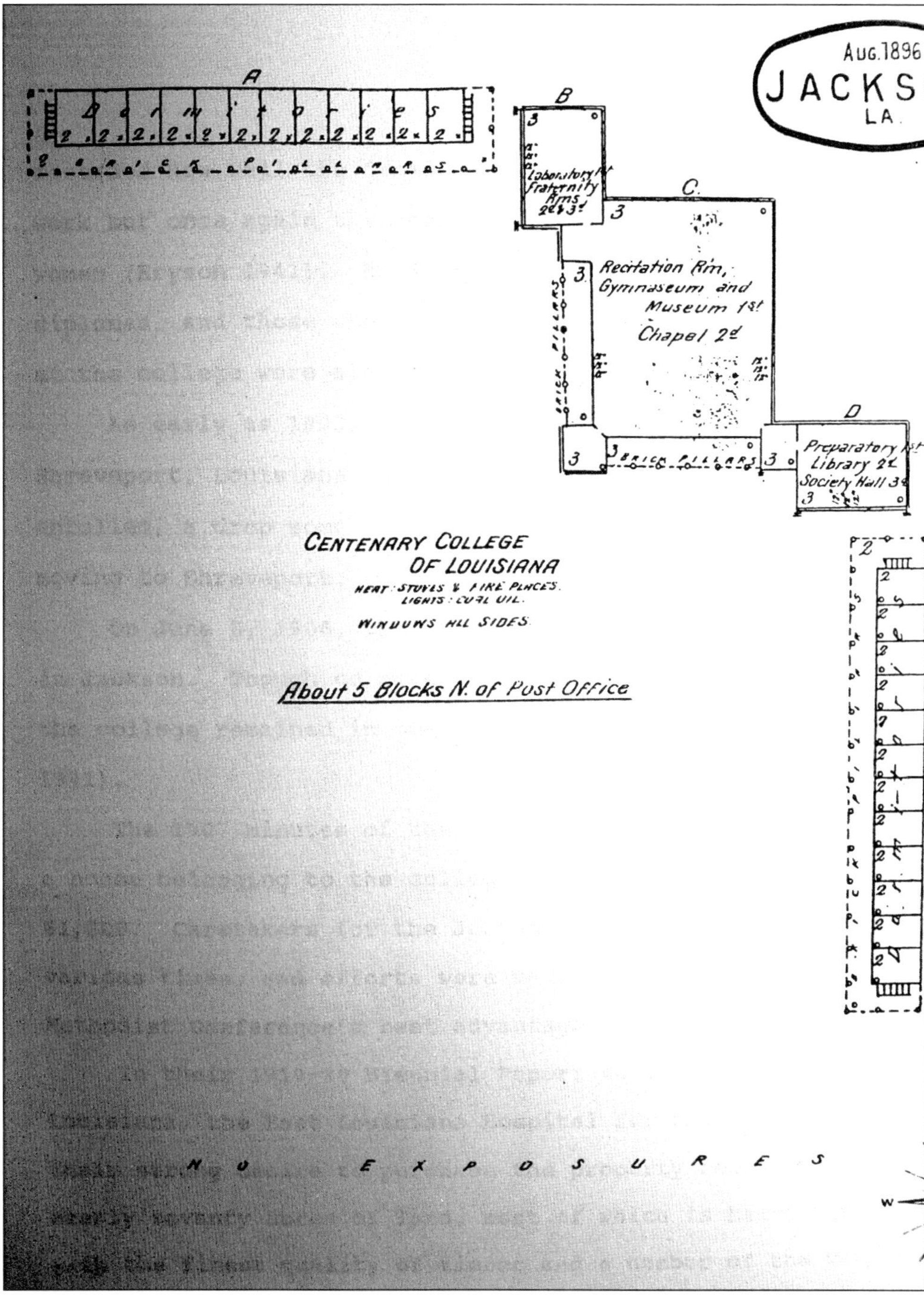

A page from the 1896 Sanborn Fire Insurance Map of Jackson, Louisiana, shows the West and East Wings and the Center Building, contrasting their scale in relation to one another. All three were built of brick, and the Center Building stood 50 feet tall.

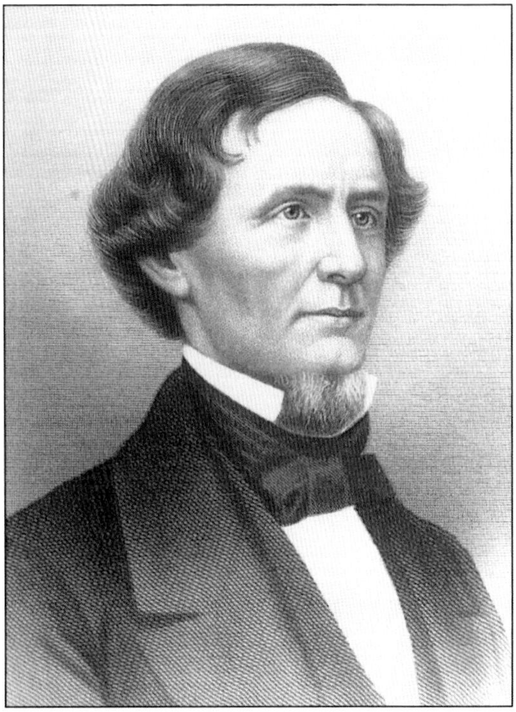

One of the students at Centenary during its Jackson days was Jefferson Davis, later a United States representative and senator, U.S. secretary of war, and the first and only president of the Confederate States of America. A graduate of Transylvania University in Kentucky, Davis studied Spanish at Centenary and married Sarah Knox Taylor, the daughter of U.S. President Zachary Taylor, who resided near the campus. Though not a graduate, Davis is certainly among the college's most notable former students.

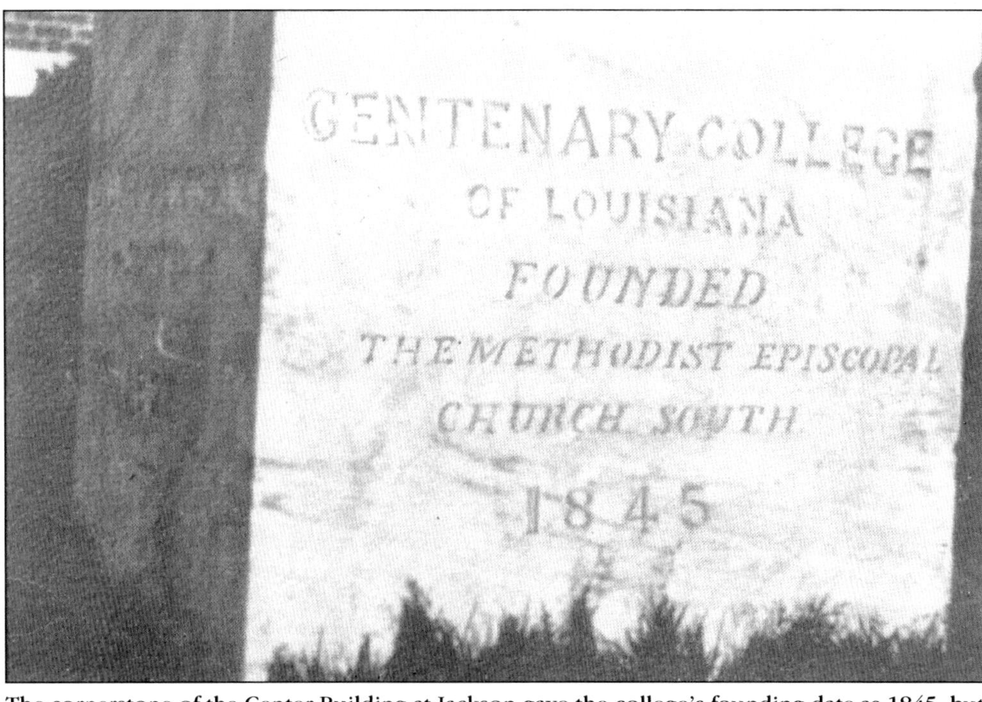

The cornerstone of the Center Building at Jackson gave the college's founding date as 1845, but, in fact, this was the date of the merger between Centenary College and the College of Louisiana. The true founding date is 1825, and the post-merger college continues to operate under the 1825 charter. After the move to Shreveport in 1908 this cornerstone was brought to the new campus, though it has since disappeared.

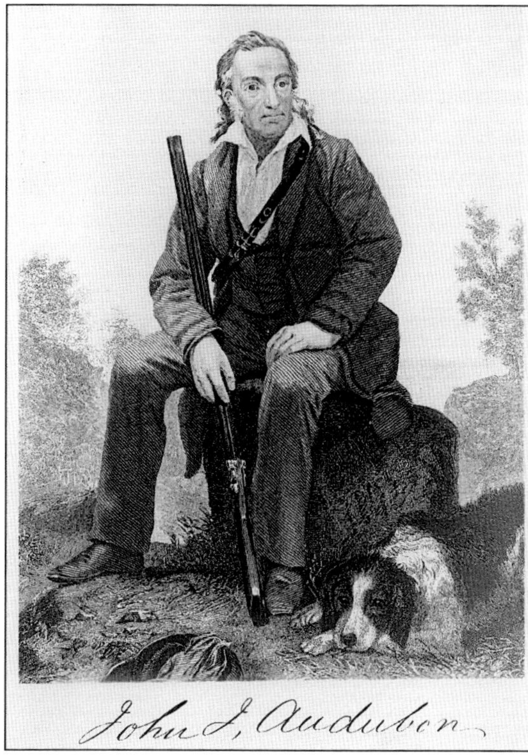

The name John James Audubon (top), celebrated ornithologist, naturalist, and artist, is one associated with early Centenary. Audubon resided close to the college's campus at Oakley Plantation near St. Francisville for a time. Here, many of his famous bird paintings were created as well as his equally noteworthy but less famous quadruped paintings. Audubon himself presented a folio of prints of his bird paintings to Centenary College as well as a folio of prints of his quadruped images. The college later sold most of the bird prints during times of financial distress; however, the quadruped prints are still in the school's collections. An exception is the brown pelican print (bottom) now housed in Centenary's Meadows Museum. The brown pelican is the state bird of Louisiana.

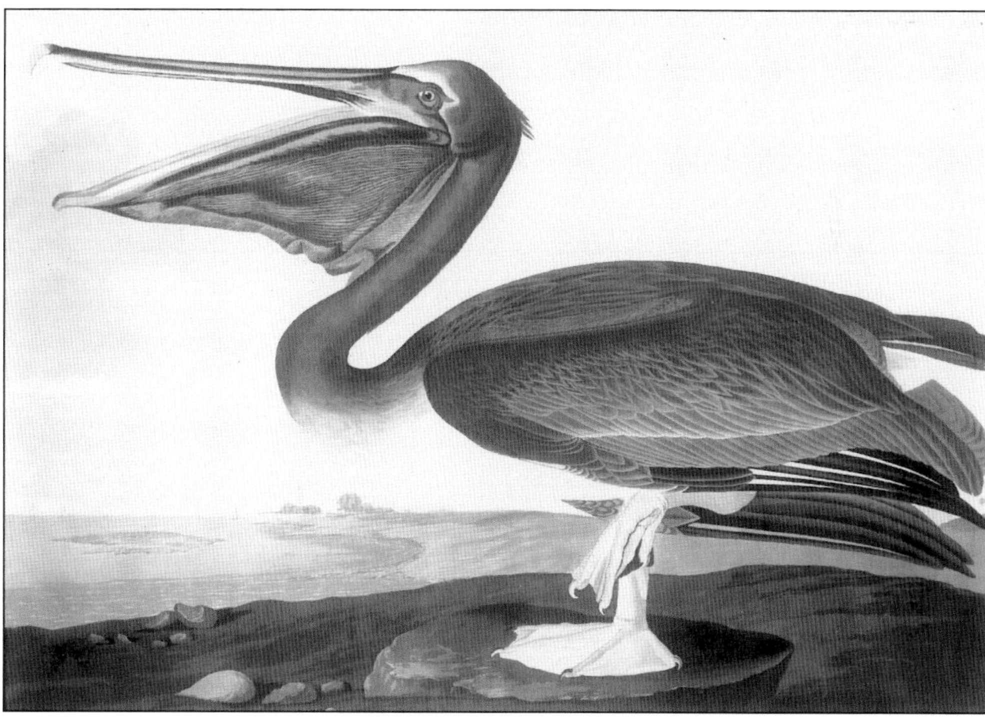

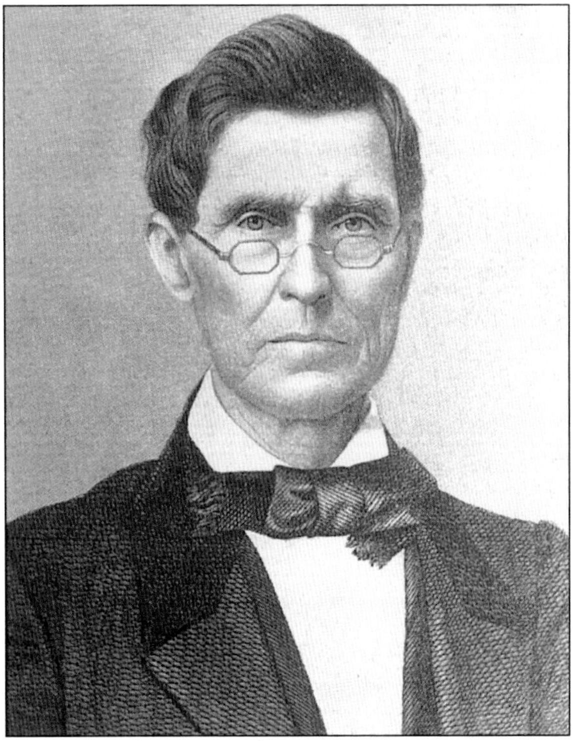

Judge Augustus Baldwin Longstreet served as Centenary's president in 1848 and 1849. A prominent figure in southern politics and education in the antebellum period, Longstreet was also a noted literary figure. His book *Georgia Scenes*, which can still be found in print, was much admired by Mark Twain, who cited it as an inspiration for some of his works. Before coming to Centenary, Longstreet was president of Emory College (now Emory University). He was later president of both the University of Mississippi and the University of South Carolina.

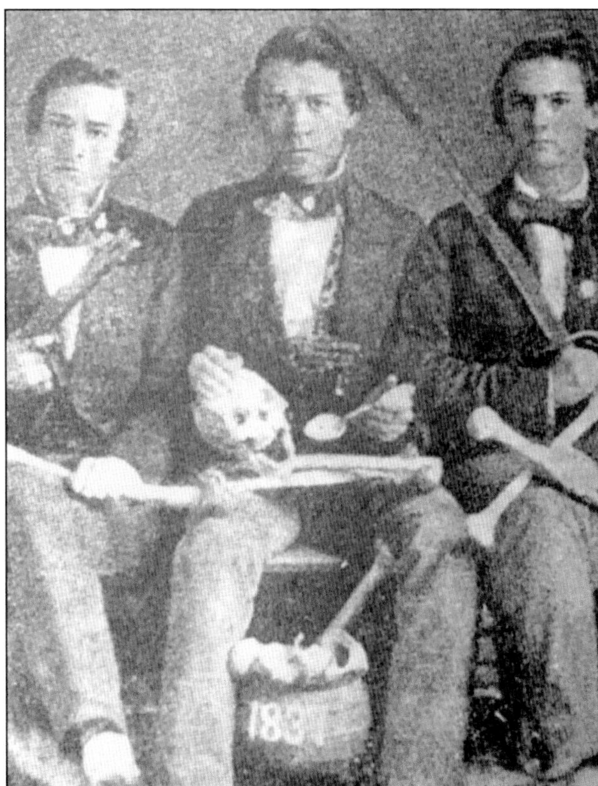

"The Temple of the Wreath," the Centenary chapter of the Mystic Seven, a secret society, was founded at Centenary in 1849. Seen here are the members in 1856, George Mayo, Thomas W. Compton, and Robert J. Perkins. A number of secret and fraternal societies arose at Centenary before the Civil War, including Delta Kappa Epsilon, Chi Phi, Phi Kappa Sigma, and the Mystic Palladians. All disbanded at the outbreak of war and none were reorganized after, though other fraternities and societies would arise in their places.

Charles Gayarre, considered to be the first important historian of Louisiana, received his undergraduate degree from Centenary's forebear, the College of Orleans, and in 1852 was awarded the M.A. degree by Centenary. In his commencement address, Gayarre predicted a long and distinguished future for Centenary, a prediction that has proved accurate.

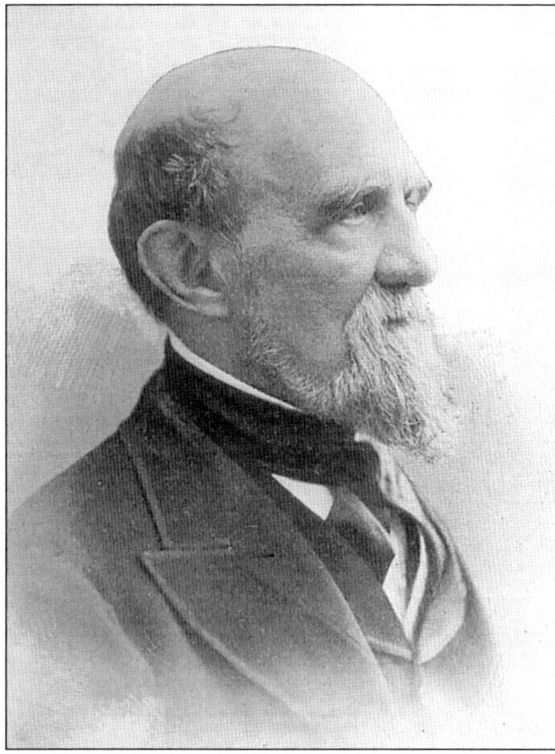

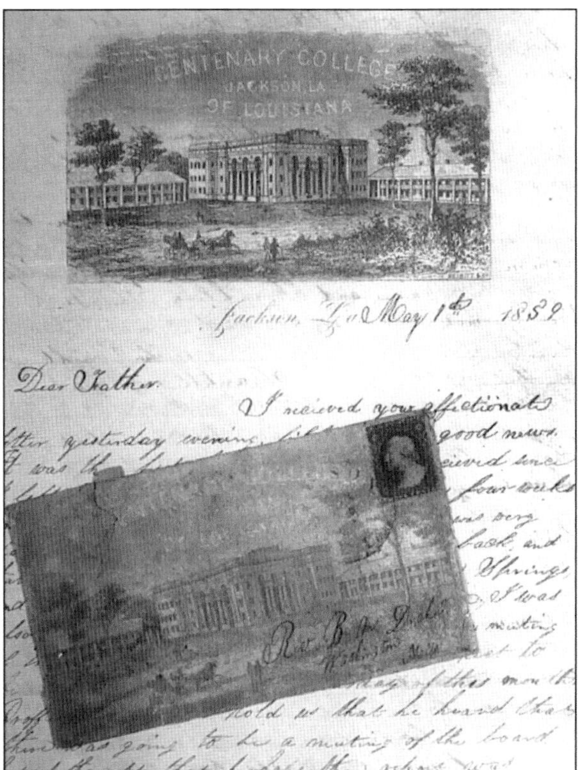

The archives of Centenary College contain many important and fascinating documents and images relating to the years in Jackson. An example is this 1859 letter to the Reverend Benjamin M. Drake from his son, William W. Drake, a Centenary student. The letterhead and envelope both depict the rendition of the campus shown on page 13. Four Drake sons were Centenary graduates, as were two succeeding generations of the family. Several families produced multiple generations of Centenary graduates in the Jackson era, most notably the Drake, Shattuck, and Scales families.

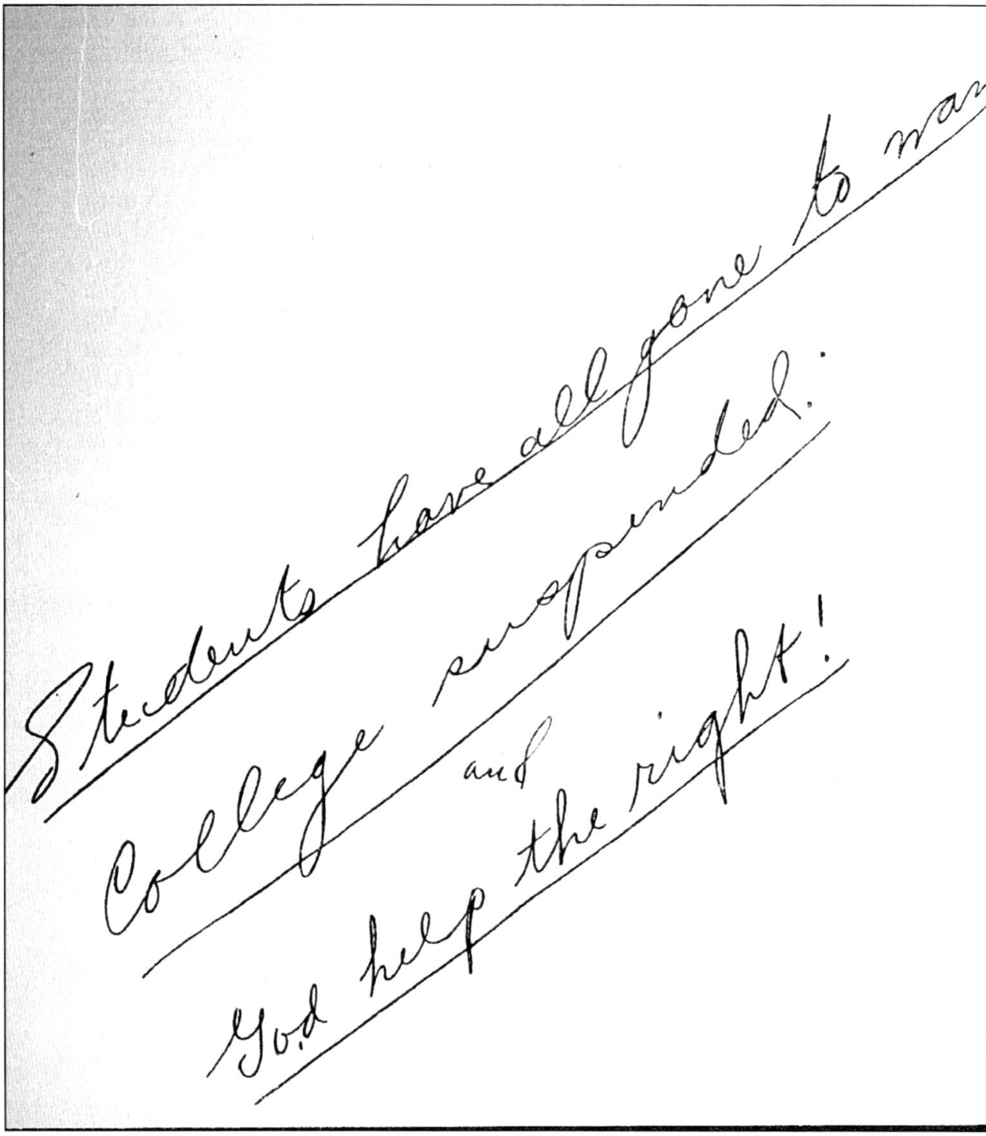

Students have all gone to war.
College suspended:
and
God help the right!

The minutes of the meeting of the board of trustees on October 7, 1861, contains this remarkable entry, written in a large hand across an entire page of the minute book. Legend has it that the entire senior class of 1861 marched away together and that all perished in battle. While it is a fact that the entire class did serve in the Confederate Army, as did many alumni and undergraduates as well, it is not true that all died in the service of their country. Nevertheless, their sacrifices and those of their college, which suffered at the hands of Union troops who occupied the campus, were great. The seniors of '61 who returned at the end of the war had not completed their course of study but were awarded their diplomas anyway, the board and faculty acknowledging that their education in the field was far greater than any they would have received in the classroom.

After the war, fraternities and societies gradually made their reappearance at Centenary. The first revived was the Union Literary Society, whose rooms and books had survived the Yankee vandalism that wrecked much of the rest of the college. The society remained active into the early Shreveport era. Pictured above are its debate team members of 1882; standing are S.J. Davies and M.A. Bell, and seated are James H. Fore and C.F. Smith.

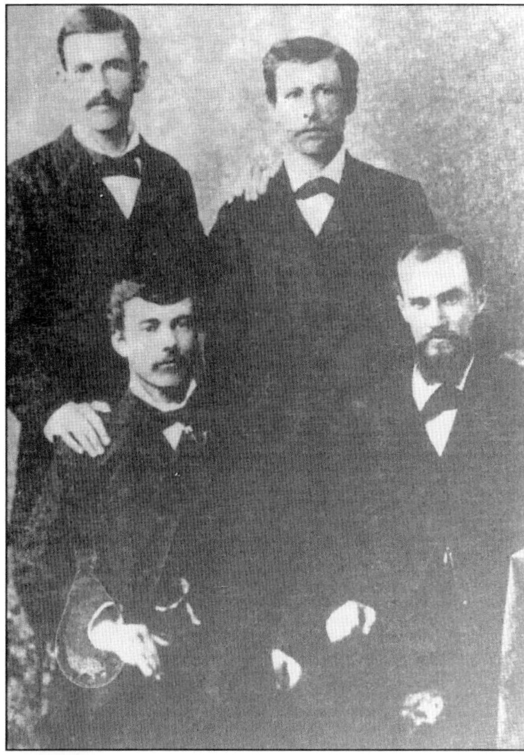

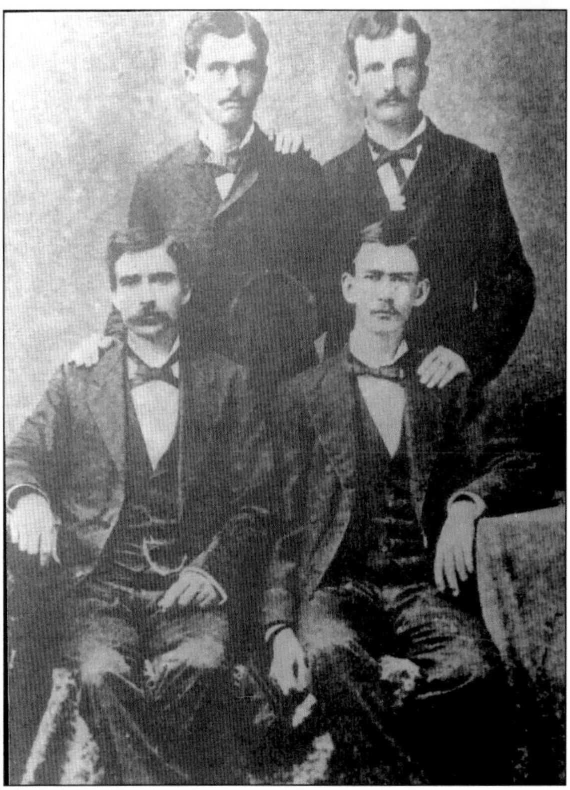

The Franklin Institute was formed in 1843, a year after the Union Literary Society, and was the school's other important debating group, save for the short-lived Lafayette Society of the 1850s, which debated in French. Seen here are the Franklin debaters of 1882. C.C. Miller (later to become the college's president) and Charles McDaniel are standing. Seated are B.J. Jones and R.H. McGimsey.

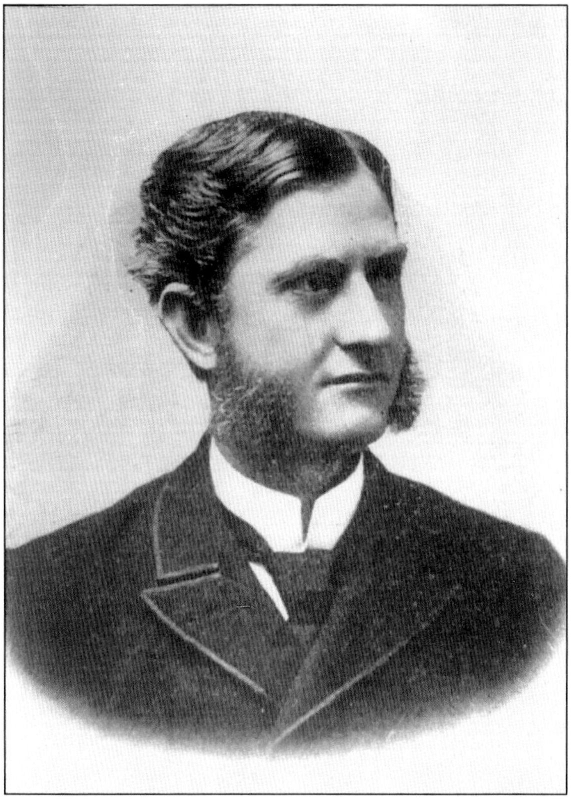

Newton Crain Blanchard, a planter's son from Rapides Parish, attended Centenary after the Civil War. He also took classes at the Louisiana Seminary of Learning (now LSU), but graduated from neither. Still, he obtained a law degree from the University of Louisiana in 1870 and became a state representative, a U.S. representative and senator, and from 1904 to 1908 was governor of Louisiana. Long a supporter of Centenary, he was a strong proponent of the move to Shreveport. Many of his books were left to the college after his death in Shreveport in 1922.

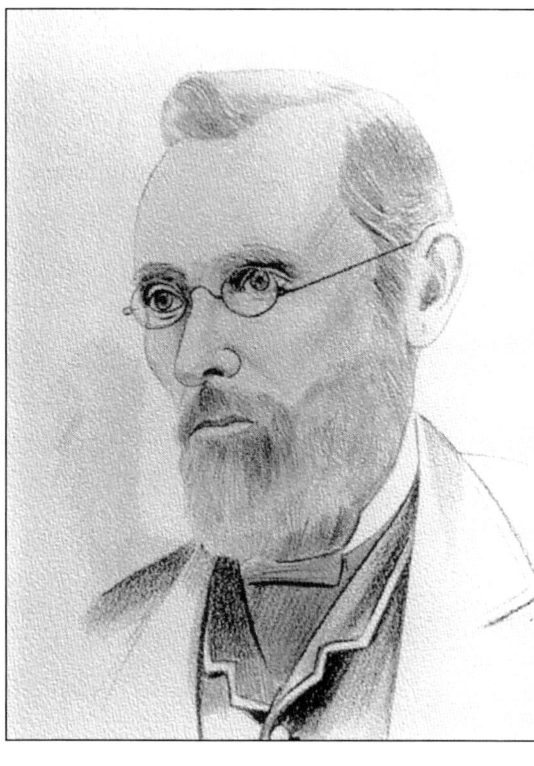

The Reverend C.W. Carter, a longtime professor at Centenary, was also editor of the *New Orleans Christian Advocate* newspaper. He received the degree of Doctor of Divinity from Centenary in 1879, and was elected president of the college in 1894, serving through 1898. Dr. Carter led Centenary through troubled times and helped keep the college in operation after the Mississippi Methodist Conference abandoned interest in Centenary, following its establishment of Millsaps College in Jackson, Mississippi. Millsaps was modeled after Centenary, as was Southern Methodist University in Dallas.

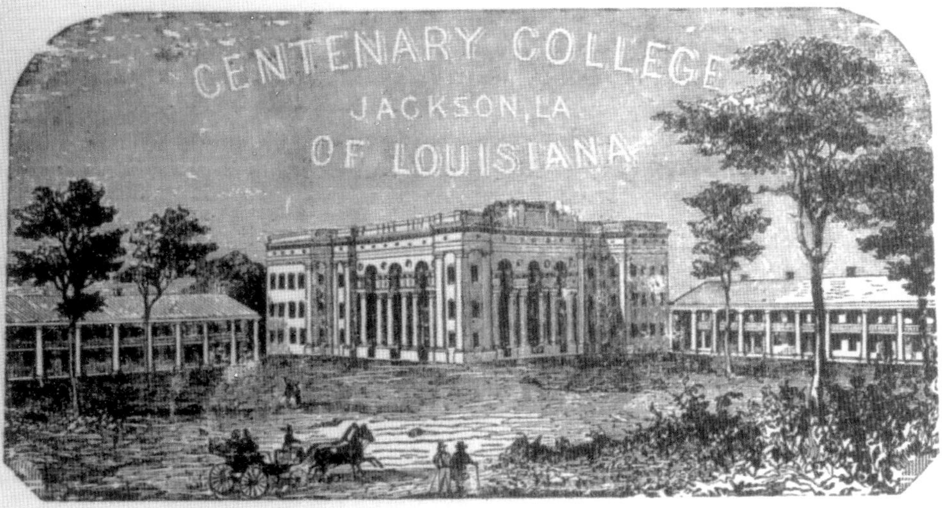

Centenary * College,

REV. W. L. C. HUNNICUTT, D. D., PRESIDENT,

JACKSON, LA.

FACULTY.

Rev. W. L. C. HUNNICUTT, D.D.	*Professor of Mental and Moral Science.*
G. H. WILEY, A. M.,	*Professor of Ancient and Modern Languages.*
R. H. McGIMSEY, A. B.,	*Professor of Mathematics.*
J. M. SULLIVAN, B. A.	*Professor of Chemistry and Physics.*
A. R. HOLCOMBE, M. D.	*Professor of Physiology and Hygiene.*
Rev. B. M. DRAKE, A. B.	*Professor English Law and Literature.*
Rev. ROBERT H. WYNN, B. A.	*Principal of Preparatory Department.*
Mrs. E. M. HUNNICUTT	*Assistant in Preparatory Department.*
Mrs. R. H. McGIMSEY,	*Teacher of Vocal Music.*

CHARGES.

College Classes, 5 months,	$30 00
Preparatory Classes, 5 months,	20 00
Contingent Fee, 5 months,	2 50
Matriculation (College Class)	5 00
Table Board, per month,	10 00
Board in Private Families, all things furnished, $13.00 to	16 00

Pictured is a page from the Centenary Catalogue of 1892. The tuition and board rates speak for themselves. It was at this time that athletics began to play a role in the life of the college. Tennis and baseball were the first sports sponsored by the school, though not all the powers in charge approved. In 1893, Centenary awarded an honorary Doctorate to Gov. Murphy J. Foster, largely for his role in driving the lottery out of Louisiana. Also during this era the first post-war fraternities were established on campus: Kappa Sigma in 1885 and Kappa Alpha in 1891.

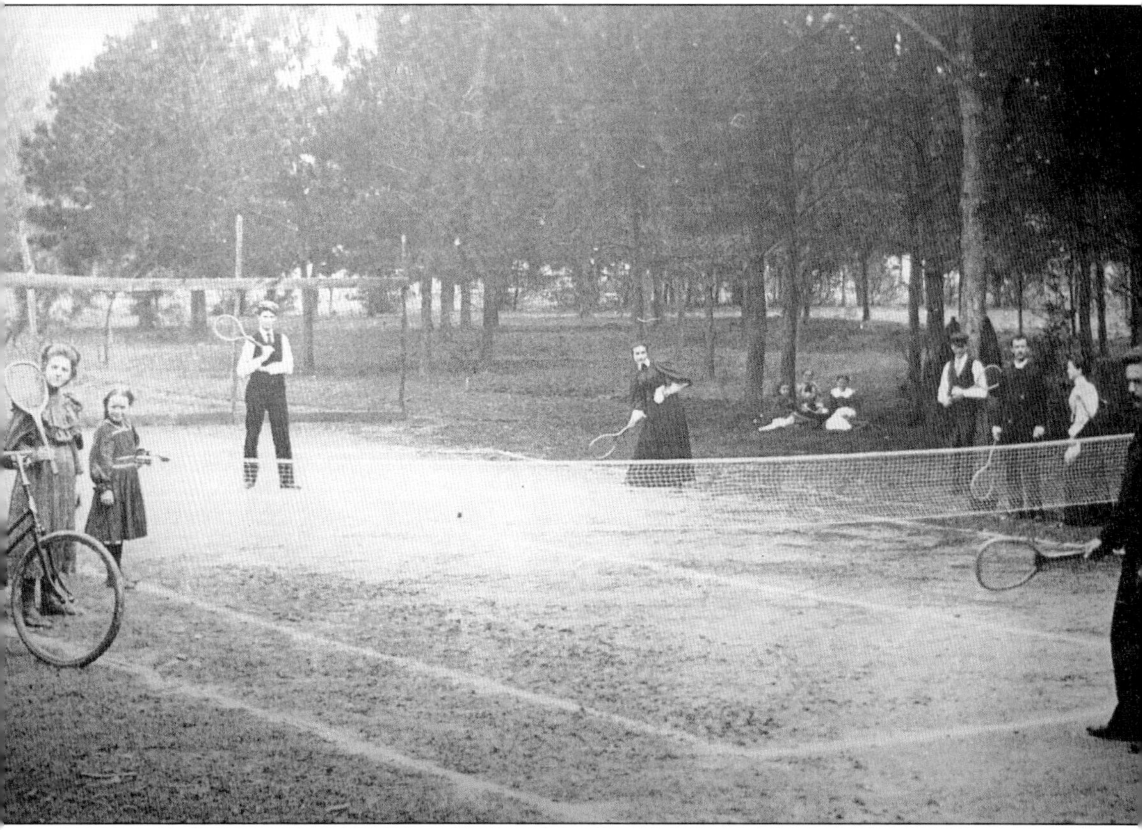

Tennis was first played on the rough clay court built behind the Center Building. Notice that the students playing in this 1899 photograph are wearing street clothes and the men wear ties. Women had been allowed into the classrooms of the formerly all-male college beginning about 1890, but not until 1900 would they graduate alongside the men. Prior to that time the women were awarded "Certificates of Completion," and not until 1947 were the pre-1900 female graduates given the diplomas they had worked for and rightfully deserved.

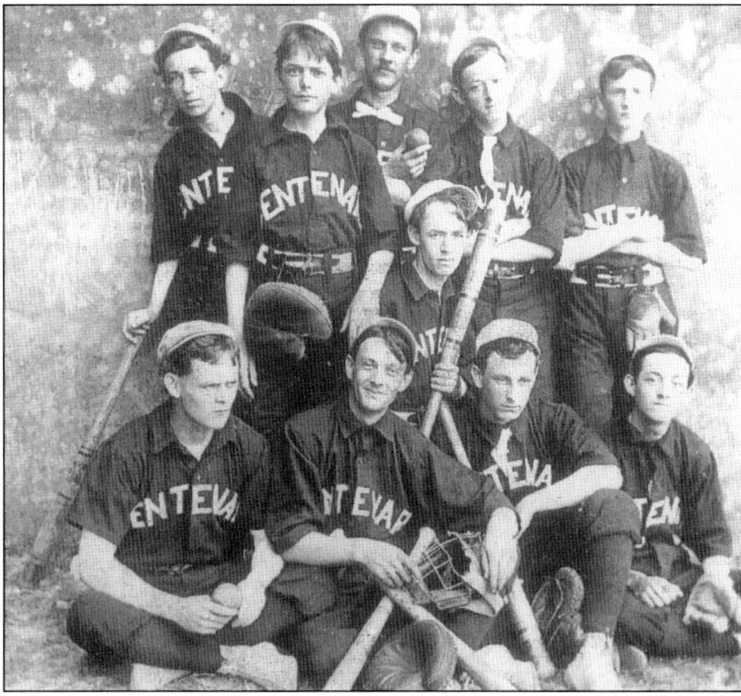

Centenary's baseball team is seen in 1897. Bishop J.C. Keener, longtime member of the board of trustees, and its president in the late 19th and early 20th century, opposed varsity sports as a bad influence that encouraged rivalries with other schools and took students' minds off academics. Thus, in 1898 intercollegiate baseball and football (which had just begun at Centenary) were abruptly banned, and students had to be content with intramural games. The team shown here was the last one Centenary fielded before the move to Shreveport a decade later.

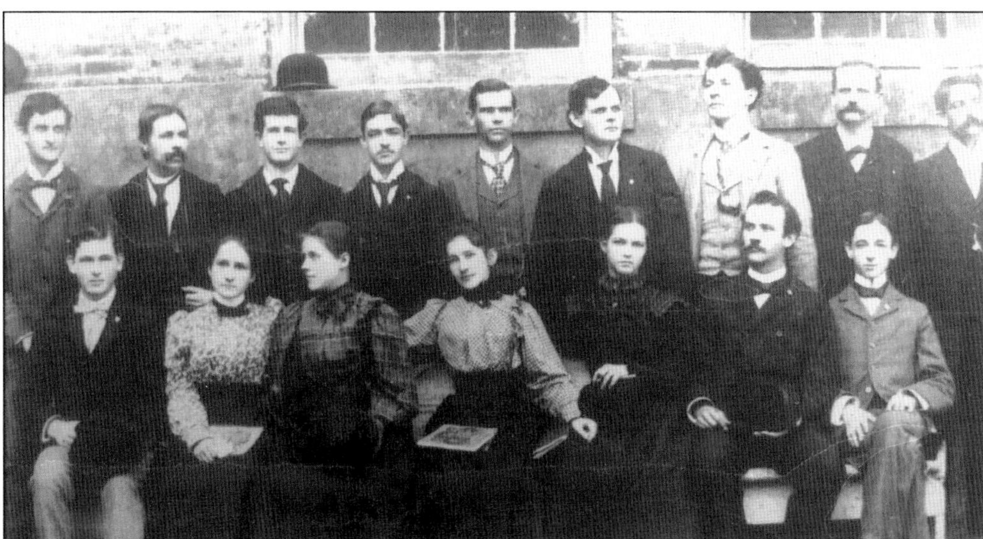

The class of 1900 was the first to include women among its graduates. The first four female graduates of the college are shown on the front row of this 1900 photograph, twin sisters Carrie and Willie Schwing, Maria Mason, and Mary Hill Taylor.

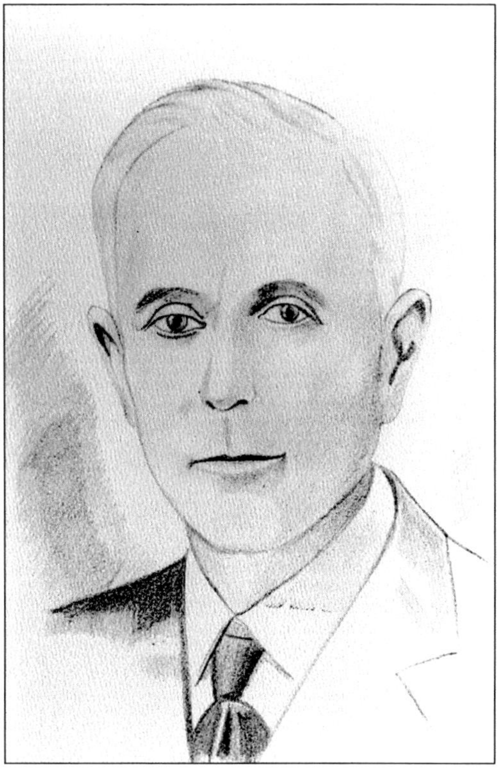

Dr. Charles C. Miller, class of 1883, became president of Centenary 20 years after graduating. It was during his presidency that agitation to move the campus from Jackson to Shreveport began. In 1903, the Rutherford-Atkins Realty Company offered a 40-acre tract south of Shreveport for the new campus. The city sweetened the deal with an offer of $110,000 to the financially strapped school. The Louisiana Conference and much of the board approved the move, but the townspeople of Jackson and Bishop Keener bitterly opposed it. Dr. Miller sided with Keener and the town, and ended up resigning as president of the college. Nevertheless, he remained an ardent supporter of the school throughout his life.

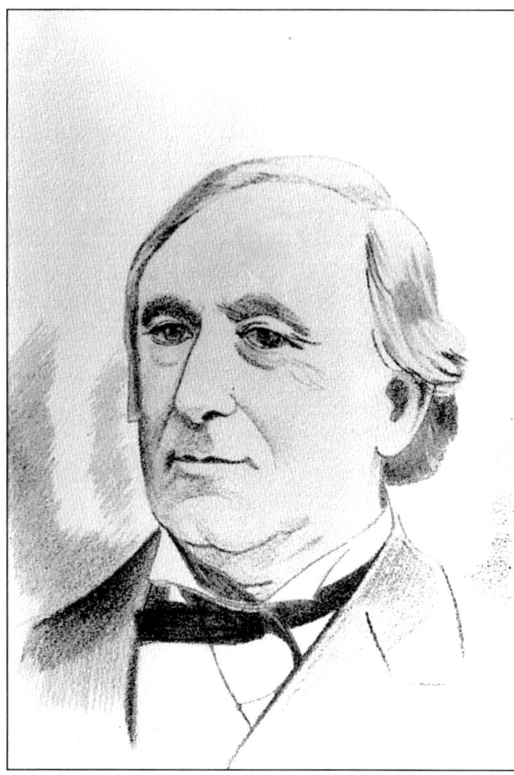

Bishop John C. Keener was active in the life of Centenary from the time of the Civil War until his death in January of 1906. During the period of financial distress following the war's end, Keener rode from house to house throughout south Louisiana raising money to keep the school afloat. A pastor in Mobile and New Orleans and editor of the *New Orleans Christian Advocate* for years, Keener was a supporter of Centenary for his entire adult life but was a bitter opponent of the move to Shreveport—he even sued to keep it from happening. His death in New Orleans at age 87 eliminated the sole major obstacle to relocating.

Two

THE EARLY SHREVEPORT ERA

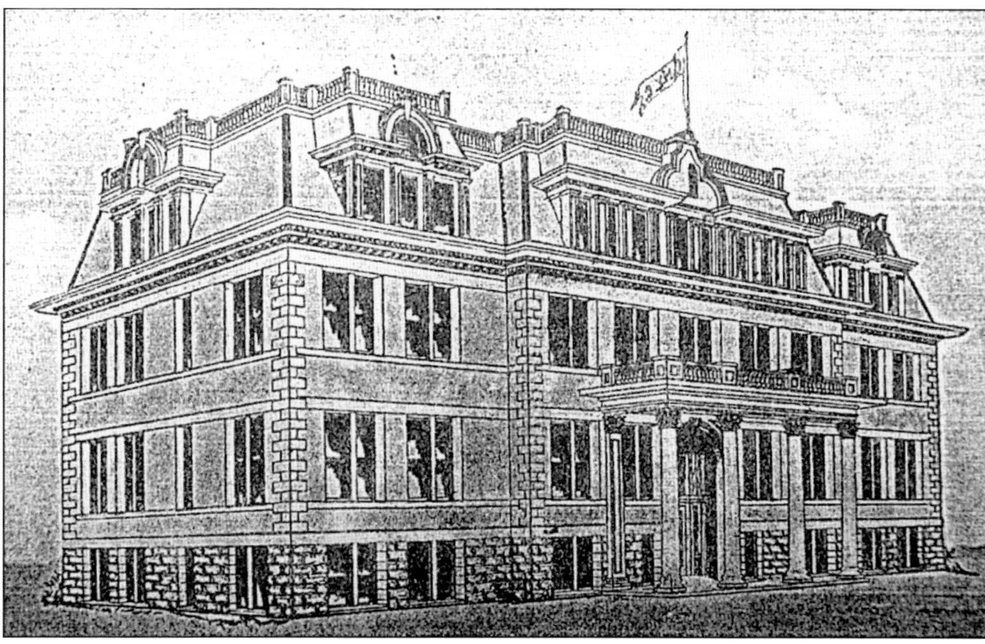

The last meeting of the board of trustees in Jackson in 1906 saw the college with only $118.11 in liquid assets. The move to Shreveport instantly gave the school a new campus and $110,000. Plus, Shreveporters voted for a special property tax to pay for the college's maintenance during the readjustment period. The first building constructed on the new campus was Jackson Hall, named in honor of the old campus location. It cost $33,000 to build and initially housed every element of the school's operations. Construction delays prevented the final move from occurring until 1908, so classes continued to meet at the old campus throughout 1907. The image above shows the original architect's design for Jackson Hall. It was built largely as shown, minus the Second Empire roof treatment of the top story. Beginning around 1910, several temporary frame structures were constructed close to Jackson Hall, alleviating the spatial stresses on the original building. These are all long gone, but Jackson Hall, though much altered, still stands today.

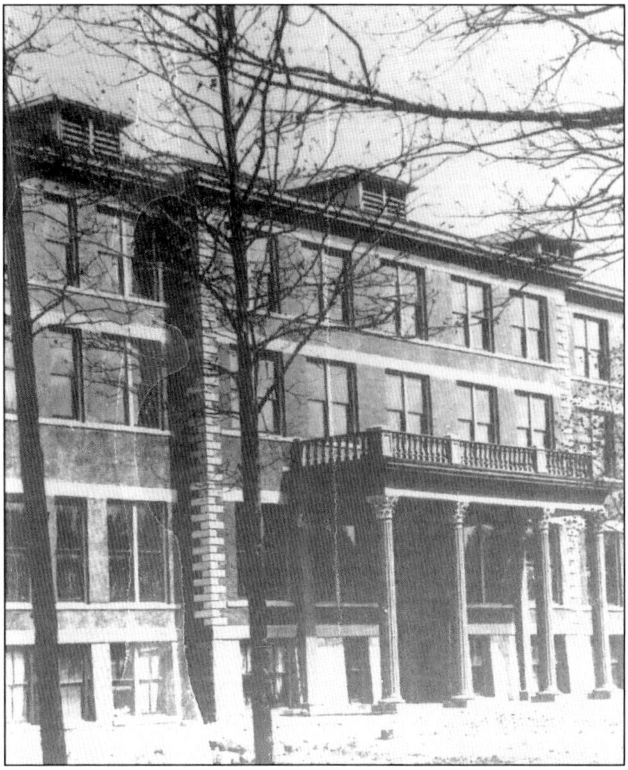

Jackson Hall is shown as it appeared shortly after completion. It opened for classes on September 16, 1908, and despite having cost $3,800 over budget, it still did not have electricity, running water, or heat. The college's new president, Dr. William Lander Weber, took as his first order of business the raising of $35,000 to equip the building with basic utilities. Almost four years later, in 1912, the new campus held its first commencement exercises here.

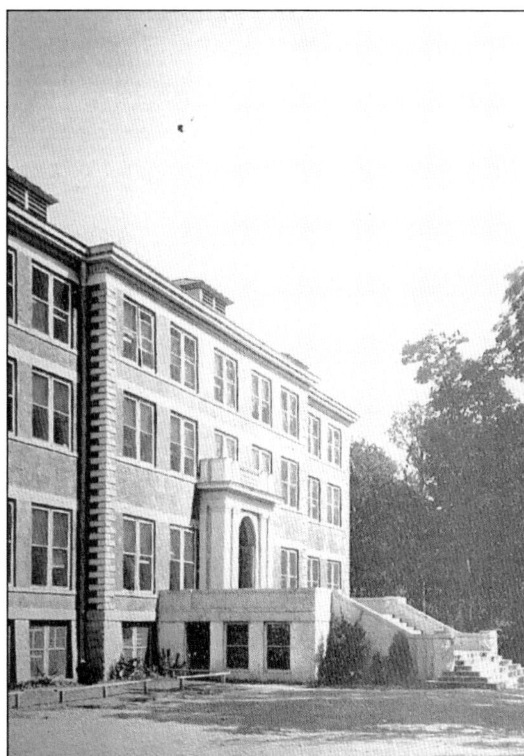

A somewhat later view of Jackson Hall shows the entrance as remodeled around the era of World War I. The main entry was now on the first floor instead of the basement, and a new classroom was added beneath the steps and terrace. The building was badly damaged by a tornado that swept across Shreveport on March 12, 1940. Afterward the top floor and roof had to be demolished, leaving the building at two stories above the basement, as opposed to its original three.

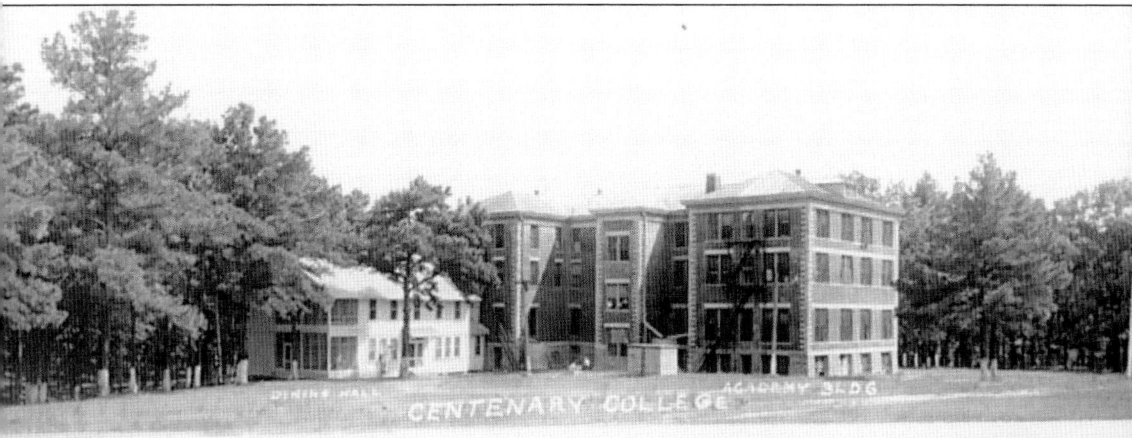

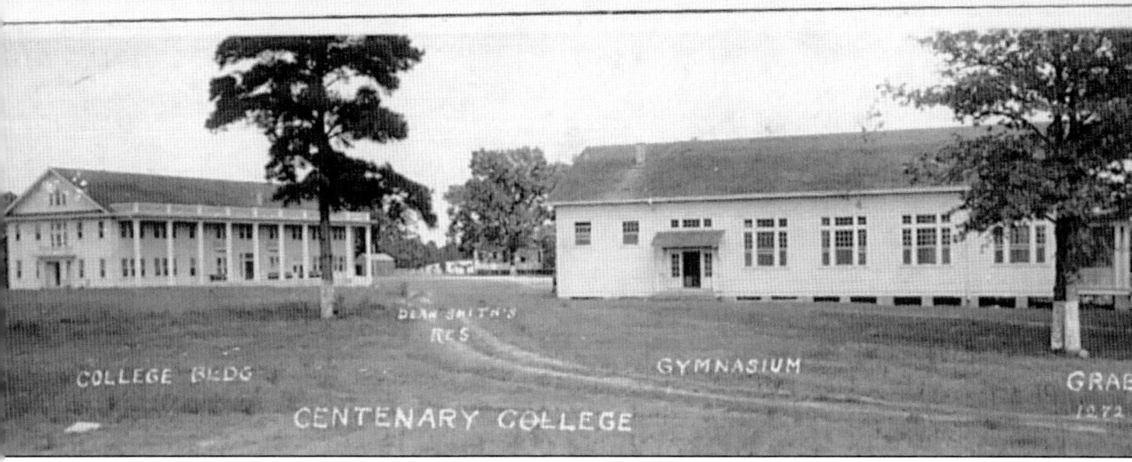

Two parts of a panoramic view show the campus as it appeared in 1921. The bottom section fits to the left of the top section. The back of Jackson Hall is seen in the top section, with the wood frame dining hall, built in 1918. The chapel (mislabeled "gymnasium" here) and College Hall were completed in 1921. College Hall, constructed as a classroom building to alleviate spatial stresses on Jackson Hall, later became the women's dormitory and was re-named Colonial Hall. In-between is the residence of Dr. R.E. Smith, dean of the college and longtime professor of religion. His home was among a dozen small frame houses built to the east of College Hall in an enclave that came to be known as "Faculty Row."

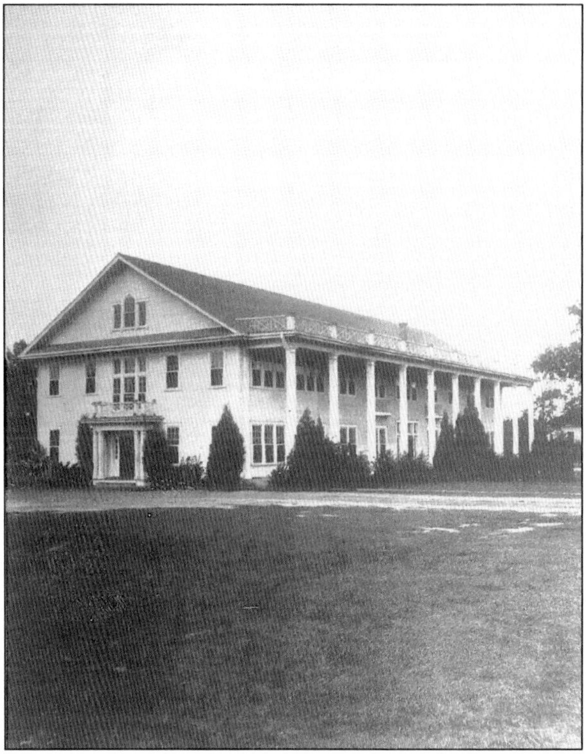

College Hall, the largest campus building after Jackson Hall, was built in 1921. Under the campus expansion program of President Sexton in the 1920s, it became Colonial Hall and the nearby chapel later became the dramatics building. Colonial Hall was long a Centenary landmark and from the mid-1920s into the early 1950s was the college's sole women's dormitory. In 1954, it was replaced by the T.L. James Dormitory, constructed on the same site.

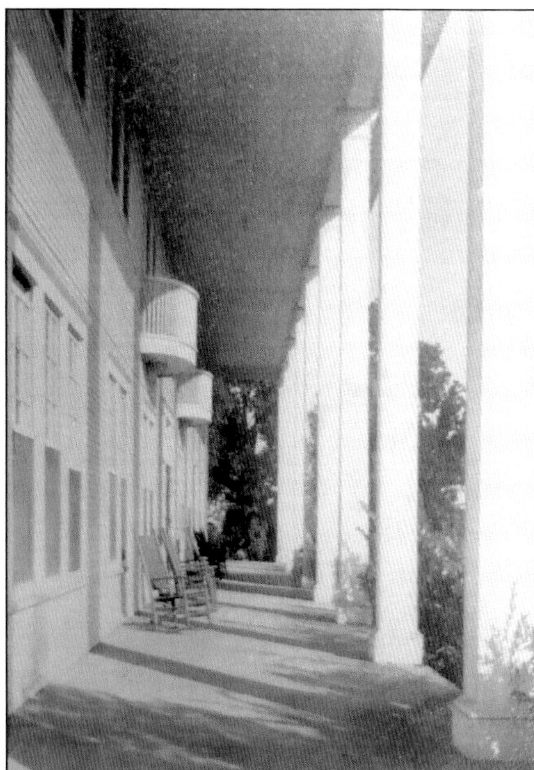

This view looking east along the front gallery of Colonial Hall is from the 1920s. It is vaguely reminiscent of the view along the front gallery of the old dormitory buildings at Jackson many decades before (see page 15).

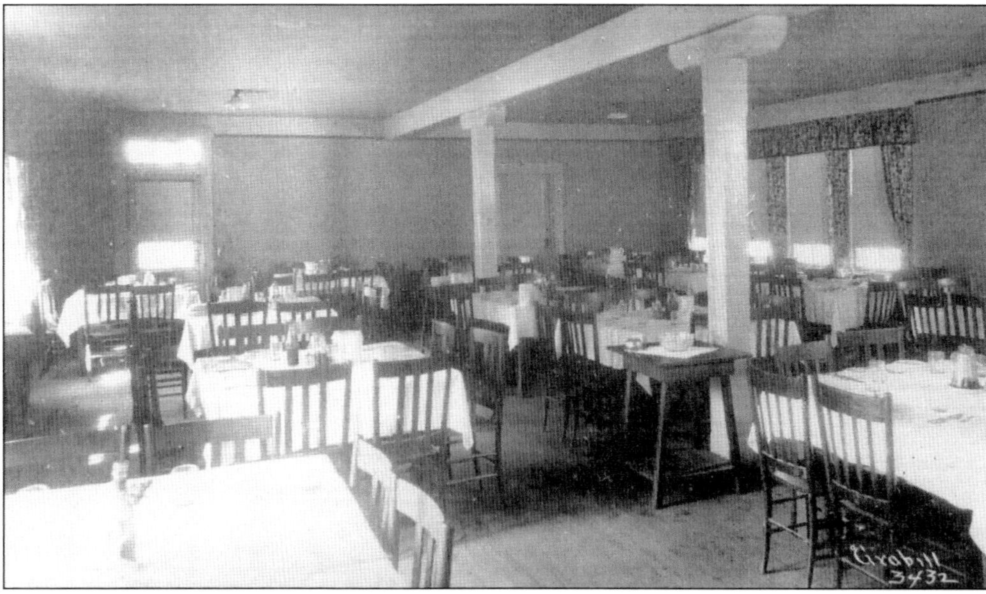

Seen here is the interior of the dining hall, the outside of which is seen in the view on page 35. This view was made around 1920. The dining hall building also housed the college's kitchen and larder.

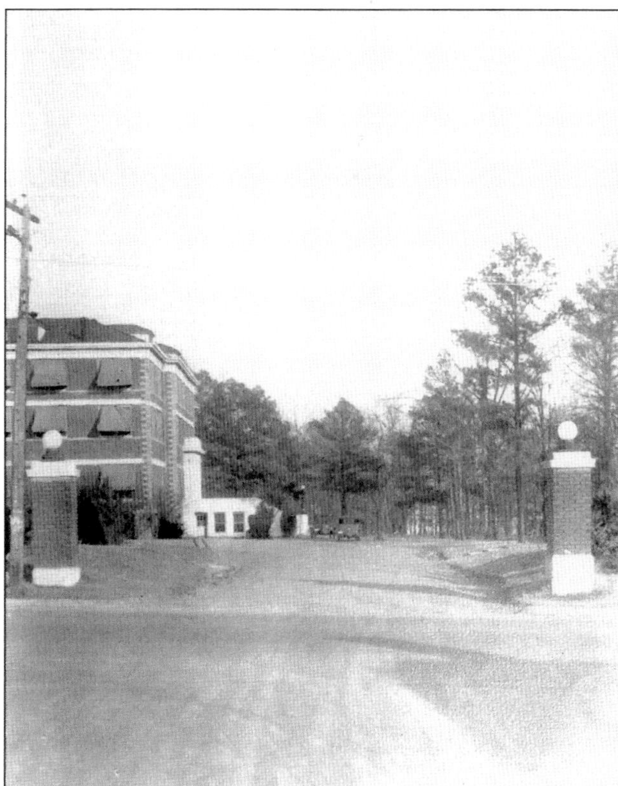

For many years, the main entrance to the college was along Centenary Boulevard at the end of Rutherford Street. Around 1920 the main gate looked like this, with brick pillars crowned by light fixtures on either side. Jackson Hall is at left, and the grounds to its east and south are entirely wooded. Rotary Hall, which today would be just to the right of Jackson Hall from this perspective, was yet to be built.

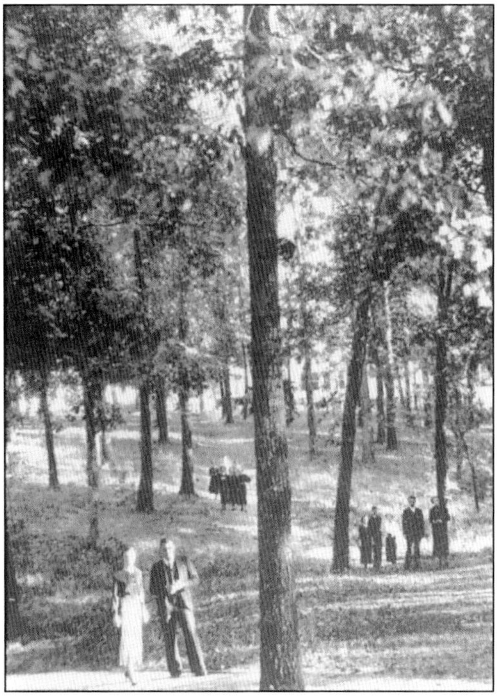

In the 1900s, 1910s, and 1920s, much of the Centenary campus was still thickly wooded and had a wilderness appearance punctuated by streamlets and thick growths of wildflowers. This view is of the southwest part of the campus across from Jackson Hall. Today, this is the site of Crumley Gardens and is still sylvan in nature and filled with foliage—though now the hand of man is much more evident in the scenery.

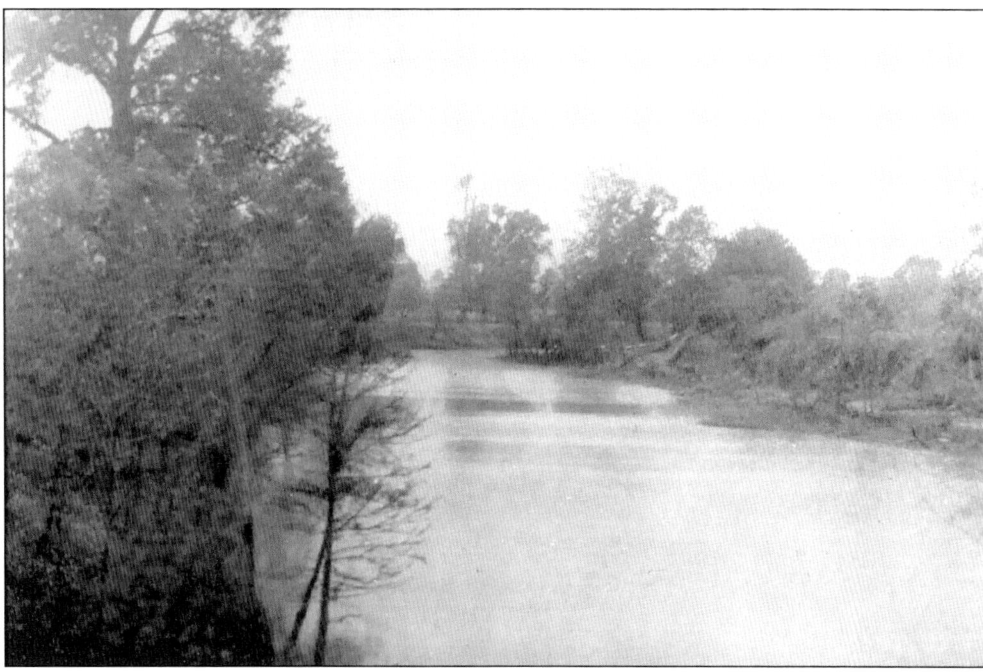

Also in its natural state during Centenary's early Shreveport days was Bayou Pierre, which flowed along the southern edge of the campus, across Kings Highway from the main cluster of college buildings. Unfortunately, the bayou was prone to overflowing its banks during heavy rains. As the city and college grew this became a significant problem. After World War II it was paved, and today is little more than a drainage canal, though the inspiration for the first lines of Centenary's Alma Mater poem and song is clearly evident in this early image of "the sleepy silver bayou."

After the move to Shreveport, varsity sports again became a part of student life at Centenary. Homer Norton, seen here, became athletic director in 1917; Bo McMillin was head football coach. In 1921, Norton became head coach both of the football and baseball teams, as well as coach of the basketball team. It was under his leadership that Centenary's football squad grew to become one of the nation's foremost college teams. Norton remained at Centenary until 1934.

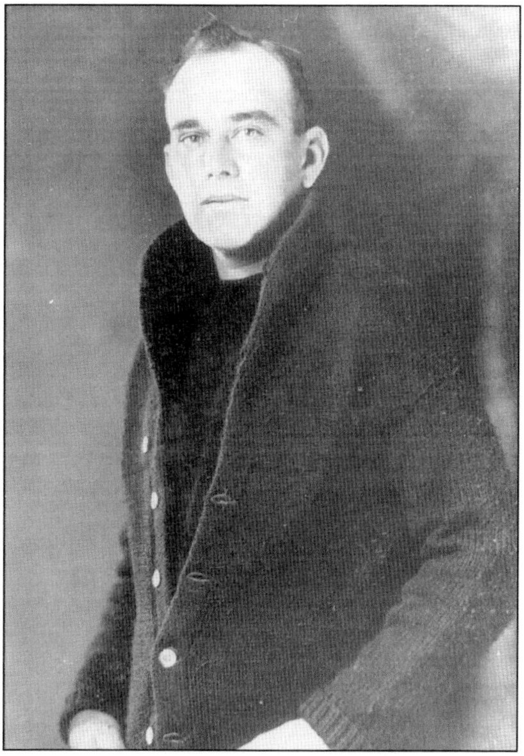

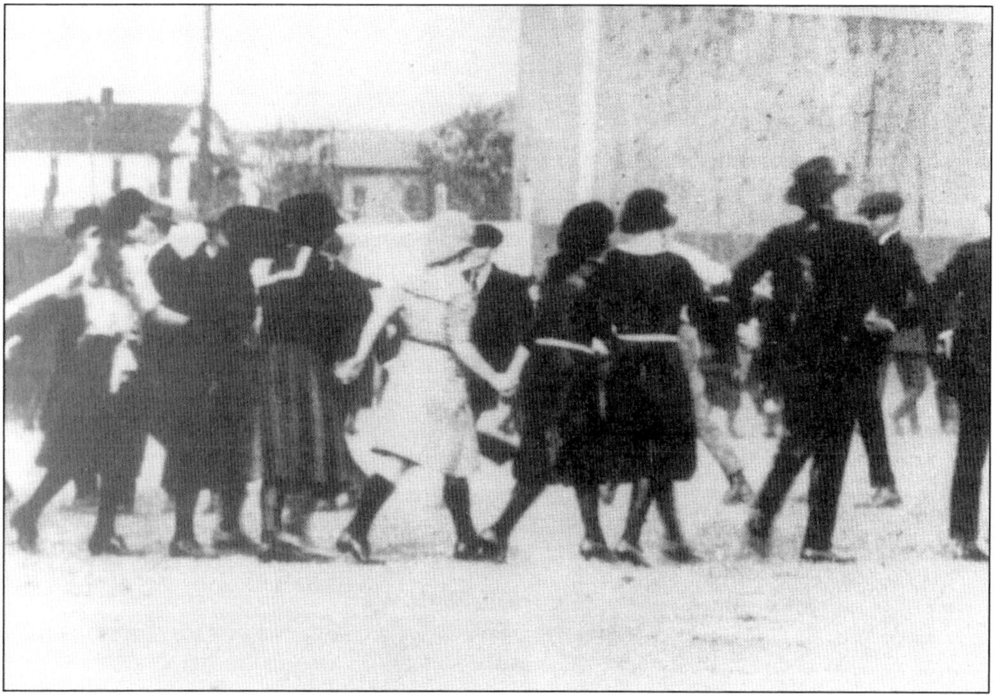

In the 1910s, a football victory was celebrated by a "snake dance" on the field. Here, Centenary students line up to dance across the field of the state fairgrounds in Shreveport following a rival's defeat on the gridiron.

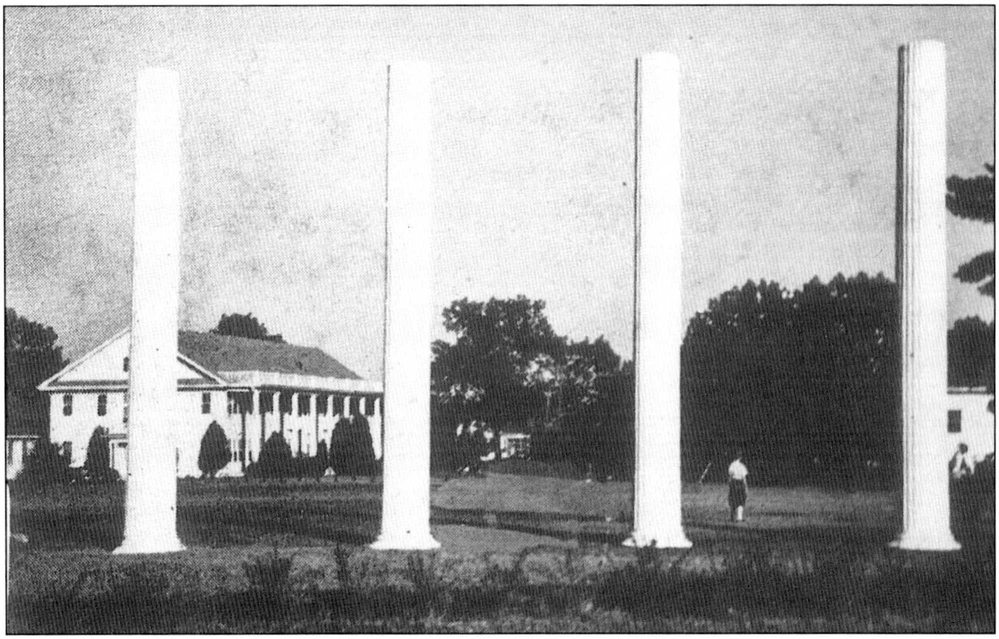

The link between the old Centenary campus at Jackson and the new Centenary campus at Shreveport was symbolized by four columns from the old campus buildings re-erected along the Centenary Boulevard side of the Shreveport campus. These were toppled by the same tornado that so badly damaged Jackson Hall in 1940, and were never replaced.

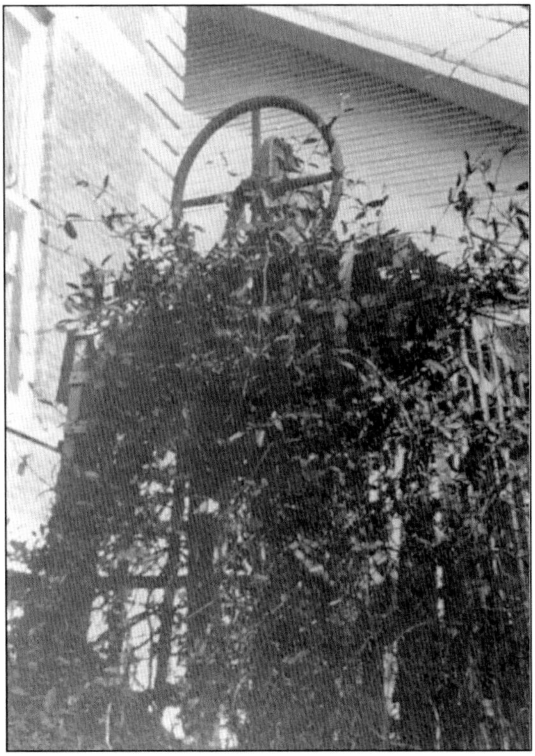

Also brought from Jackson was the college bell and its stand, which once had been located just to the south of Jackson's East Wing. At Shreveport it was originally placed near the northeast corner of Jackson Hall, close to the dining hall. Seen here covered with ivy in the 1920s, it was eventually removed from its decaying stand and restored. Today the bell is housed inside Centenary's administration building, Hamilton Hall.

S.L. Riggs had been a student at Centenary's Jackson campus in the late 1890s but left to fight in the Spanish-American War. Although he never graduated, Mr. Riggs remained active at Centenary for the rest of his life. He was instrumental in laying out the grounds at the Shreveport campus in the 1900s and 1910s, and worked at maintaining them through the 1930s. Mr. Riggs is seen here by the Jackson columns; houses along Centenary Boulevard are visible in the distance.

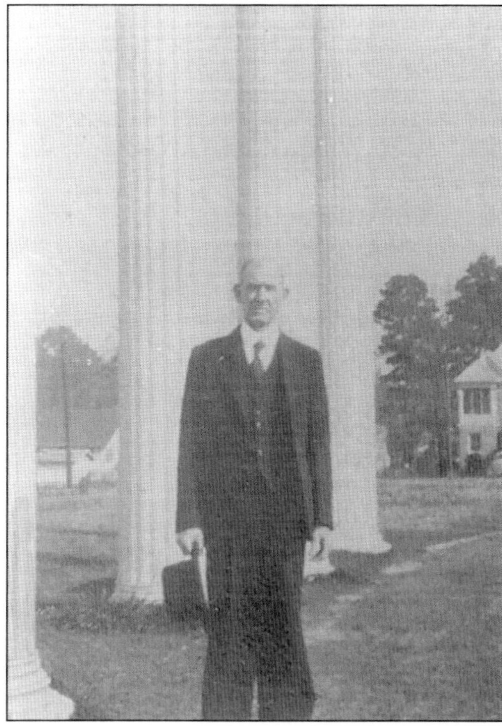

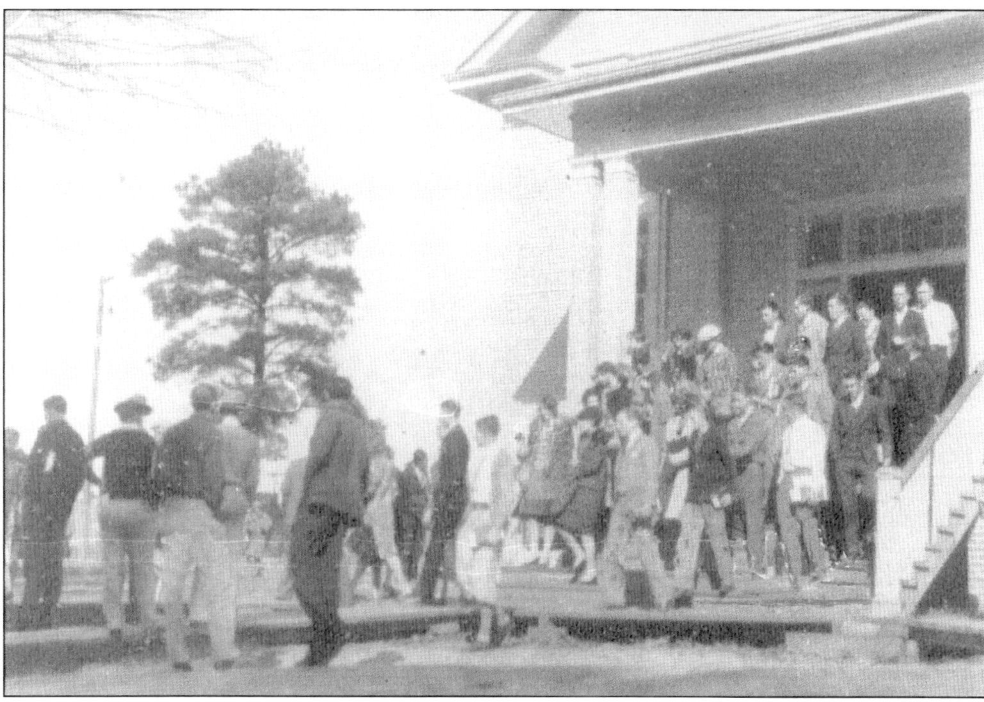

Students exit the chapel in the 1920s. The old frame chapel stood in the center of the campus, just west of where the garden in front of the Student Center is located today. Religious services, convocations, assemblies, and, in some years, commencements, were held here. In its later years the building would house the Centenary dramatics department.

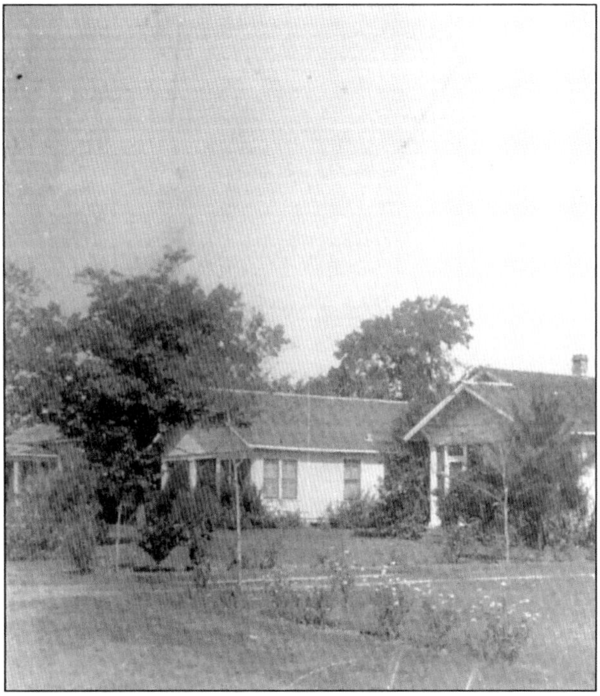

Faculty Row is pictured in the 1920s—a series of small frame houses for faculty members and their families, located in the northeast part of the campus. Some faculty members lived elsewhere in town, of course, but the tradition of professors living on campus was a time-honored one and the majority continued to do so throughout the 1930s. Today, the area once occupied by Faculty Row is the site of Bynum Commons and the parking lot just to its east.

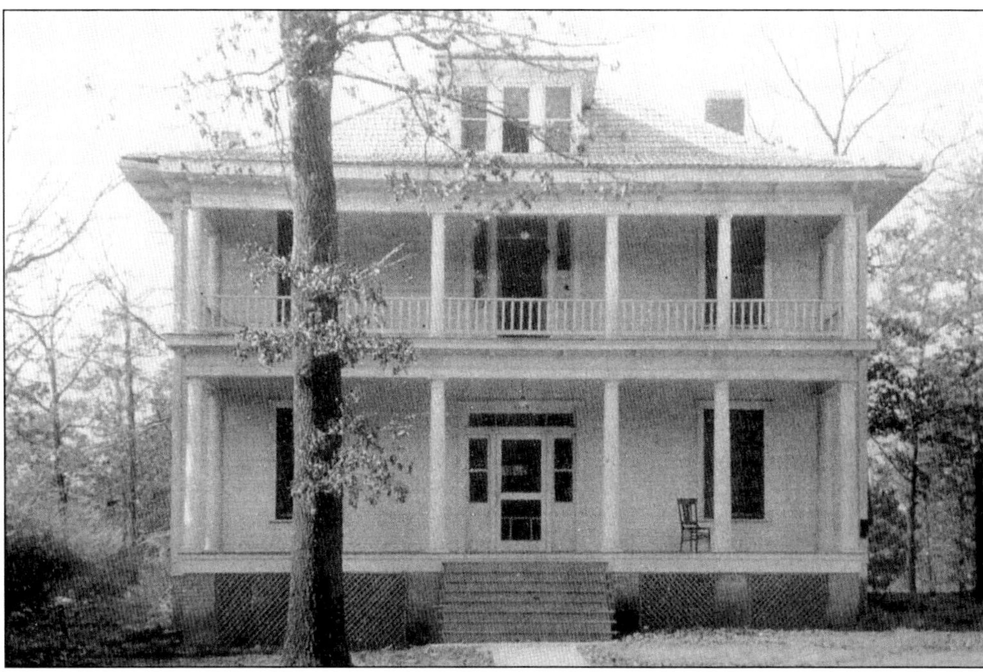

The Theta Kappa Nu fraternity house is seen in the 1920s. Only two fraternities came to Shreveport from Jackson—Kappa Sigma, first established at Centenary in 1885, and Kappa Alpha, established in 1891. Others formed on the Shreveport campus following World War I, namely Theta Kappa Nu, Sigma Phi, Pi Theta Upsilon, and Lambda Theta Chi. No sororities were formed at Centenary before the late 1920s.

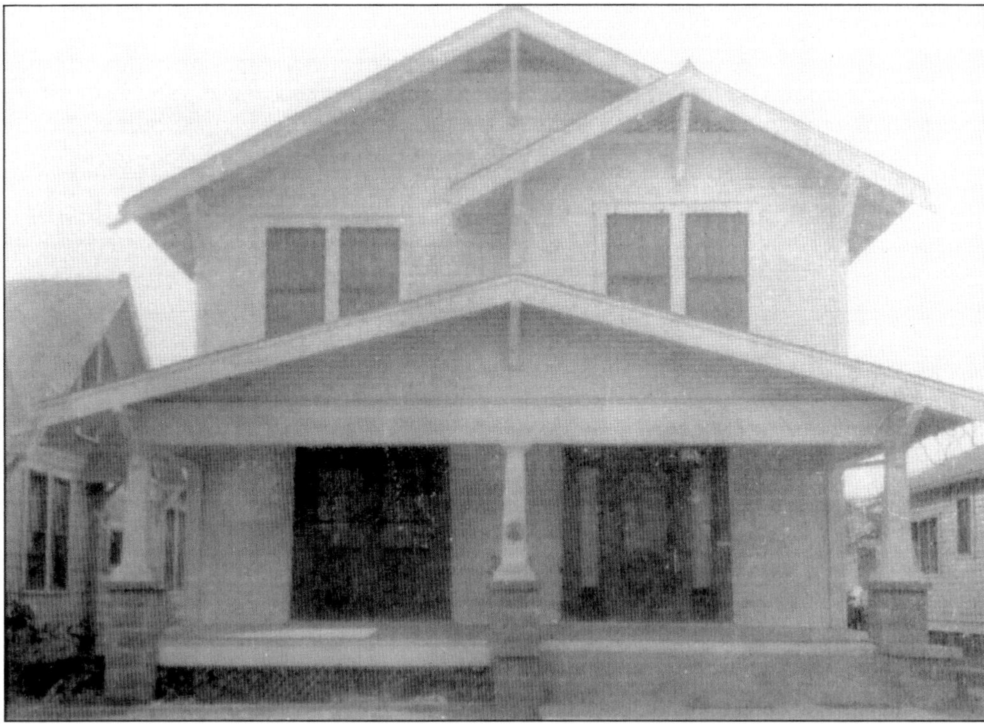

Above: The Kappa Alpha fraternity house in the 1920s was located on Centenary Boulevard, midway between Rutherford and Columbia Streets. It was severely damaged by fire in the late 1940s, and afterward moved to its present location on East Washington Street. The house still stands, though much altered from its original appearance, and today houses the Centenary Center for extended learning, as well as a few other school offices. Below: The Sigma Phi house was located near the campus on Robinson Place. The area along the west edge of the campus housed virtually all the fraternities during the early years at Shreveport, and Centenary Boulevard from Rutherford to Wilkinson came to be called "Fraternity Row."

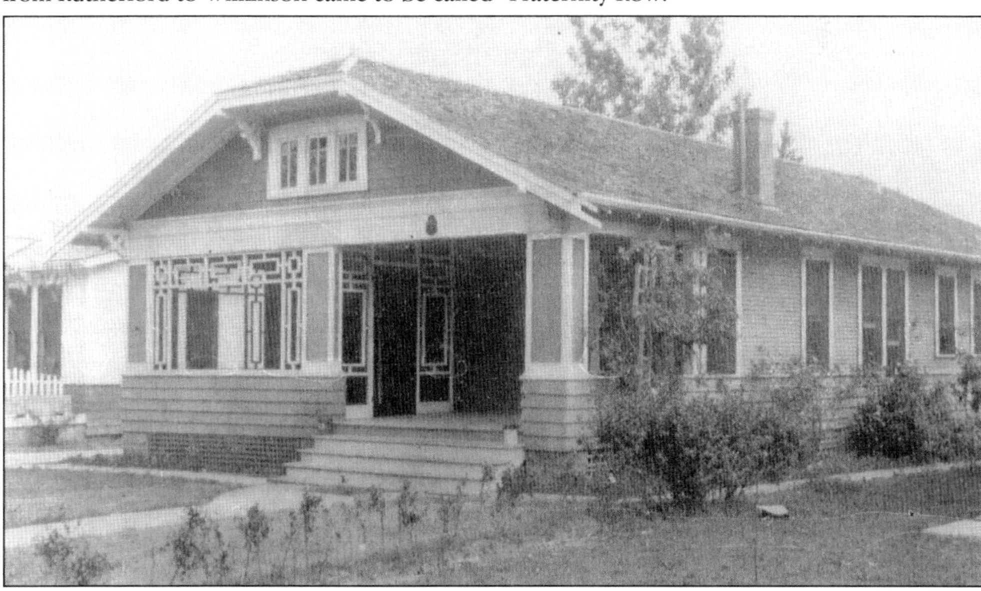

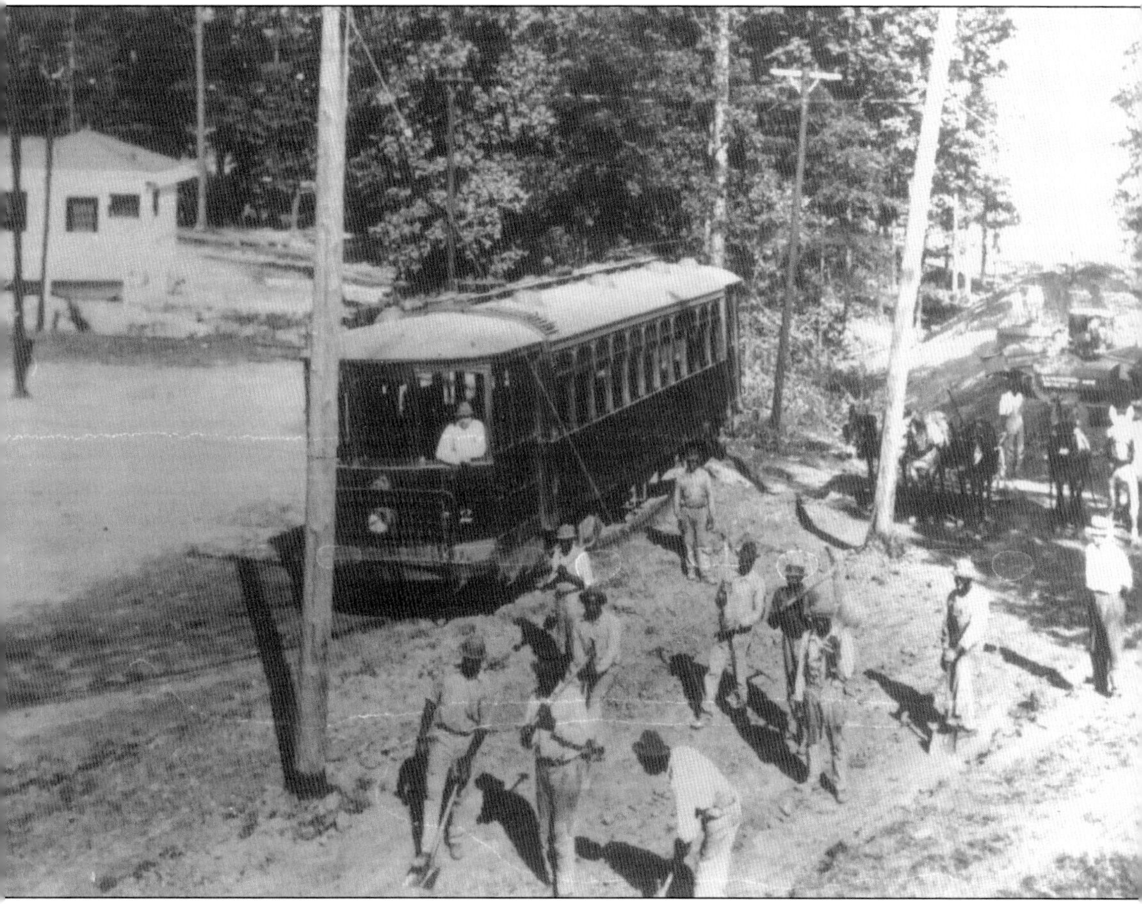

In Centenary's earliest days at Shreveport, the campus was located outside the city limits. By 1912, however, it had been brought into the city and was served by most public utilities. As the college grew during the 1910s and 1920s, so too grew the neighborhoods surrounding it. To the north and west was Highland, to the south and west, Gladstone. The area to the east remained undeveloped for many years, but came to be regarded as part of the Broadmoor neighborhood. The area to the immediate south of the campus came to be called, appropriately enough, the Centenary neighborhood. Streetcar service, not only to and from the campus but also serving these developing neighborhoods, was a must. Here, the Shreveport Traction Company is opening a new line at Centenary Boulevard and Kings Highway, on the campus's edge. Fares from the campus to downtown Shreveport, just three miles away, cost 5¢; the ride took 35 minutes.

Three

The 1920s and 1930s

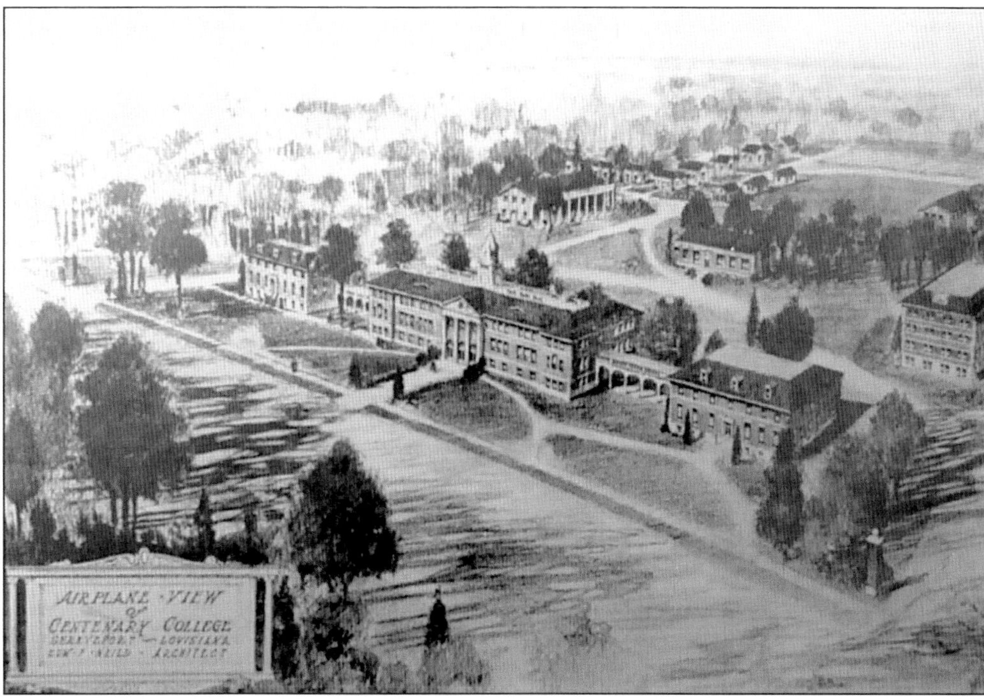

In 1917 Dr. George S. Sexton, pastor of the First Methodist Church of Shreveport, joined Centenary's board of trustees and the college would never be the same. In 1921 Dr. Sexton was asked to serve temporarily as Centenary's president. He accepted and the temporary appointment turned into an 11-year career and a wholehearted commitment to the school for the rest of his life. Dr. Sexton's great ambition was to turn Centenary's then rather impermanent-looking campus into a state-of-the-art institution of higher education. Ambitious plans for the future campus were commissioned of a Shreveport architect named Edward F. Neild, who later would be nationally recognized in his field. Neild's plans called for a campus filled with Colonial Revival buildings of red brick. In this 1922 drawing by Neild, a large classroom building facing Centenary Boulevard is flanked by smaller buildings. Only the Arts Building, at right, was actually built, though Sexton's dream of a grand and first-rate campus did, in fact, come true.

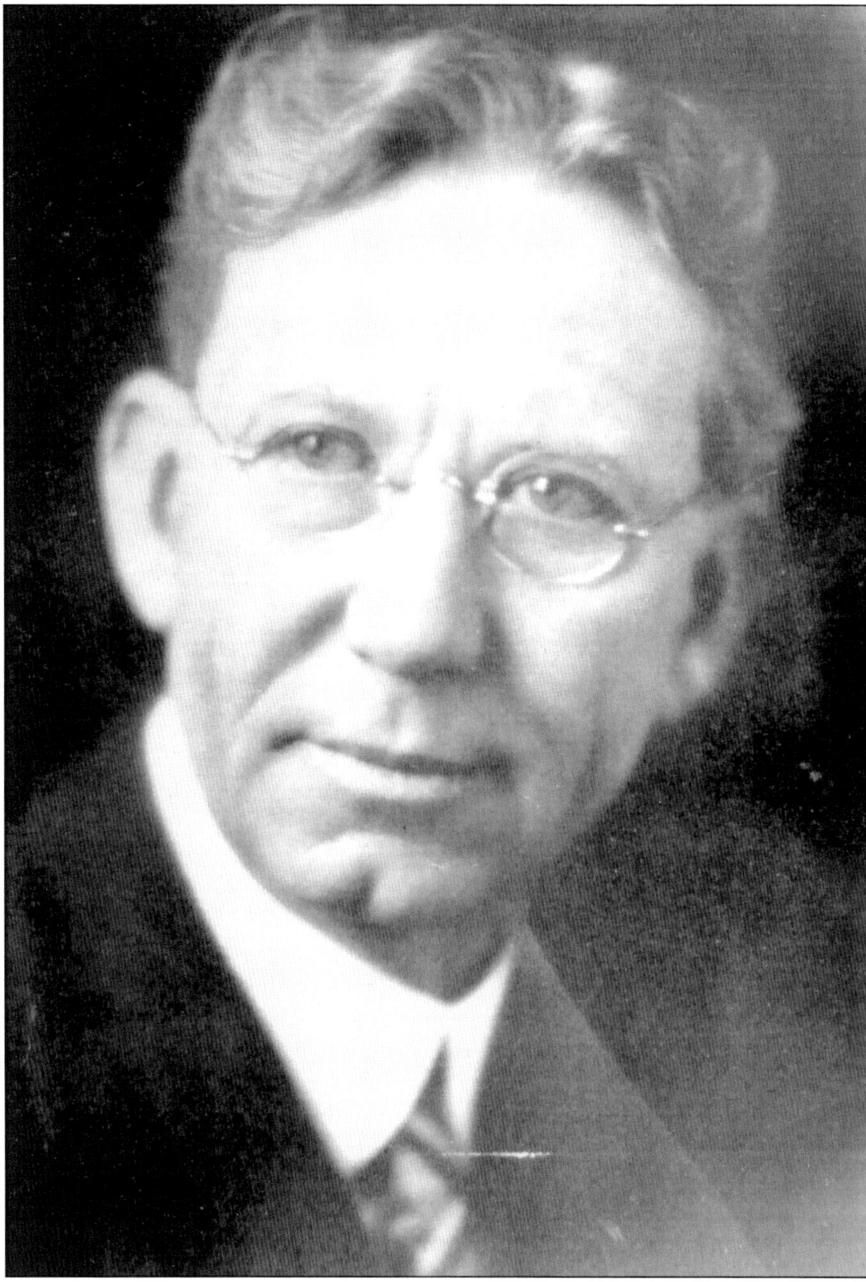

Probably no one in Centenary's history has had a greater role in its development than George Samuel Sexton. Born in Tennessee in 1867 and educated at Hendrix College in Conway, Arkansas, he was ordained a minister at 21. Among his congregations were churches in Texarkana, Galveston, Houston, and several other Texas cities. He came to Shreveport in 1914. As Centenary's president from 1921 to 1932, he oversaw the beginnings of the modern campus and Centenary's return to national prominence in academics and its rise to national prominence in sports. Even after retiring from the presidency, he and his wife, Sallie, continued to reside on the campus, where he remained actively involved right up until his death on July 4, 1937.

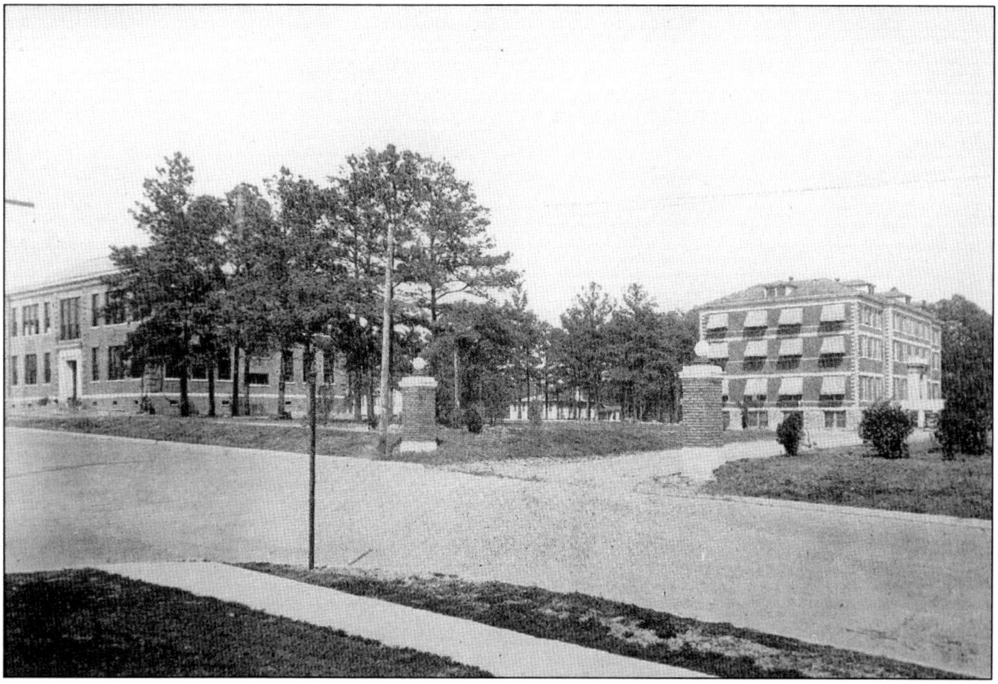

By 1923, the campus has already begun to change as this view of the old main gate shows. Jackson Hall is at right, and the new Arts Building, designed by architect Ed Neild, is at left. The Arts Building, housing liberal arts classes, would later become the library, then the administration building, and finally the Meadows Museum of Art, which it remains today.

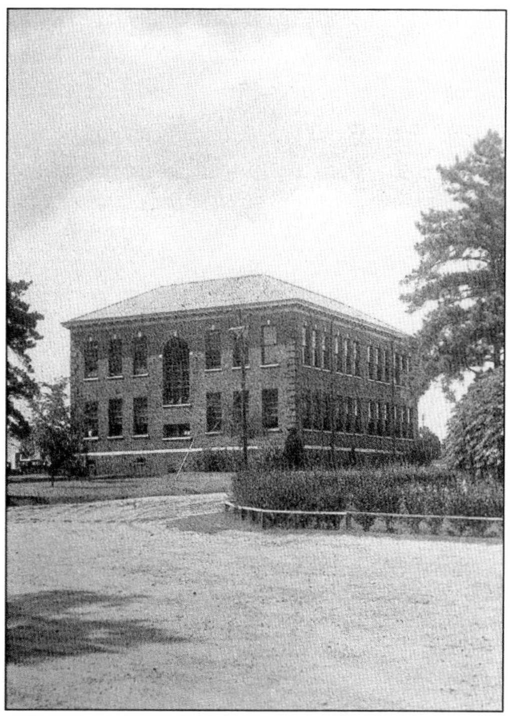

Another view of the new Arts Building was photographed in 1923 or 1924. Here the south and east elevations are seen from the driveway in front of Jackson Hall, which is just outside the photograph to the right. Today, the Peters Building stands on the lawn on the south side of the former Arts Building, obscuring this view.

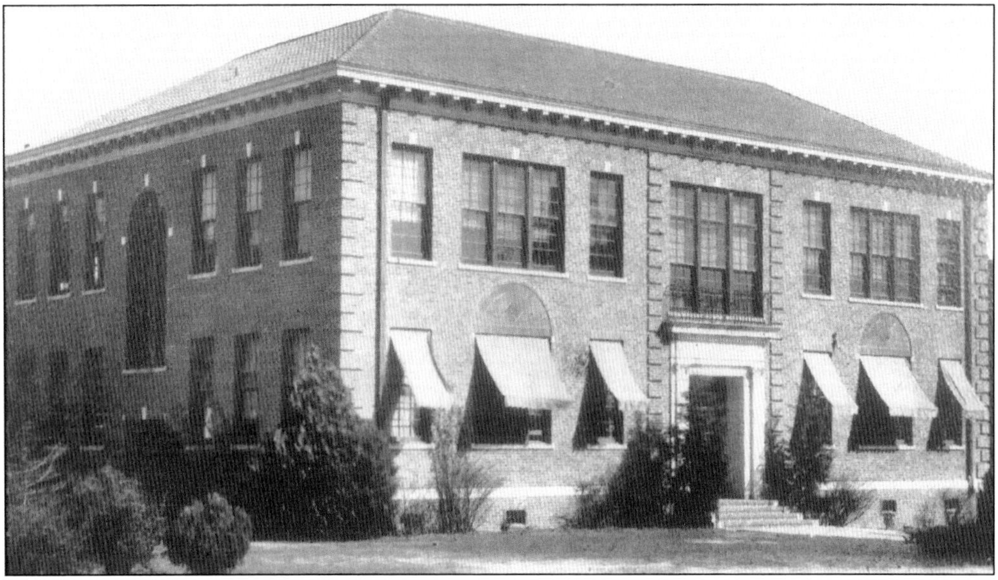

The Arts Building is shown as it appeared about 1925. After the Arts Building opened, it housed the majority of the college's classrooms. Jackson Hall was converted into the men's dormitory and College Hall was converted into the women's, becoming Colonial Hall. Jackson Hall remained a dormitory until 1930 when Rotary Hall was built. After that, Jackson Hall and the Arts Building were both used for classroom space.

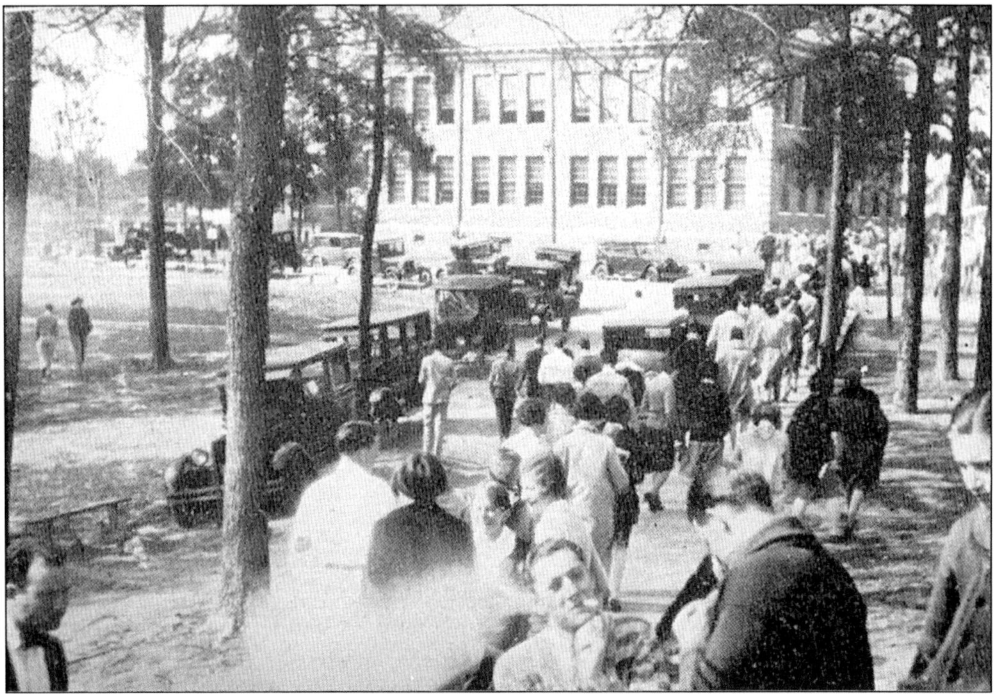

The campus event shown in this mid-1920s photograph may be registration day. Although the main campus roadway (today called Sexton Drive) is lined with automobiles, the long line leading to the Arts Building and the dress of the students would seem to rule out a commencement. Perhaps it is a convocation; the original print is unlabeled.

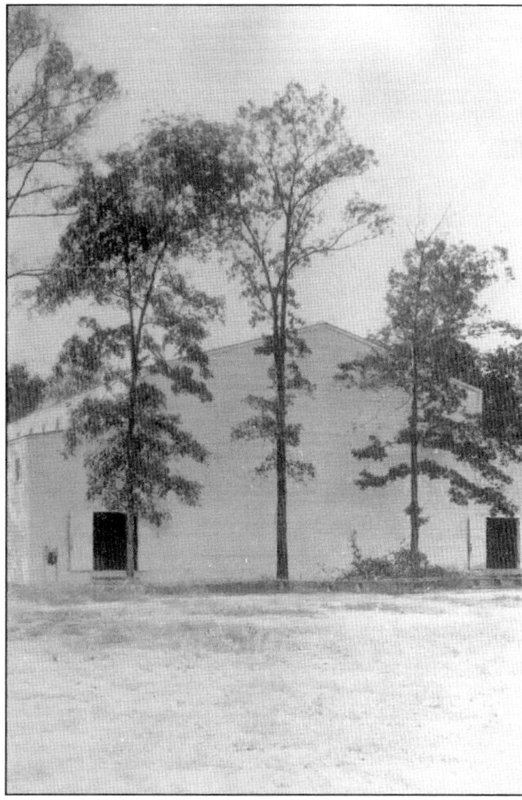

The gymnasium, completed in late 1925, was built with funds raised by Dr. Sexton and the Shreveport Kiwanis Club. It was first used on January 8, 1926, for a basketball game between Centenary and Texas A&M. Dr. Sexton was an avid proponent of college athletics, and it was he who chose the name by which Centenary's teams are known today—"Gentlemen" for the men's teams, "Ladies" for the women's. Dr. Sexton stressed that Centenary students should always be ladies and gentlemen first and foremost, on the court and field or off. The top image shows the gymnasium's exterior, the bottom image its interior. It stood on part of the site of today's Mickle Hall. Little more than a decade after its construction, it was replaced by the larger Art Deco-style Haynes Gymnasium, itself extensively refurbished in 1999.

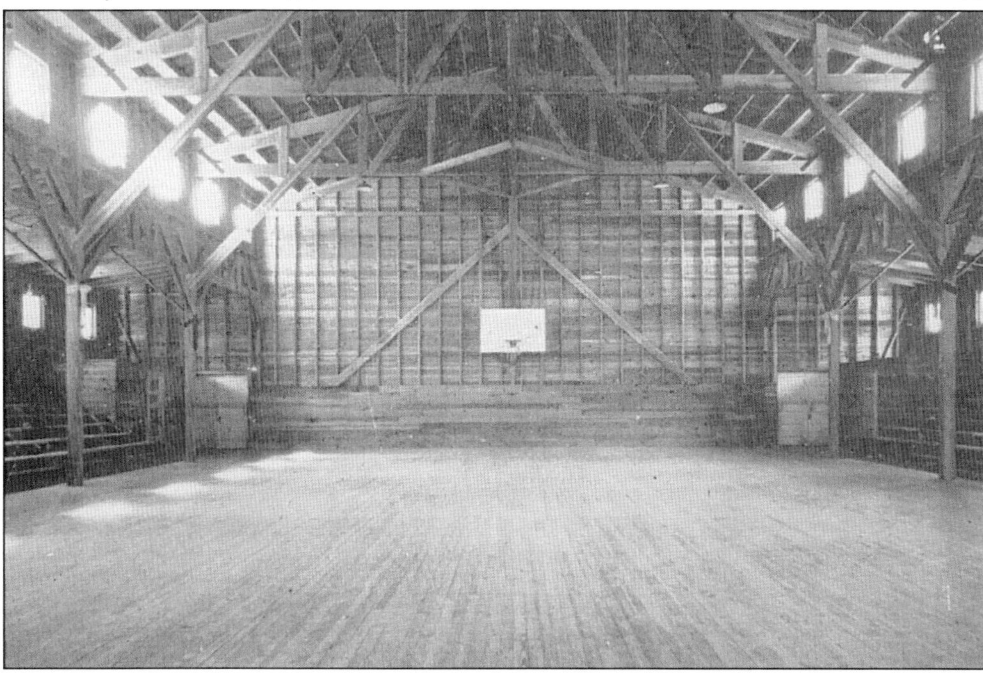

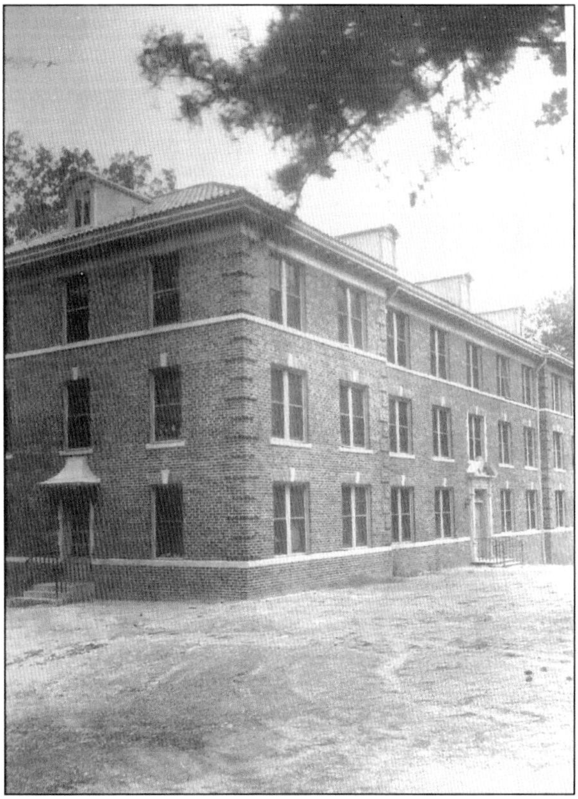

Left: Rotary Hall, first planned in 1926 and completed in 1930, was the first campus building constructed specifically as a dormitory, which it remains to this day. It was built with funds raised by the Shreveport Rotary Club—of which Dr. Sexton was an active member—as its share of Centenary's 1929 financial drive. It was enlarged and extensively refurbished in 1996, though its north and west facades, seen in this photo taken shortly after its completion, still look very much the same today. Below: The Rotary International seal carved in stone is seen above the west entrance to Rotary Hall. A wing was added to Rotary in 1953 and further renovations occurred in 1965. The 1996 remodeling was done by the Newman Partnership, a Shreveport architectural firm.

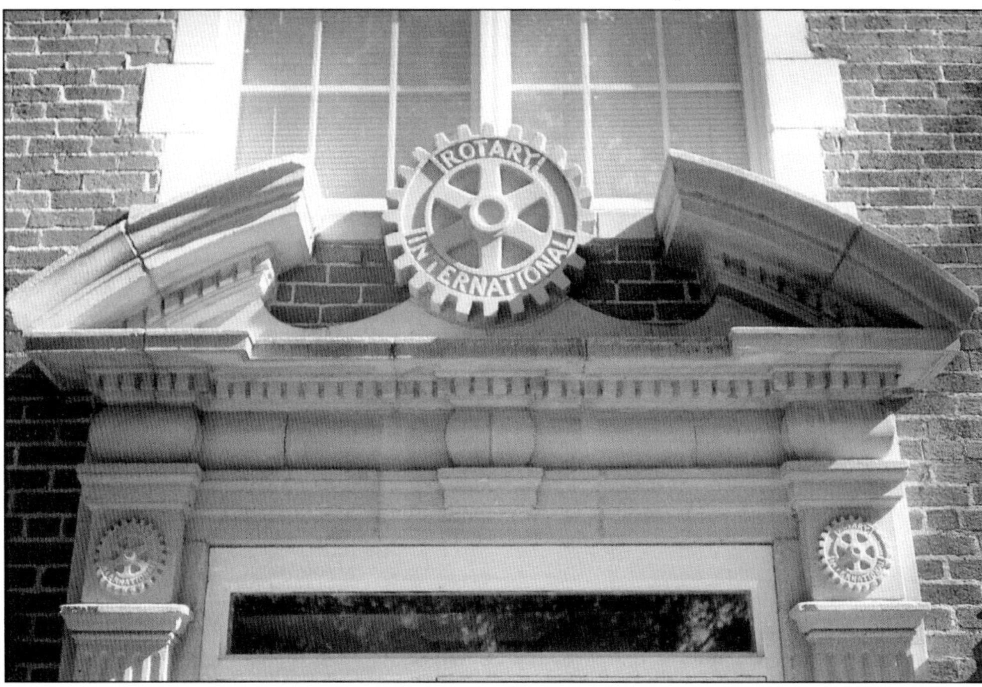

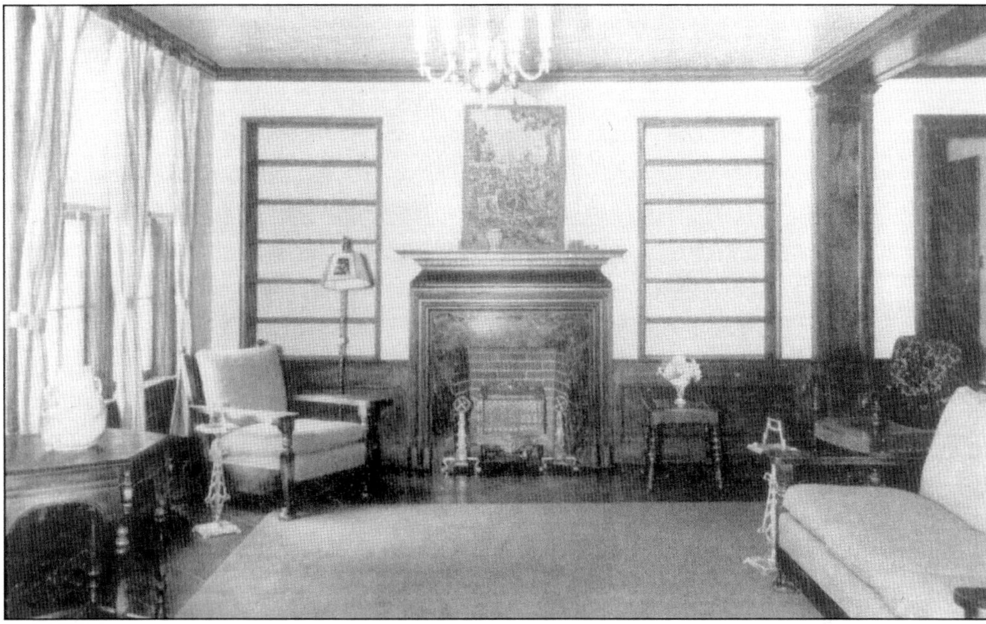

The living room, or reception room, of Rotary Hall is seen as it appeared shortly after the dormitory's completion. Rotary Hall today is Centenary's only co-ed dorm.

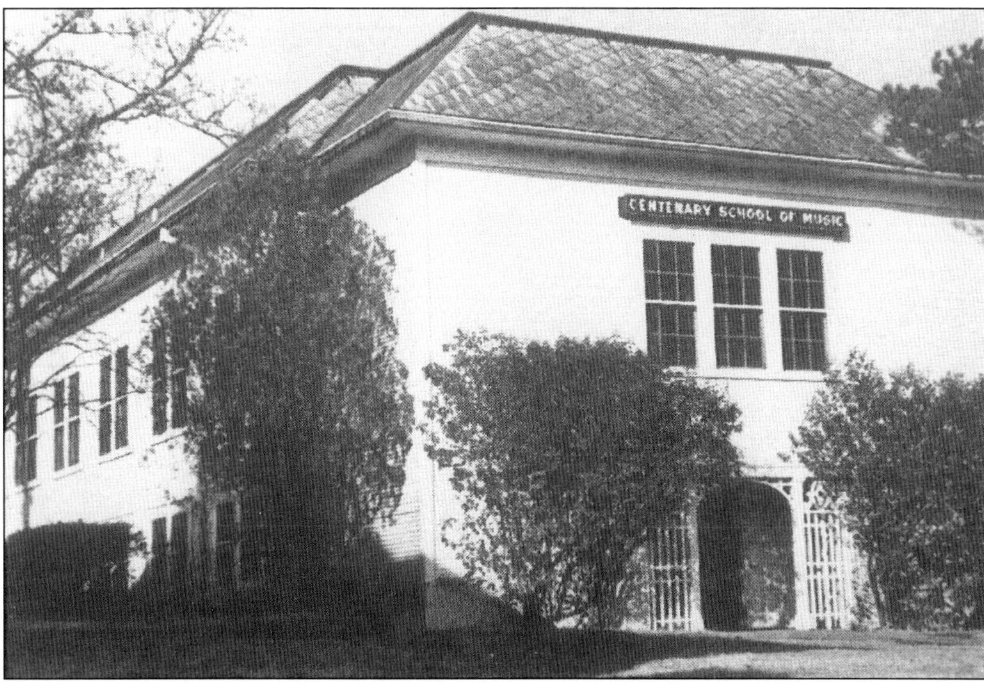

During the early 1920s, the music building or lyceum, together with the religion building or South Hall, were the first academic buildings constructed on the east side of the campus. Here the college's choir, now known the world-over, was formed in 1942. Before this, the college orchestra, glee club, and sextette were organized here, and gave regular concerts over Shreveport's KWKH radio station during the 1930s. The buildings stood on the present site of the Smith Building and adjacent parking lots.

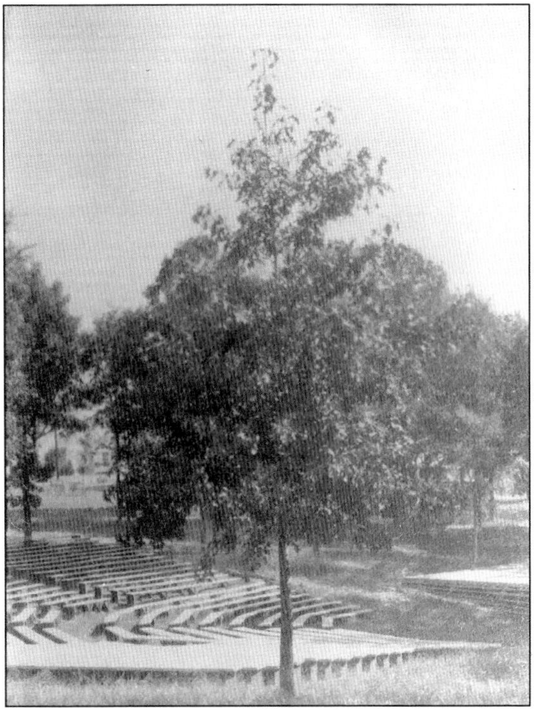

Another campus amenity added during the 1920s was the amphitheater, built in a natural basin near the center of the campus. Originally equipped with wooden benches and an open-air platform stage, it was located where today's amphitheater, with its permanent concrete benches and band shell, now stands.

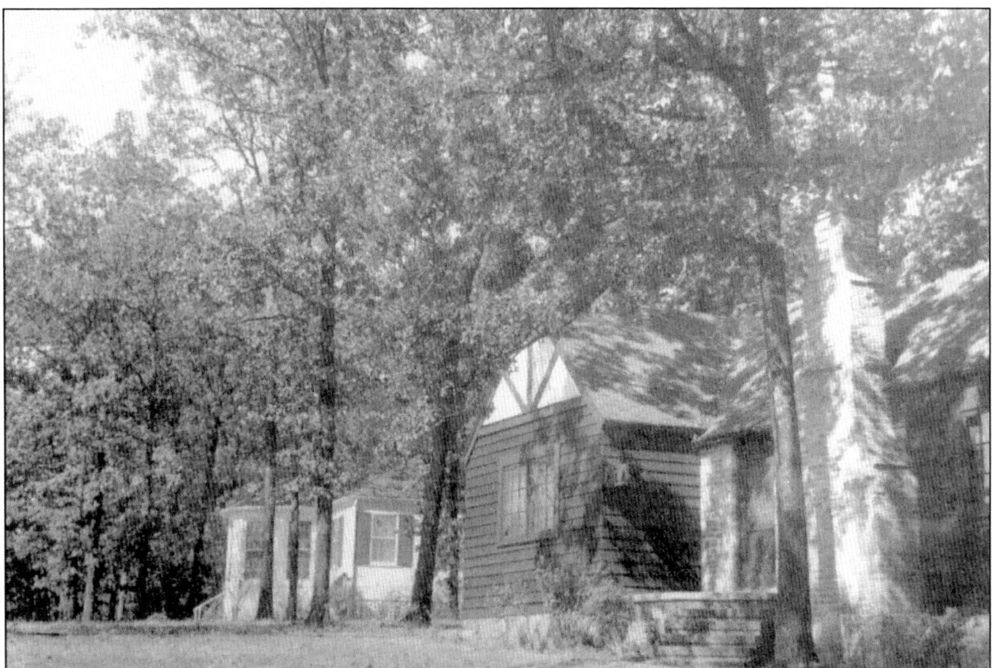

"Sorority Row" was originally located along Kings Highway, on the campus's south side. The first sorority established at Centenary was Zeta Tau Alpha, in 1927. Chi Omega followed in 1929 and Alpha Xi Delta in 1931. Seen here are the Zeta Tau Alpha house (left) and the Alpha Xi Delta house (right) in the 1930s. Both stood where Cline Hall stands today.

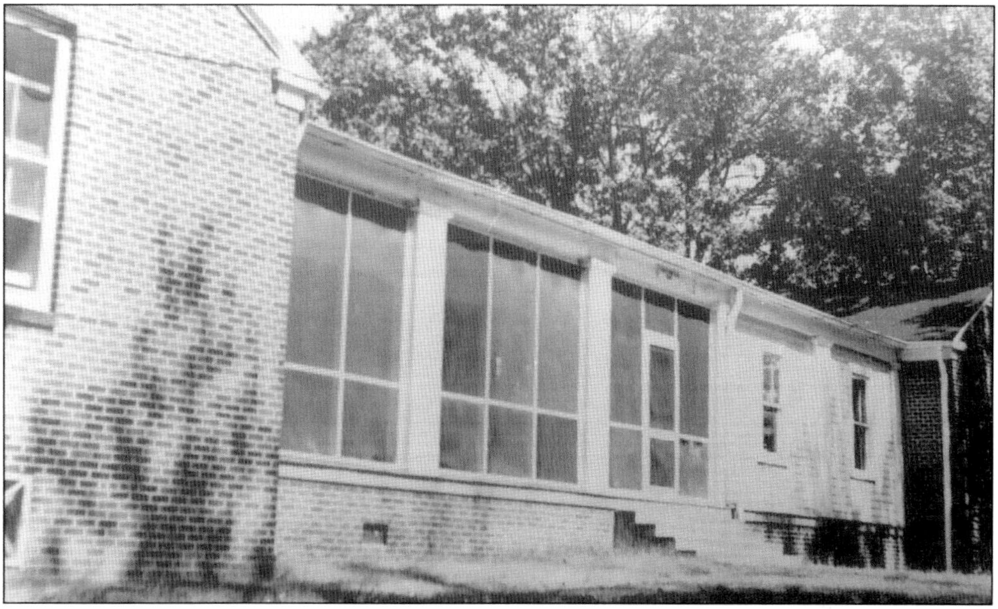

The late 1930s brought plans for a student union building to be constructed at the center of Centenary's campus, just to the east of the amphitheater. The resulting building, seen here in the 1940s, was later incorporated into the Moore Student Center, constructed in 1958.

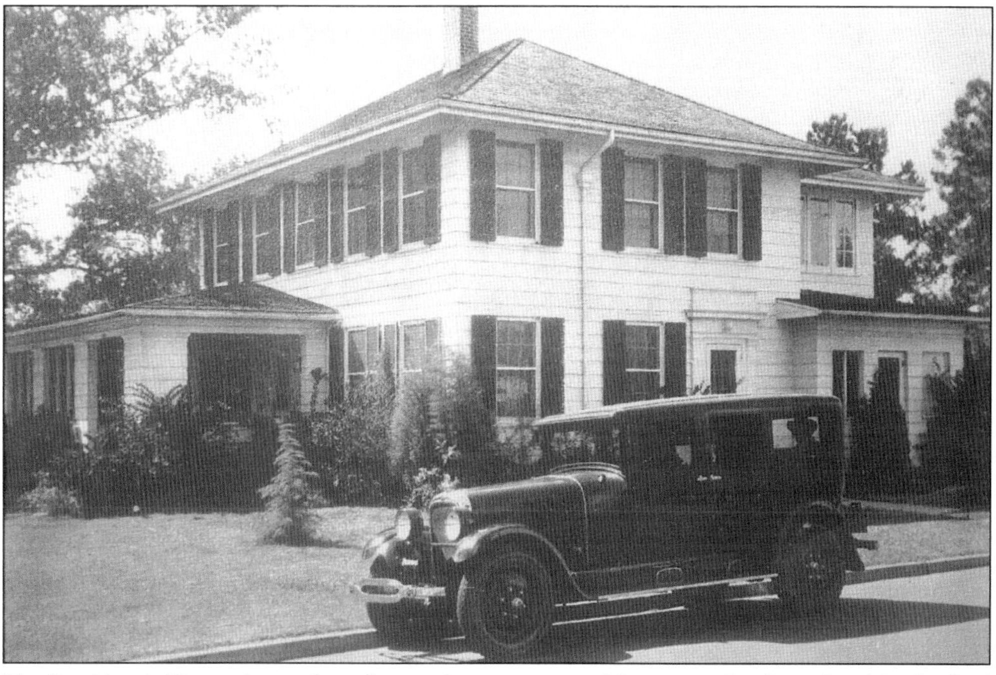

The President's House, located on the southwest corner of Centenary Boulevard and Rutherford Street, was built in 1922. George and Sallie Sexton were its first occupants. In 1965, the college acquired a new house for the president's use and this one was later remodeled and leased to an arts organization called the Craft Alliance. In 1985 it was enlarged and extensively remodeled, and an auditorium was constructed on its south side. The resulting facility now houses the Centenary Art Department and is known as the Sidney R. Turner Arts Center.

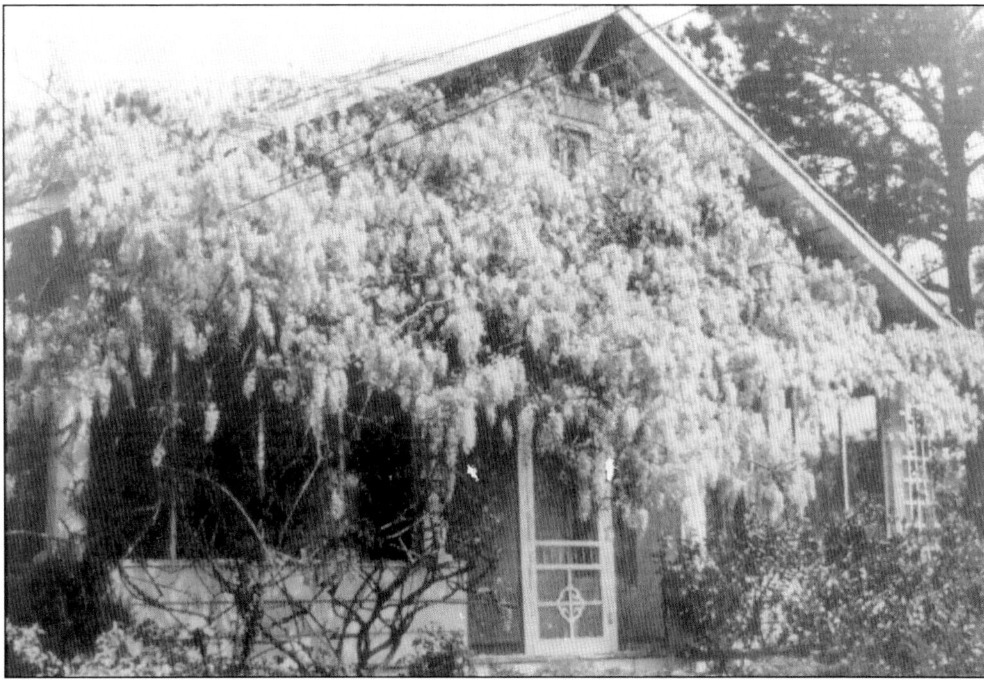

After stepping down from the presidency of Centenary College in 1932, Dr. and Mrs. Sexton moved from the President's House to this small wisteria-covered cottage on faculty row. Here, Dr. Sexton resided until his death in 1937; Mrs. Sexton lived here several years longer. In 1960 the George S. Sexton Memorial Residence Hall, a women's dormitory, was constructed where the house formerly stood.

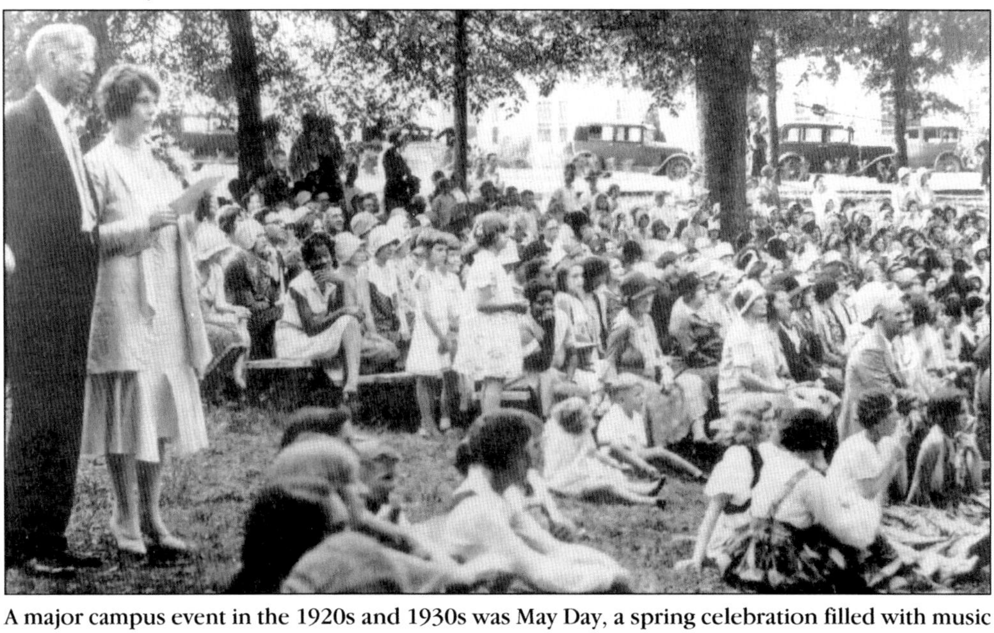

A major campus event in the 1920s and 1930s was May Day, a spring celebration filled with music and dramatic performances and the selection of a campus "May Queen." Here, an audience of both college students and Shreveport citizens watch a play in the amphitheater as Dr. Sexton and dramatics instructor Mrs. H. R. Nickerson observe at far left. The date is May 1, 1930.

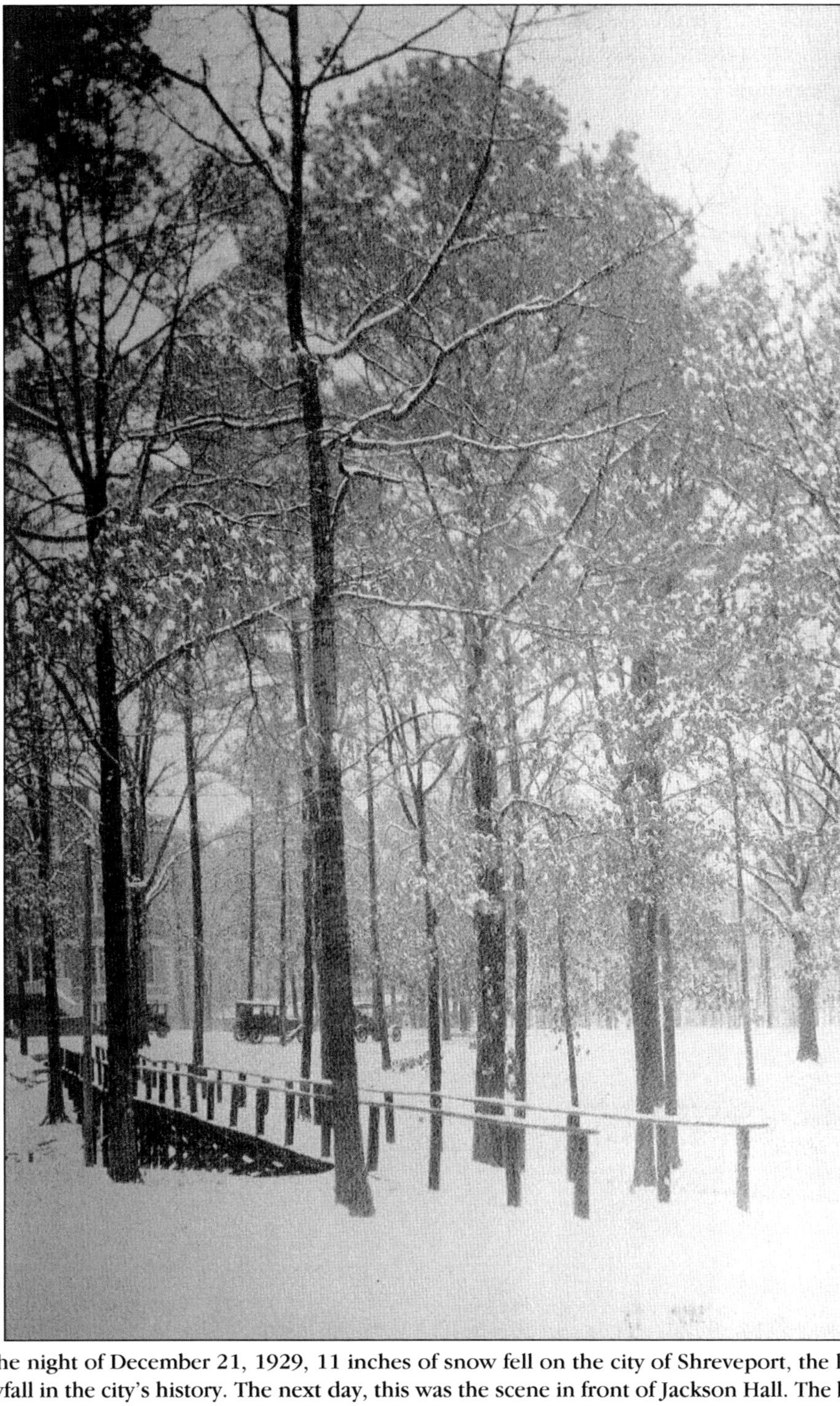

On the night of December 21, 1929, 11 inches of snow fell on the city of Shreveport, the largest snowfall in the city's history. The next day, this was the scene in front of Jackson Hall. The bridge in the foreground crossed the stream that now runs through the Crumley Gardens—the little stream was undoubtedly frozen that day. Jackson Hall is barely visible through the trees at left.

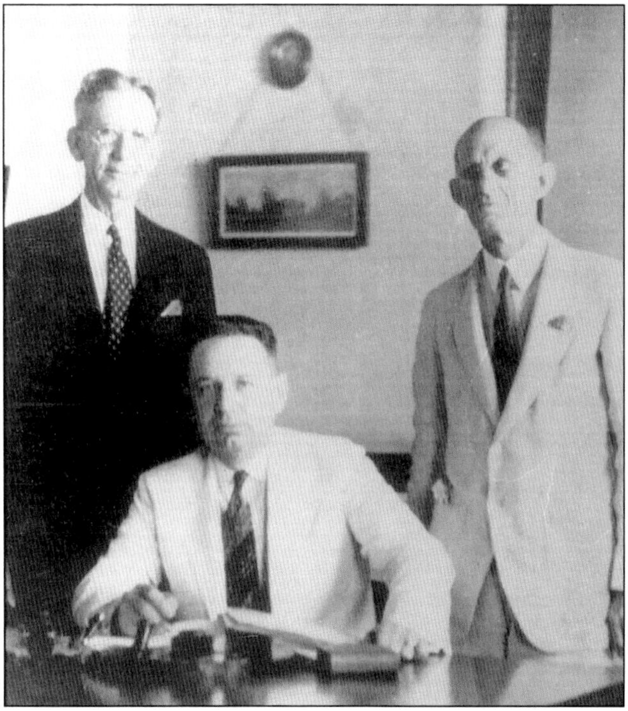

In 1932, Dr. Sexton stepped down as Centenary's president so that his time might be devoted more fully to promoting the college and raising funds for its development, without the encumbrances of day-to-day administrative concerns. Seen here in 1932, Dr. Sexton (left) hands over the reigns of Centenary to Dr. Angie Smith (center) as Dr. John L. Scales (right), chairman of the board of trustees, looks on. Dr. Scales, a Shreveport physician, was an 1892 Centenary graduate. He became a board member in 1919 and served the college faithfully until his death in 1969 at age 97. Dr. Smith later became a bishop.

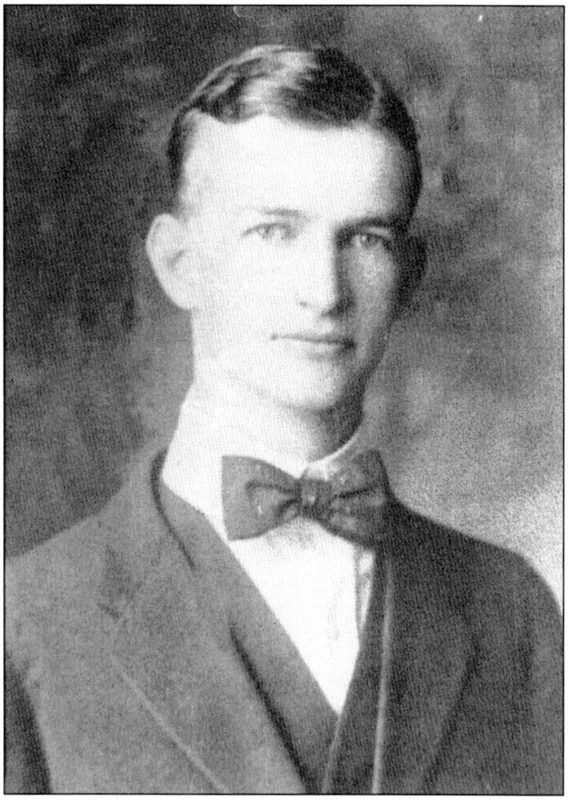

Another prominent and long-active board member was Paul Marvin Brown Jr., a 1917 graduate of Centenary who joined the board in the 1930s. When Dr. Sexton retired, Brown was offered the college presidency. He declined the position but was instrumental in pulling Centenary out of debt. During his chairmanship in the 1950s and 1960s, many of the campus's modern buildings were constructed. Brown, a Shreveport oilman, was active in Centenary's life for almost all of his. A third generation alumnus, his family has produced numerous Centenary graduates from the Jackson days to modern times. Brown Chapel is named in honor of the Brown family and an endowed chair is named in honor of Paul Brown, shown here in his student days.

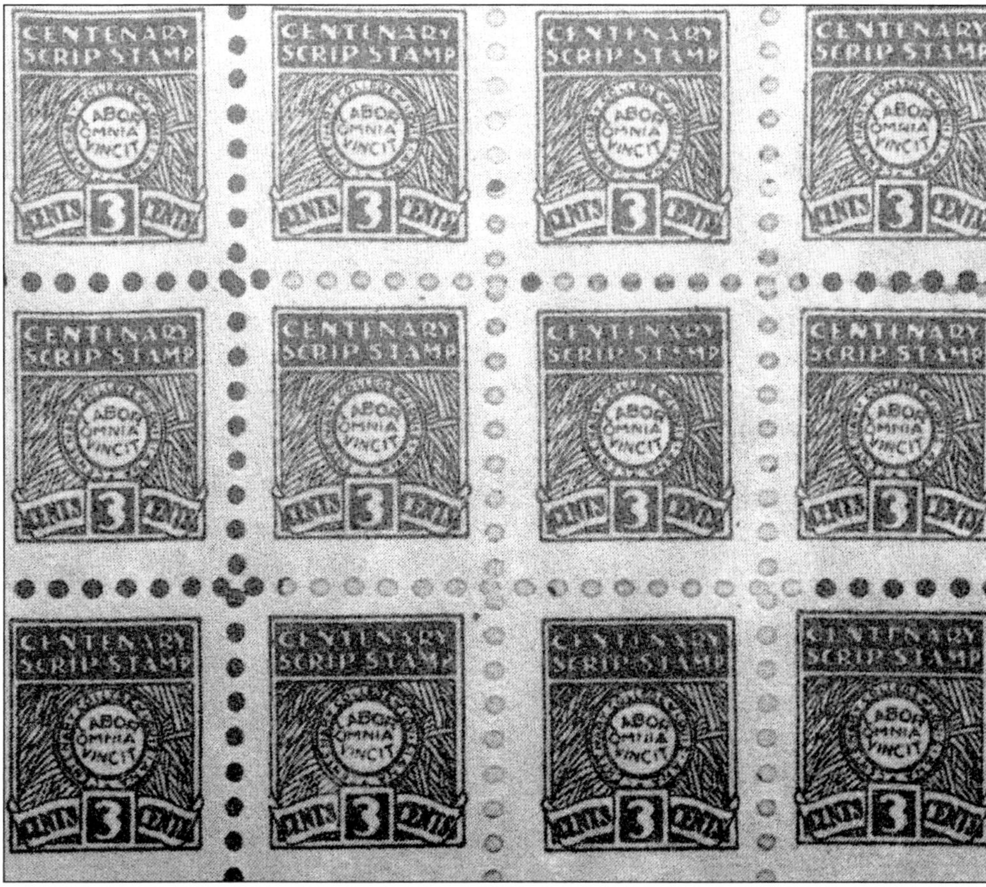

From 1933 through 1935, at the height of the Great Depression, Centenary developed a scrip system to tide it over through cash-poor times. Centenary's scrip was issued through the First National Bank of Shreveport, which would pay bearers for their stamps when presented in increments of $1 or more. The scrip was honored by most Shreveport area merchants and financial institutions during this period. Pictured above is part of a sheet of 3¢ scrip stamps; below is the cover of a redemption booklet containing a dollar's worth of the stamps.

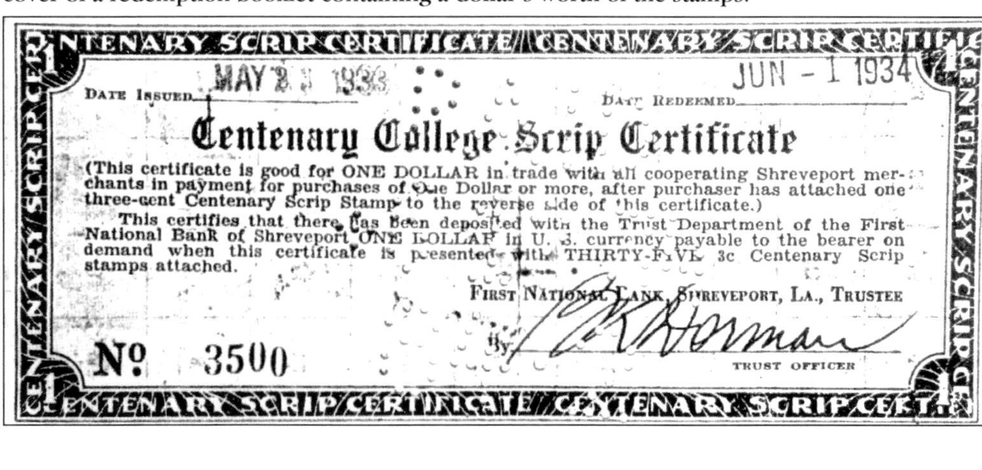

CENTENARY SCRIP CERTIFICATE

DATE ISSUED MAY 2 1933 DATE REDEEMED JUN - 1 1934

Centenary College Scrip Certificate

(This certificate is good for ONE DOLLAR in trade with all cooperating Shreveport merchants in payment for purchases of One Dollar or more, after purchaser has attached one three-cent Centenary Scrip Stamp to the reverse side of this certificate.)

This certifies that there has been deposited with the Trust Department of the First National Bank of Shreveport ONE DOLLAR in U. S. currency payable to the bearer on demand when this certificate is presented with THIRTY-FIVE 3c Centenary Scrip stamps attached.

FIRST NATIONAL BANK, SHREVEPORT, LA., TRUSTEE

By [signature] TRUST OFFICER

Nº 3500

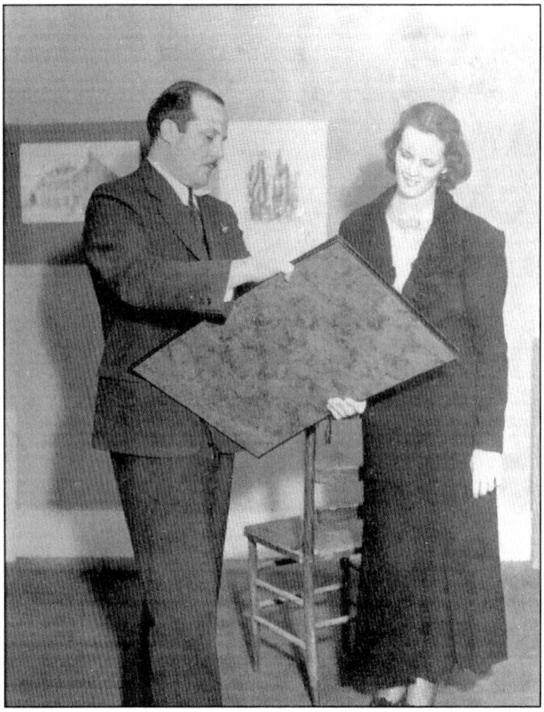

Don Brown, longtime professor of art at Centenary, was well known throughout the South for his paintings and charcoals. His unique artistic style was somewhat reminiscent of other artists working in the WPA genre of the Depression era. Here he is seen in 1934 with student Margaret Jane Taylor examining the design for the cover of the 1935 Yoncopin, Centenary's yearbook. The Yoncopin was first published in 1921. Its name, suggested by student Elizabeth Burgess, is that of a locally native water lily.

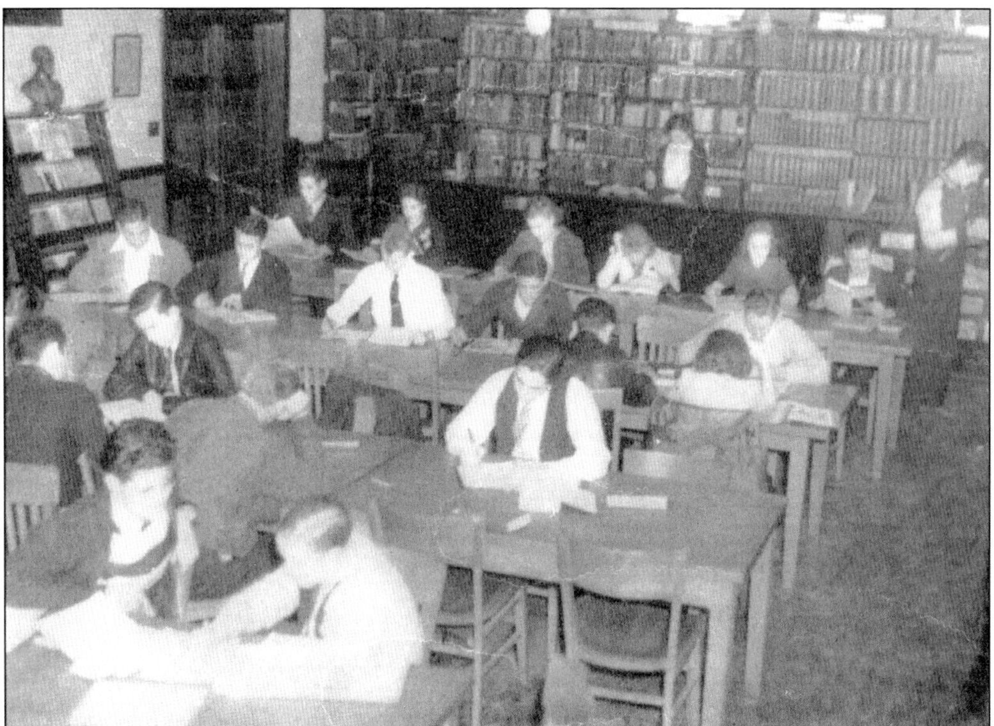

The interior of the library, housed in the former Arts Building, is seen as it appeared in the late 1930s. The main library contained some 23,000 volumes at that time, and the George Sexton Memorial Library contained many more specialized books on religious subjects.

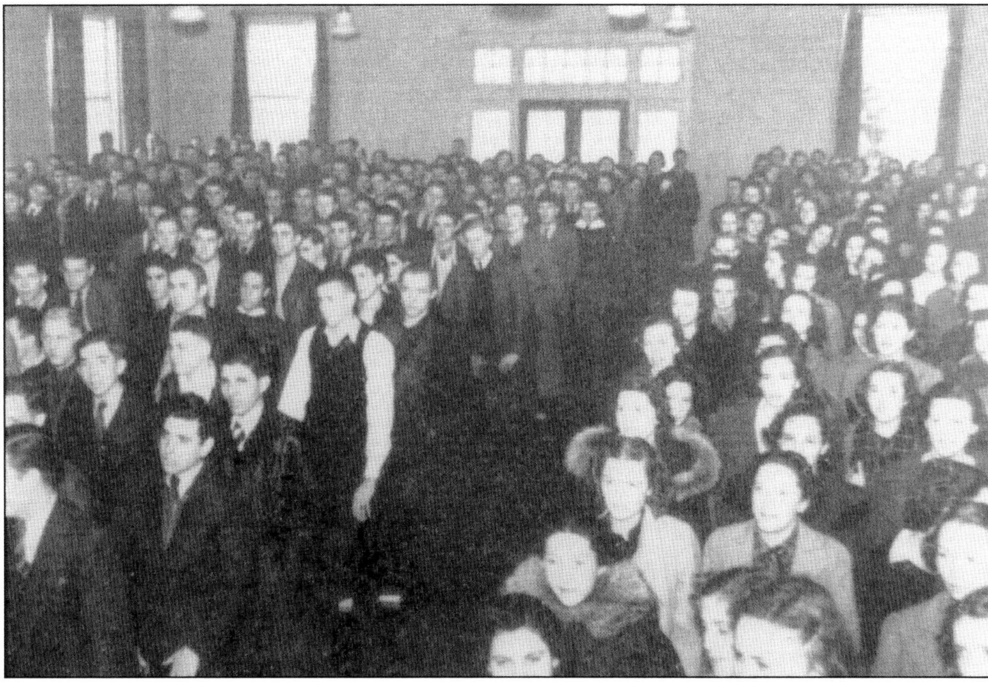

A service or convocation inside the chapel in 1937 is packed with students. In 1938, the chapel was re-named the George S. Sexton Memorial Chapel in memory of the school's late president. It was one of many memorials honoring Dr. Sexton at the college he did so much to build.

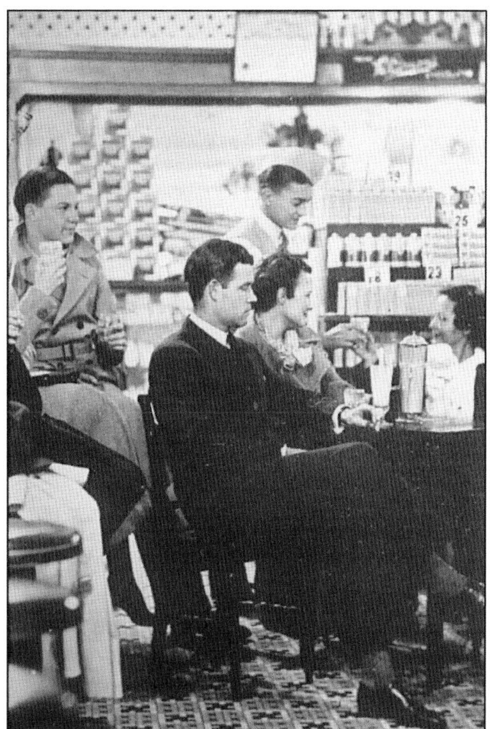

The Centenary Drug Store, across from the campus, was a popular gathering spot for students in the 1930s. Here students visit at the soda fountain in 1935. In the 1940s, the drug store's location became the Plaza Cafe, Shreveport's first Mexican restaurant. It was owned by Frank Cuellar, who co-founded the El Chico chain. Other popular close-to-campus student spots have been the P&B Drug Store in the 1930s, Strawn's Eat Shop since the 1940s, Murrell's and George's Grills since the early 1960s, Pizza King since the 1970s, and Joe's Bar and Grill since the early 1990s.

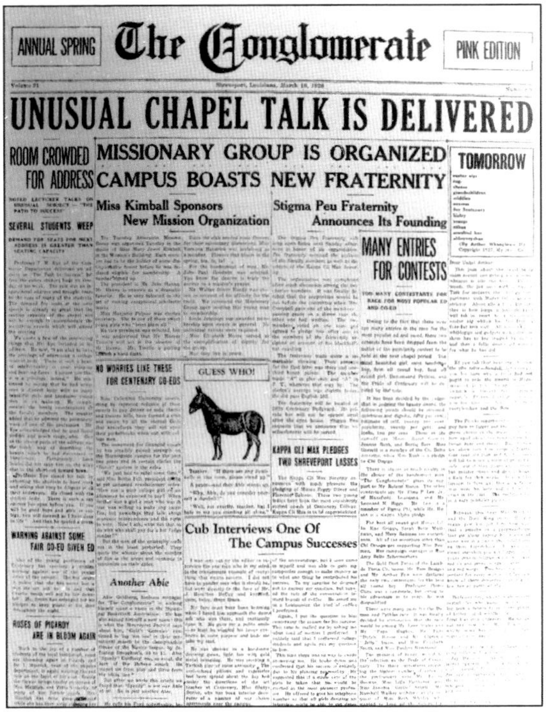

ANNUAL SPRING

The Conglomerate

PINK EDITION

Shreveport, Louisiana, March 18, 1928

UNUSUAL CHAPEL TALK IS DELIVERED

ROOM CROWDED FOR ADDRESS

NOTED LECTURER TALKS ON UNUSUAL SUBJECT — "THE PATH TO SUCCESS"

SEVERAL STUDENTS WEEP

DEMAND FOR SEATS FOR NEXT ADDRESS IS GREATER THAN SEATING CAPACITY

MISSIONARY GROUP IS ORGANIZED

CAMPUS BOASTS NEW FRATERNITY

Miss Kimball Sponsors New Mission Organization

Stigma Peu Fraternity Announces Its Founding

TOMORROW

MANY ENTRIES FOR CONTESTS

TOO MANY CONTESTANTS FOR RACE FOR MOST POPULAR ED AND CO-ED

NO WORRIES LIKE THESE FOR CENTENARY CO-EDS

GUESS WHO!

KAPPA CLI MAX PLEDGES TWO SHREVEPORT LASSES

Cub Interviews One Of The Campus Successes

WARNING AGAINST SOME FAIR CO-ED GIVEN ED

Another Abie

ROSES OF PICARDY ARE IN BLOOM AGAIN

The Conglomerate, Centenary College's weekly student-run newspaper, is the successor to *The Maroon and White*, founded at Jackson in 1890. In 1923, the name was changed to *The Conglomerate*, which it remains to this day. Shown here is the front page of the 1928 lampoon edition, long an annual tradition.

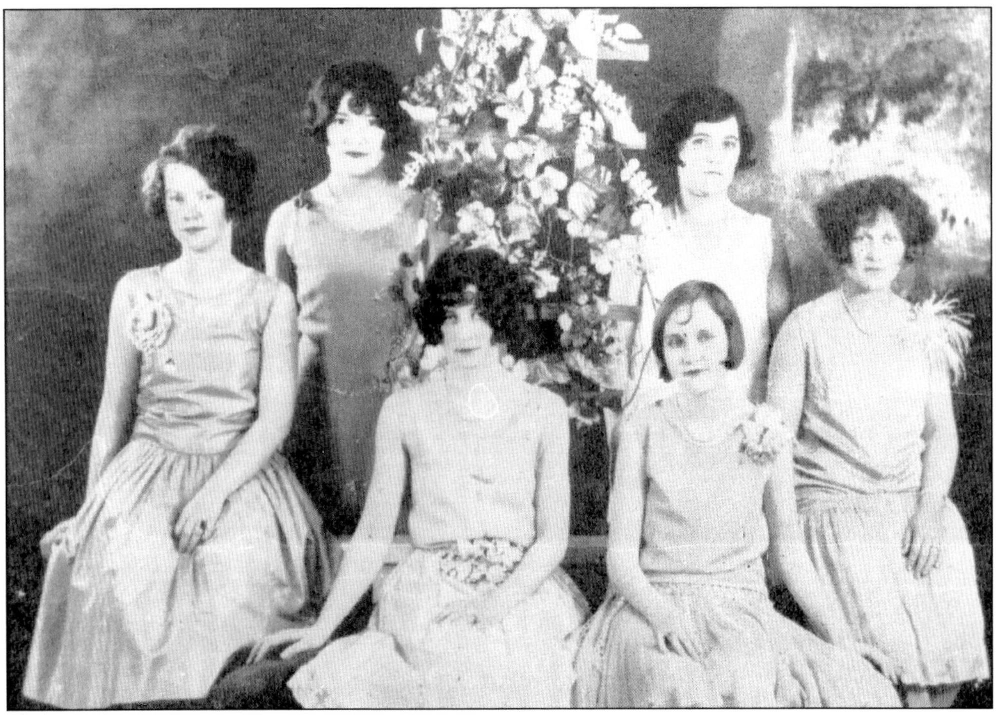

Another extracurricular activity begun in the 1920s was the college Glee Club. Established as an all-male singing club in 1922, its female accompaniment, the Sextette, was formed in 1925. Shown here is the first Sextette, which consisted of singers Bess Cargill, Mildred Webb, Annie Brown, Genevieve Reed, Hazel Smith, and Doris Bush.

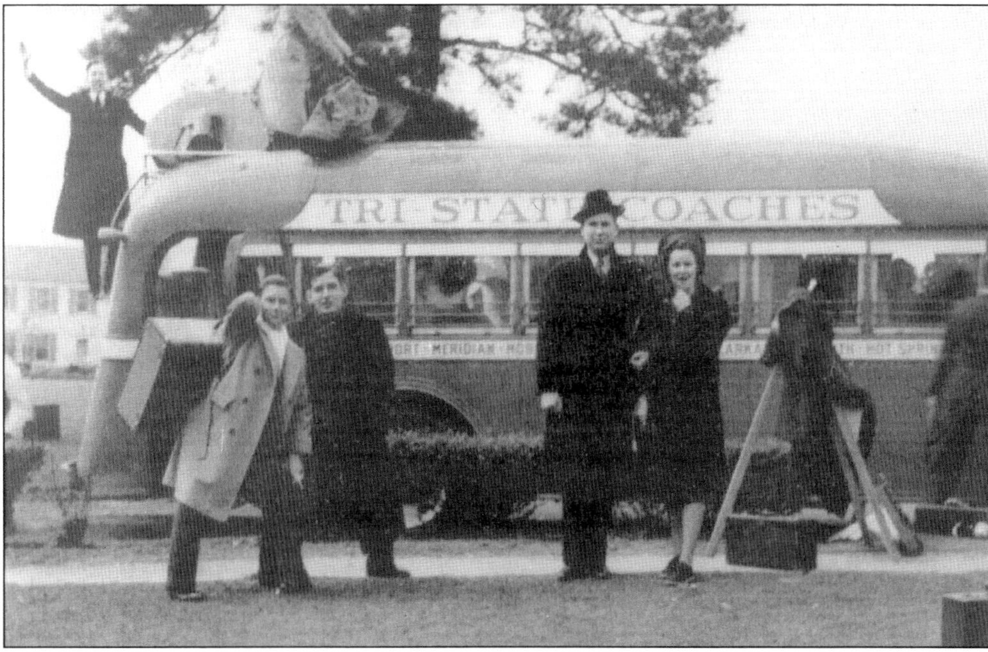

Kollege Kapers was one of the most popular clubs at Centenary during the 1930s, '40s, and '50s. A variety show put on by students, Kollege Kapers traveled around the region performing for audiences in communities with little other live entertainment, as well as in Shreveport and on campus. Founded in 1933, the Kapers crew first traveled by train and then by motor coach as seen above in the late 1930s. Below is a scene from a Kollege Kapers performance a decade later. From left to right are Louis Sicard, Fred Rogers, and Dave Freeman. Sicard was later a noted visual artist.

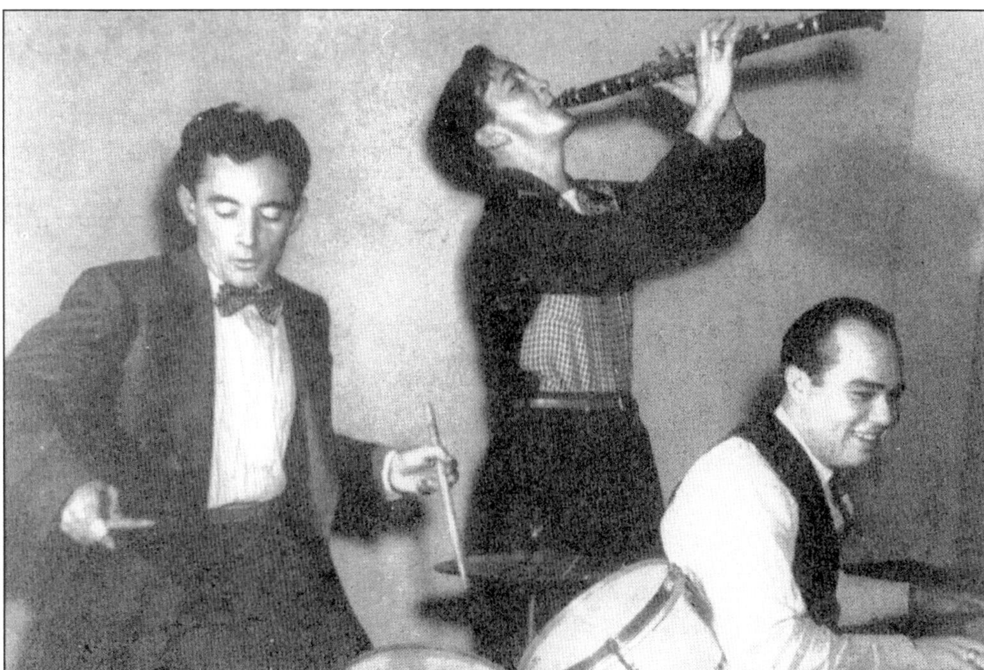

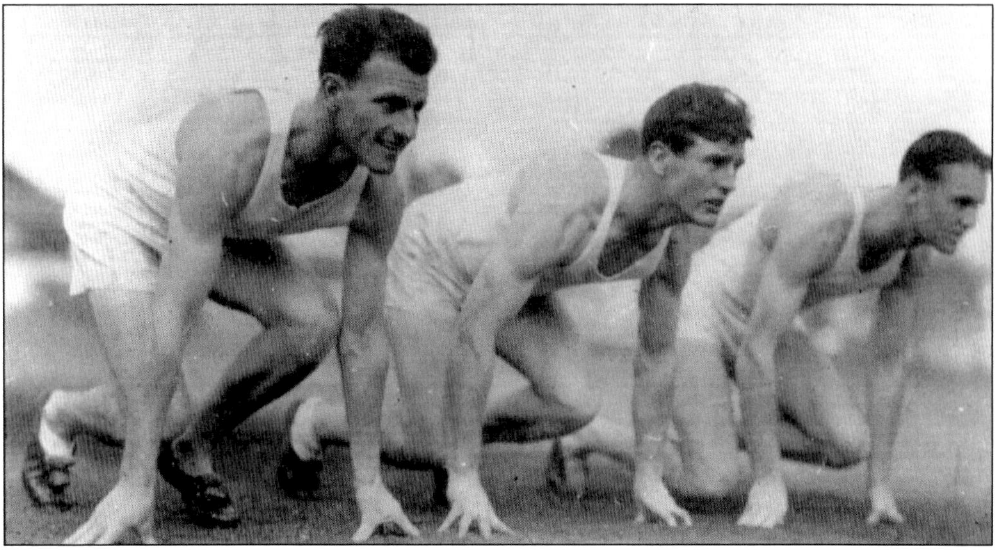

Centenary's athletic program became a major part of the school's life in the 1920s. President Sexton was as strong a supporter of intercollegiate athletics as Bishop Keener had been an opponent of them. Under Sexton's leadership, the athletic program was expanded to include such sports as track and archery. Above is the track team in 1928; seen below is women's archery in the 1930s.

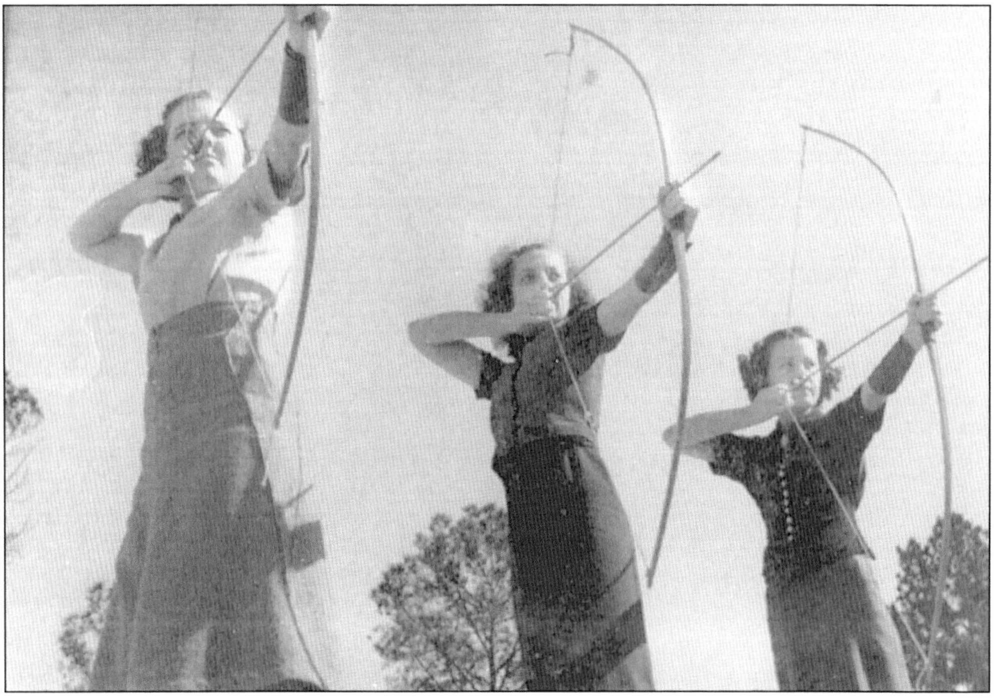

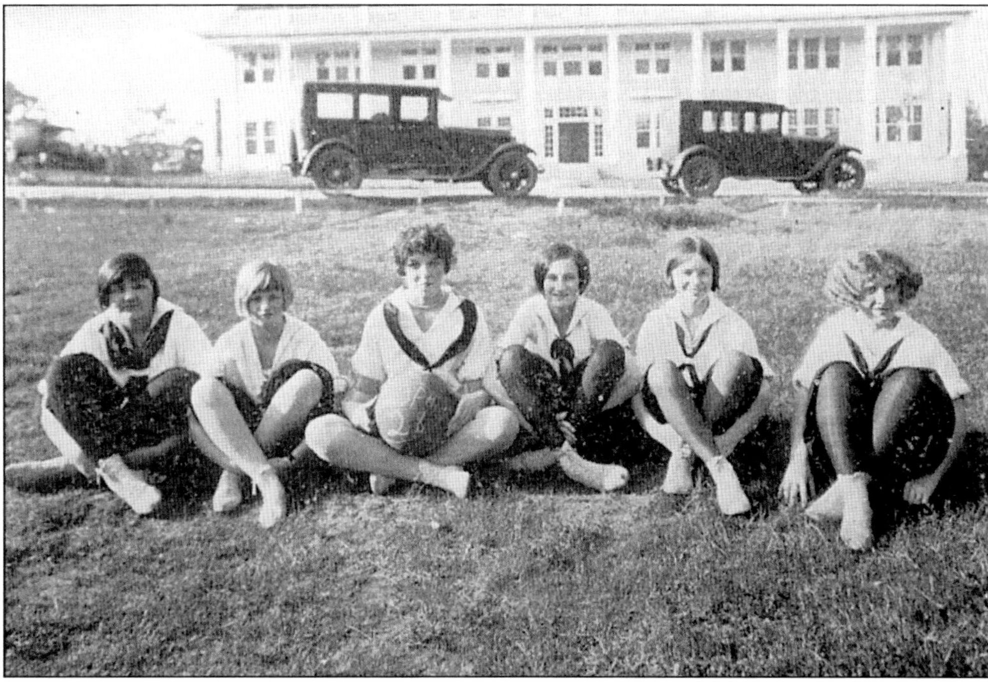

The participation of women in college sports was enthusiastically supported by the college during the Sexton era. Besides archery, golf, tennis, and marksmanship were included in the women's athletic program, as were basketball and riding. Above is the 1928 sophomore girls' basketball team in front of Colonial Hall. Below, the 1936 equestrian team lines up in almost the same location.

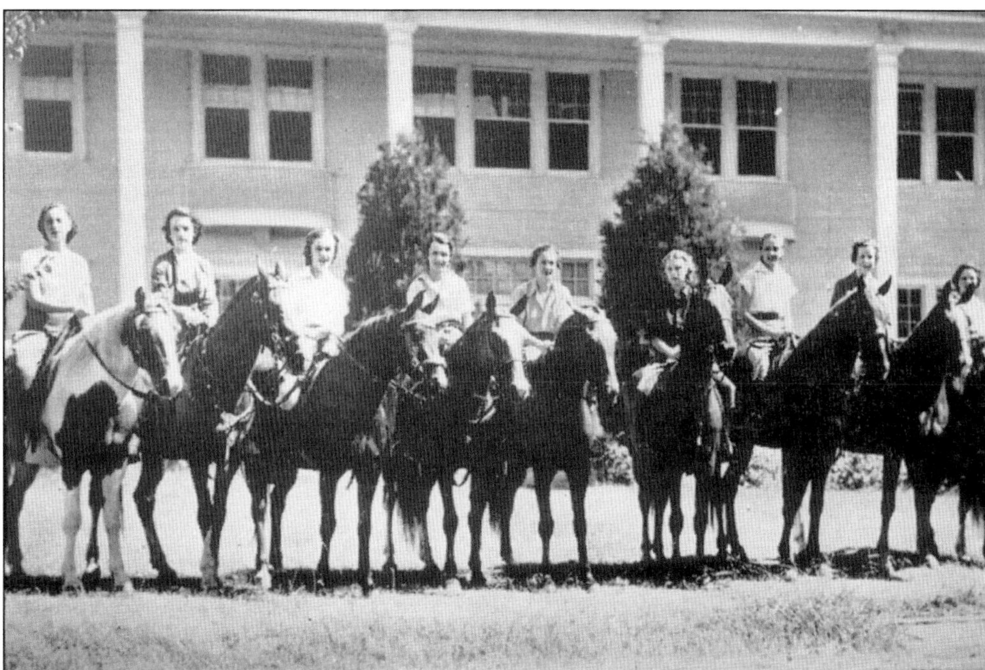

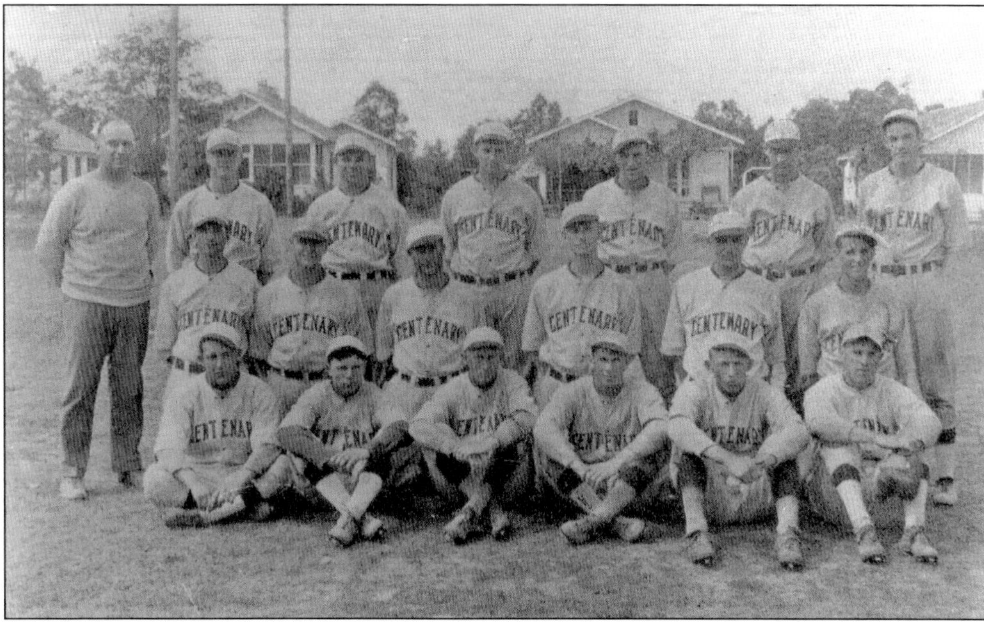

Varsity baseball returned to Centenary in the 1910s, but was not particularly well organized until the 1920s. Here, the 1928 team poses with Coach Norton (left) on the diamond, with Faculty Row in the background. The baseball diamond in those days was located where Hamilton Hall and the Magale Library are today. The gymnasium, Dr. Sexton's "wooden wonder," as it was known, stood just south of the diamond, where Mickle Hall is today.

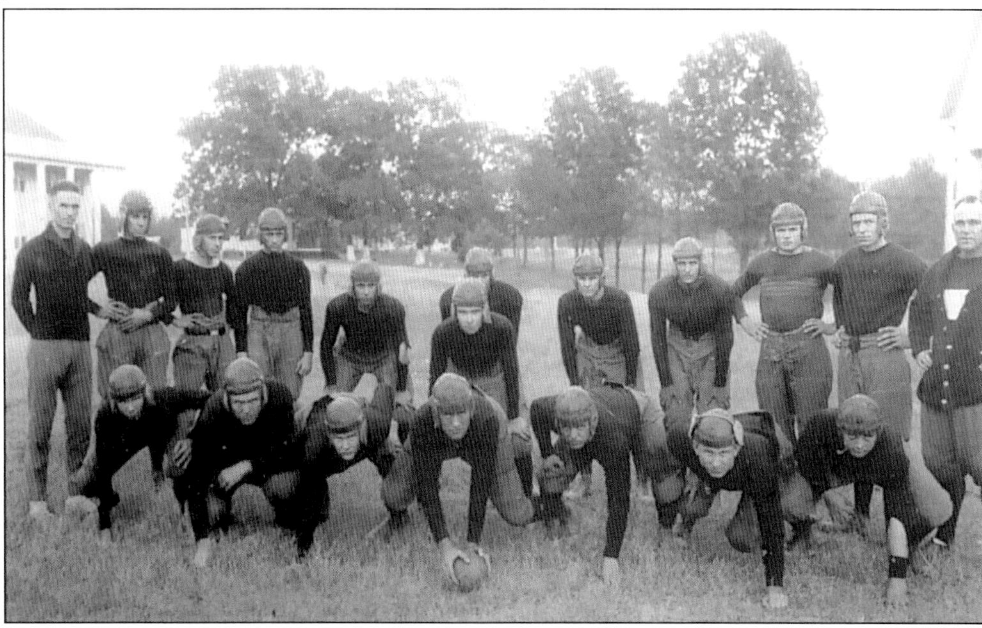

The Centenary football team of 1921 posed between Colonial Hall (left) and the chapel (right), with the site of the amphitheater just behind them. Coach Norton is pictured at far right. It was at about this time that Dr. Sexton changed the team name from "Ironsides" to "Gentlemen." This was the beginning of an unprecedented era for Centenary football, which brought national attention to the college.

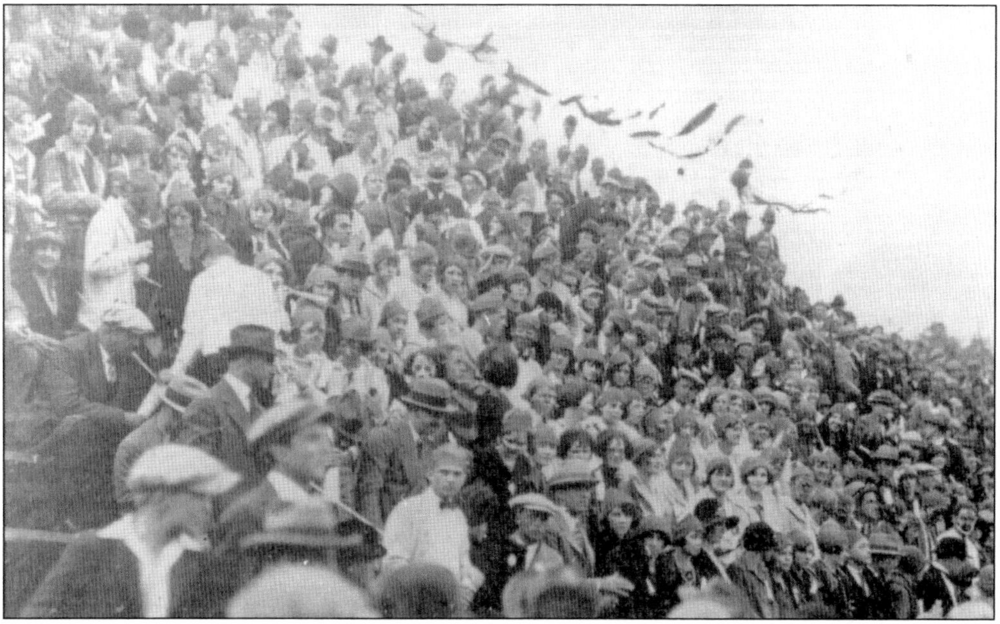

The Centenary Stadium, built across Kings Highway from the main campus, was completed in 1932 and represented the first expansion of the campus from its original acreage. It was the gift of oilman Arch Haynes, an enthusiastic supporter of Centenary athletics and of the college in general. It held 15,000 spectators and was usually filled to capacity. The stadium was demolished after World War II to build housing for returning veterans attending Centenary on the G.I. Bill; today's baseball field occupies its site. Above, a capacity crowd attends a home game in the first stadium in 1926—it stood where Hardin Field is today. Below, Centenary quarterback Manning Smith is seen in an off-tackle slant in the 1933 Centenary v. Texas A&M game, which Centenary won, 20 to 0. This game was held in the big new stadium.

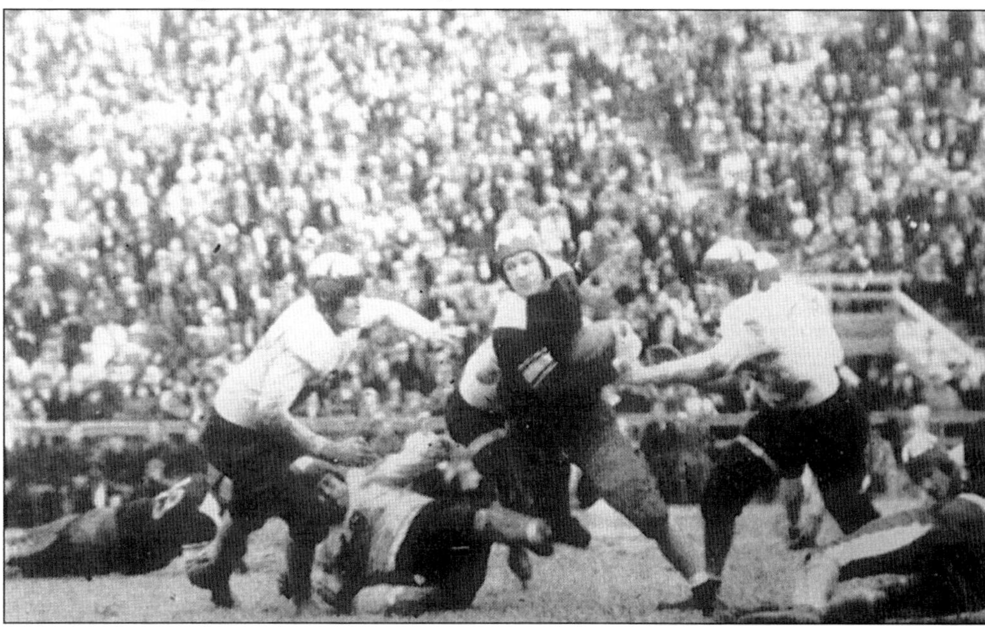

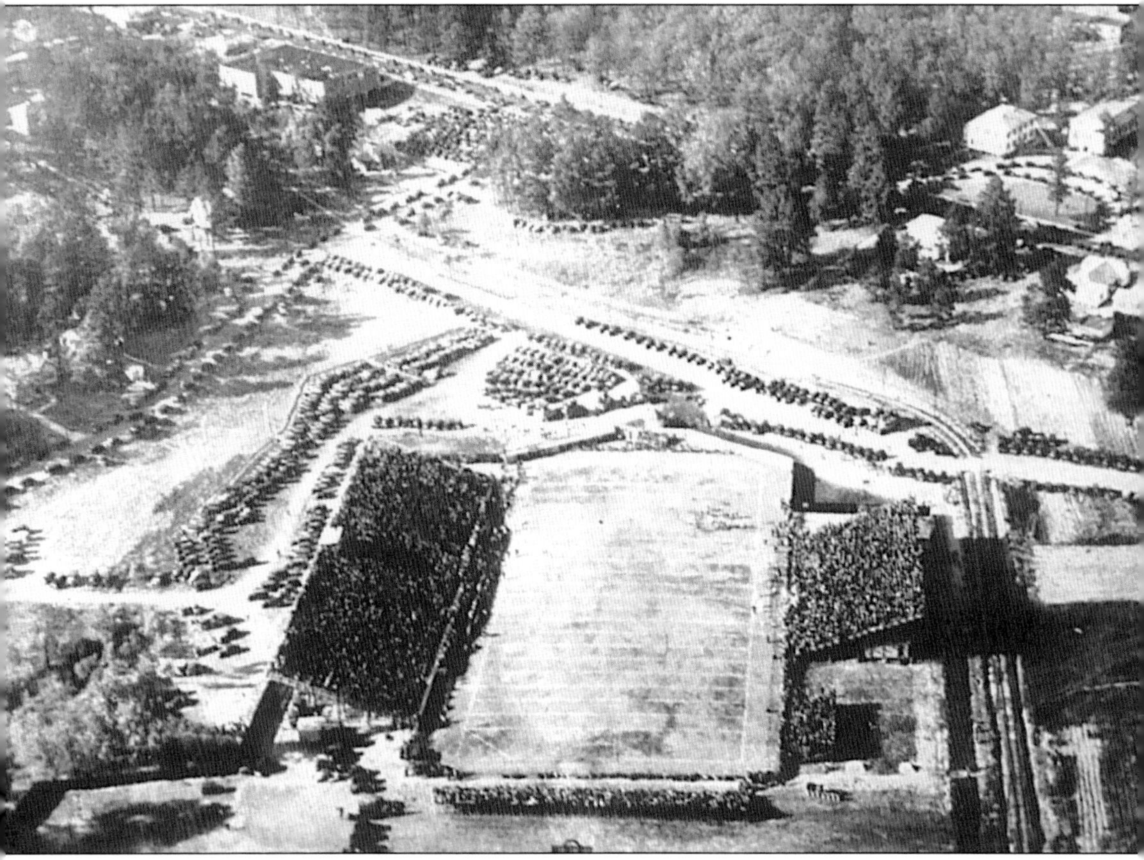

The 1932 Centenary v. LSU game was played to a packed crowd at the Centenary stadium, seen here from the air at half-time. Among those in attendance was Louisiana Governor Huey P. Long, who was responsible for building LSU's athletic program at the same time Dr. Sexton was building Centenary's. Long, who was assassinated in Baton Rouge in 1935, was one of the state's—and nation's—most controversial political figures at the time. A resident of Shreveport and, ironically, of the Centenary area (his house is now a National Register of Historic Places-listed landmark, located just two blocks from Centenary's campus), Long said he attended the game not only to see LSU win, but to see Centenary defeated on its own turf by his rival "Fighting Tigers." Instead, the game ended with Centenary undefeated. In this photograph, Kings Highway may be seen running across the top at the south edge of the main campus. The old religion and music buildings are visible at upper right.

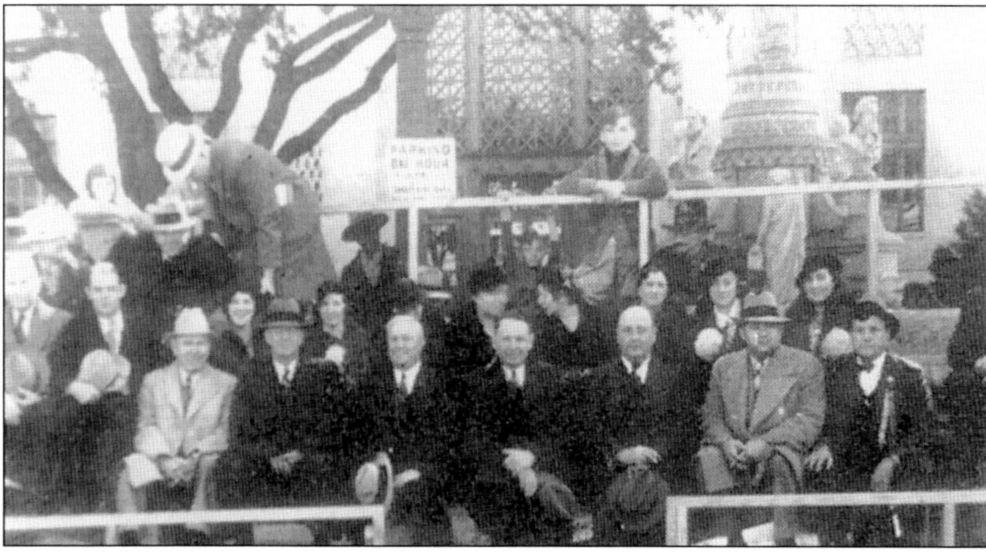

Dignitaries from Centenary, LSU, and the City of Shreveport watch the pre-game parade on Texas Street prior to the big Centenary v. LSU football game of 1932. Centenary's President Angie Smith is at front row, center, Gov. Huey Long, in a light-colored coat and wearing a hat, is seated one person away from Dr. Smith's right. The Caddo Parish Courthouse is in the background.

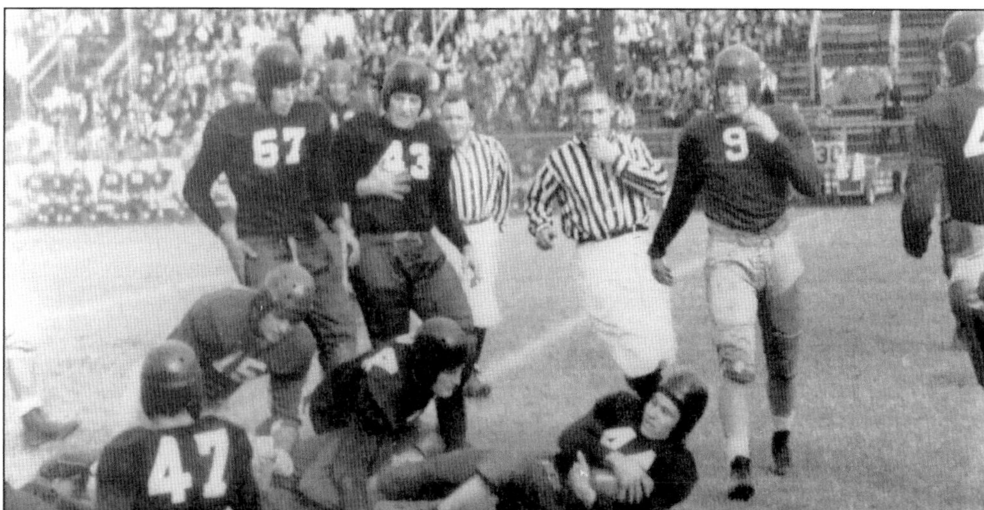

During the 1920s and 1930s, Centenary College was a terror among the powers in college football. Under outstanding coaches such as Bo McMillan, Homer Norton, and Curtis Parker, and with many equally outstanding players, Centenary's football team enjoyed numerous undefeated seasons and brought much valuable attention to the school during its halcyon days. This scene, of the Centenary v. Loyola game of 1938, is from that era. A shortage of male students during World War II followed by the post-war removal of the stadium, together with soaring expenses, brought about the end of football at Centenary. The year 1948 saw the last football season for the college when President Joe Mickle vowed that never again would Centenary fall into debt over football or put the game ahead of academic expenditures.

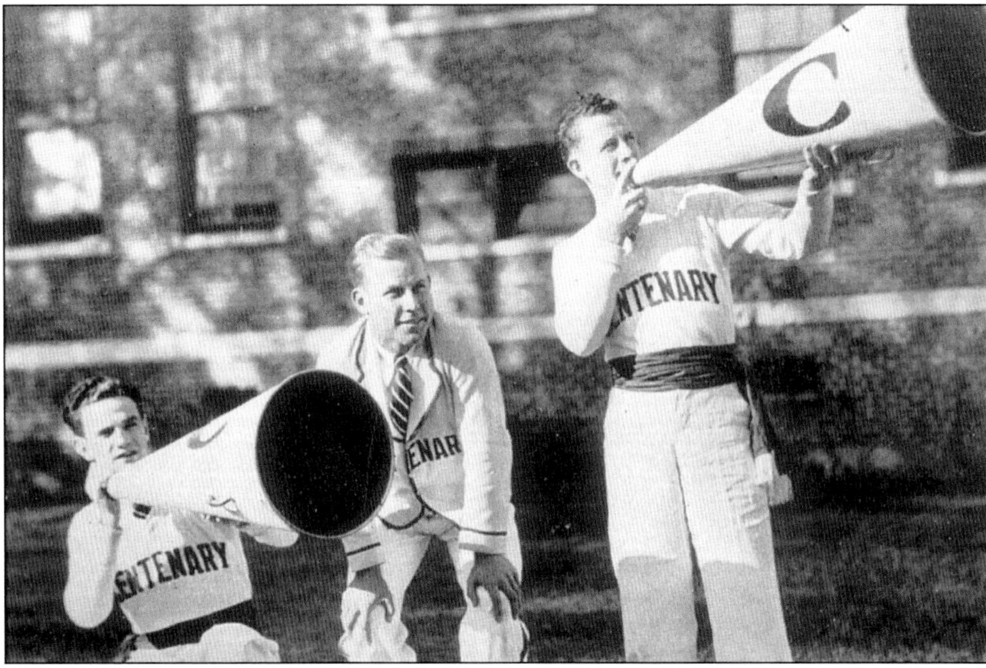

During the height of Centenary football, cheerleaders were an important element of the festivities surrounding the games, leading students and school supporters in spirited cheers of encouragement for their team. Above, three male members of the cheerleading squad pose next to the Arts Building in 1931. Below, some seven years later, members of the now-co-ed squad clap for Centenary on the field of the stadium. Today, Centenary's cheerleading squad, now all-female, still enthusiastically generate school support for the Gentlemen's basketball games.

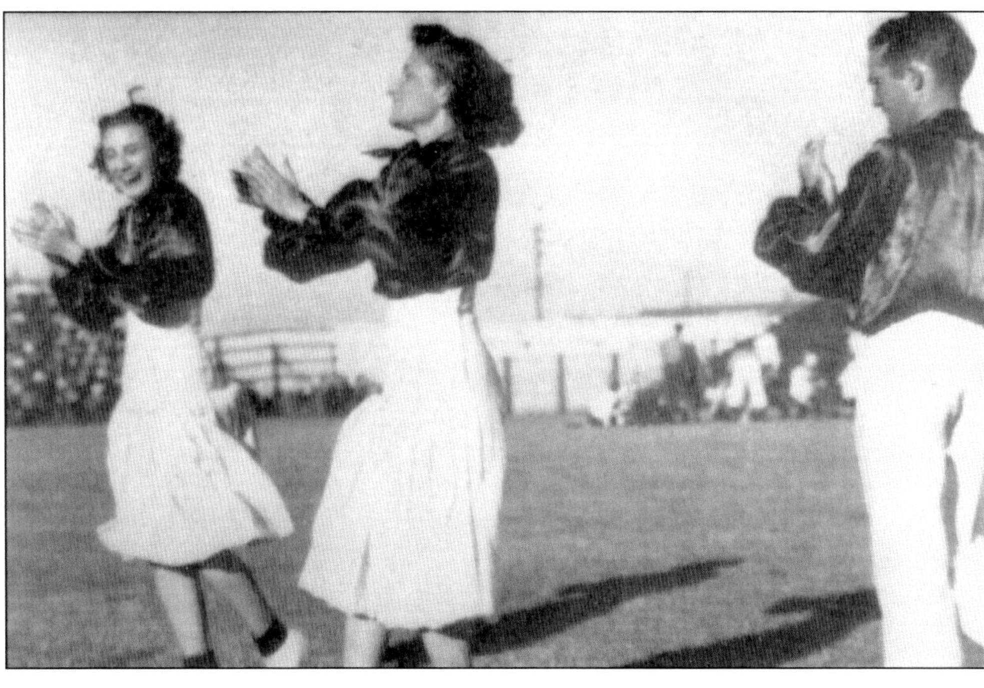

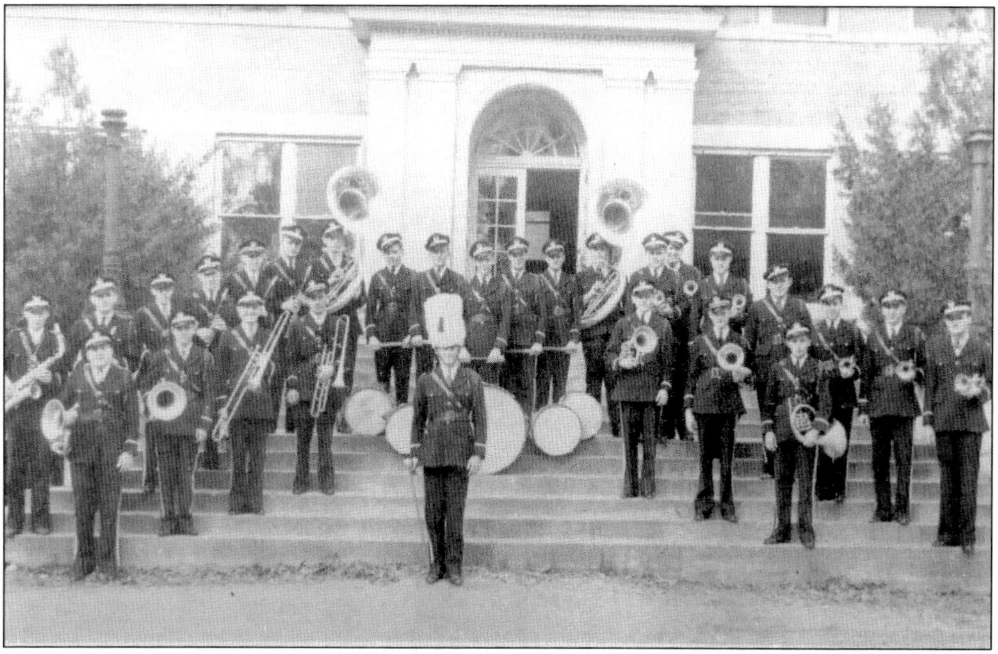

Another important element of Centenary football games was the Centenary band. Although Centenary had had a band back in the Jackson days, it was a concert band formed to entertain at school functions, much as the orchestra might. The band which began in the 1910s supported the school's athletic events, and by the 1920s had become an indispensable element at every football game. Seen above is the Centenary band of 1933 on the steps of Jackson Hall; Dr. S.D. Morehead was its leader. Below is the band at the stadium in 1938, the first year with female members.

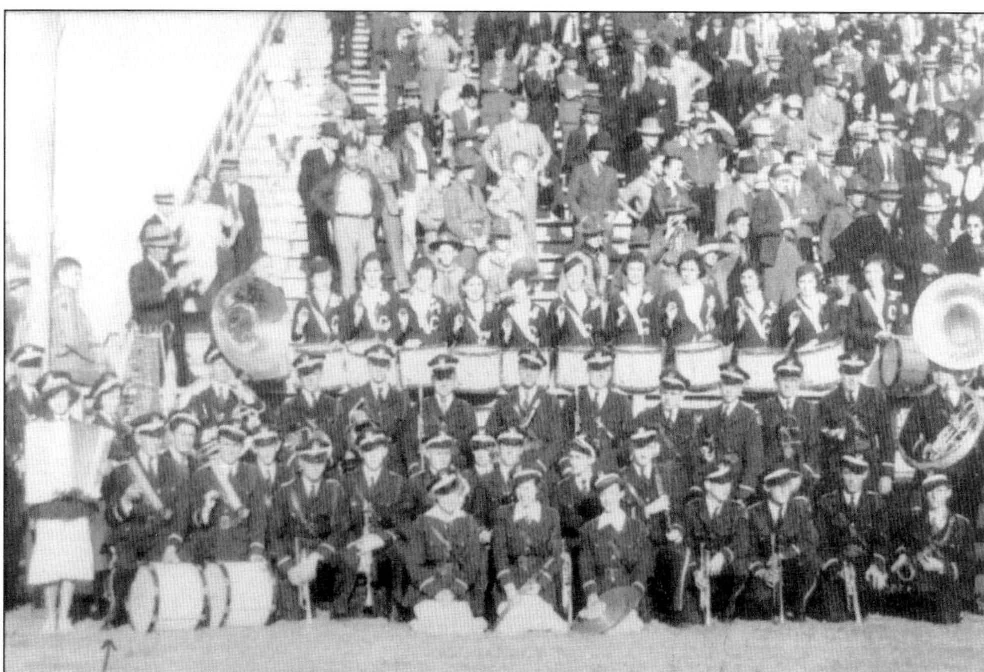

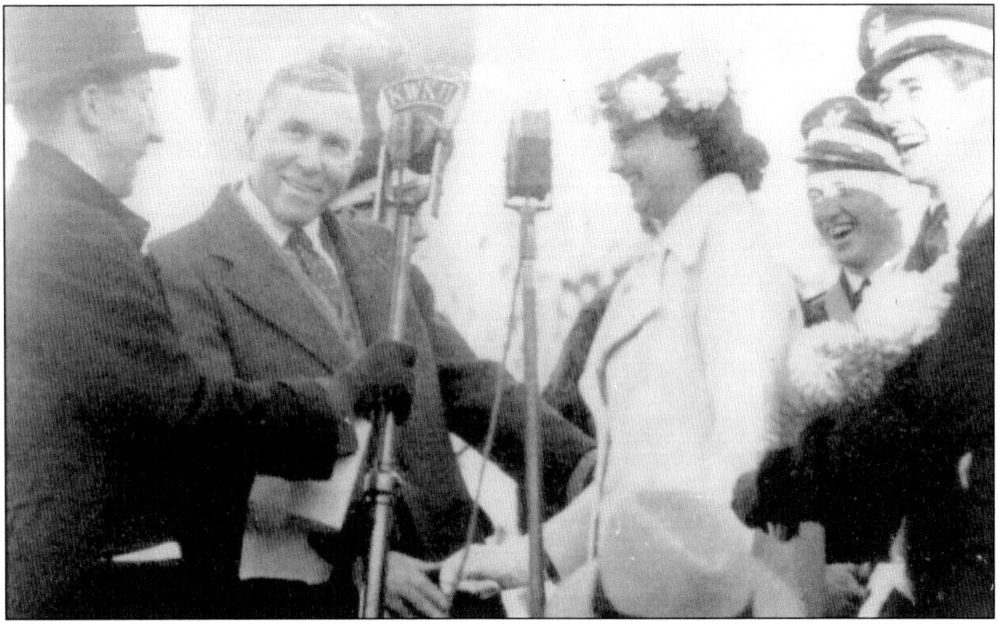

Dr. Pierce Cline became Centenary's president in 1933 and remained in office until his death ten years later. Like Dr. Sexton, Cline was a strong supporter of Centenary athletics, particularly football. At top Dr. Cline (second from left) crowns Homecoming Queen Jessie Mae Sexton at the 1938 homecoming game, which was broadcast nationwide. Below is Haynes Gymnasium, completed in 1936 and still in use today. Haynes Gym was given by Arch Haynes, who also gave the school's stadium during the Sexton era. First called the Centenary College Physical Education Building, it was re-named Haynes Memorial Gymnasium in the 1950s following Mr. Haynes' death. A monument of the Cline presidency at Centenary, it is still in use today, having undergone extensive refurbishing in 1985 and again in 1999–2000.

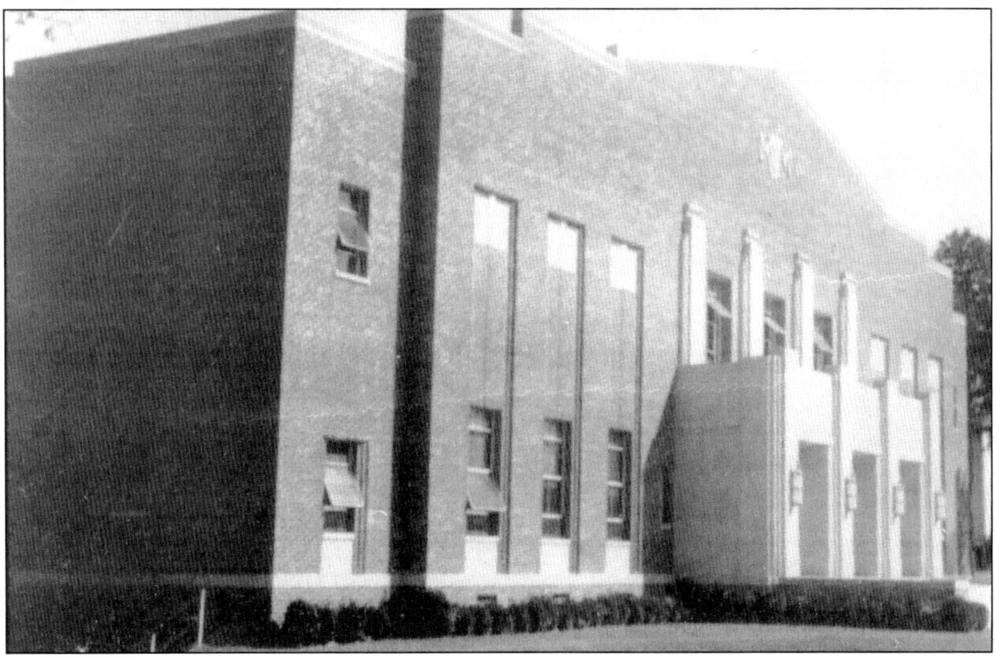

Four

The 1940s and 1950s

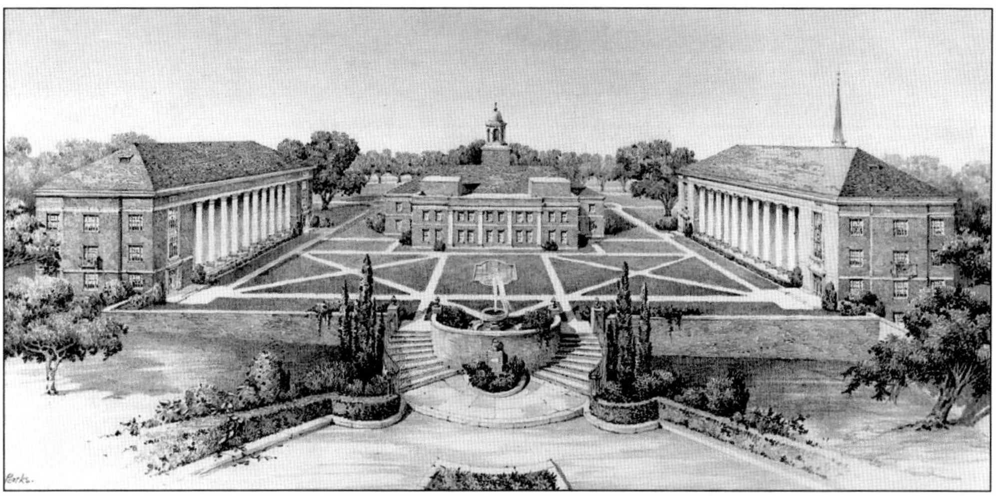

After World War II, Centenary embarked upon a new building program, one even more ambitious than that commenced in 1922. The ultimate result of this new program would be the campus of today. J. Cheshire Peyton was called upon to develop a plan for several large buildings on the campus's eastern side, facing Woodlawn Avenue. A prominent Shreveport architect, Peyton was formerly employed by the Neild firm, which had designed the first large-scale campus building program. The original scheme, shown here, called for a Colonial Revival-style library to be flanked by two massive Neo-Classical classroom buildings. In the view above, seen from a vantage point above the present Student Union Building, the back of the proposed library is at center with the proposed liberal arts building at left and the proposed science building at right. The spire of the proposed chapel rises above the science building. Except for the liberal arts building, the plan was eventually executed much as depicted in this rendering.

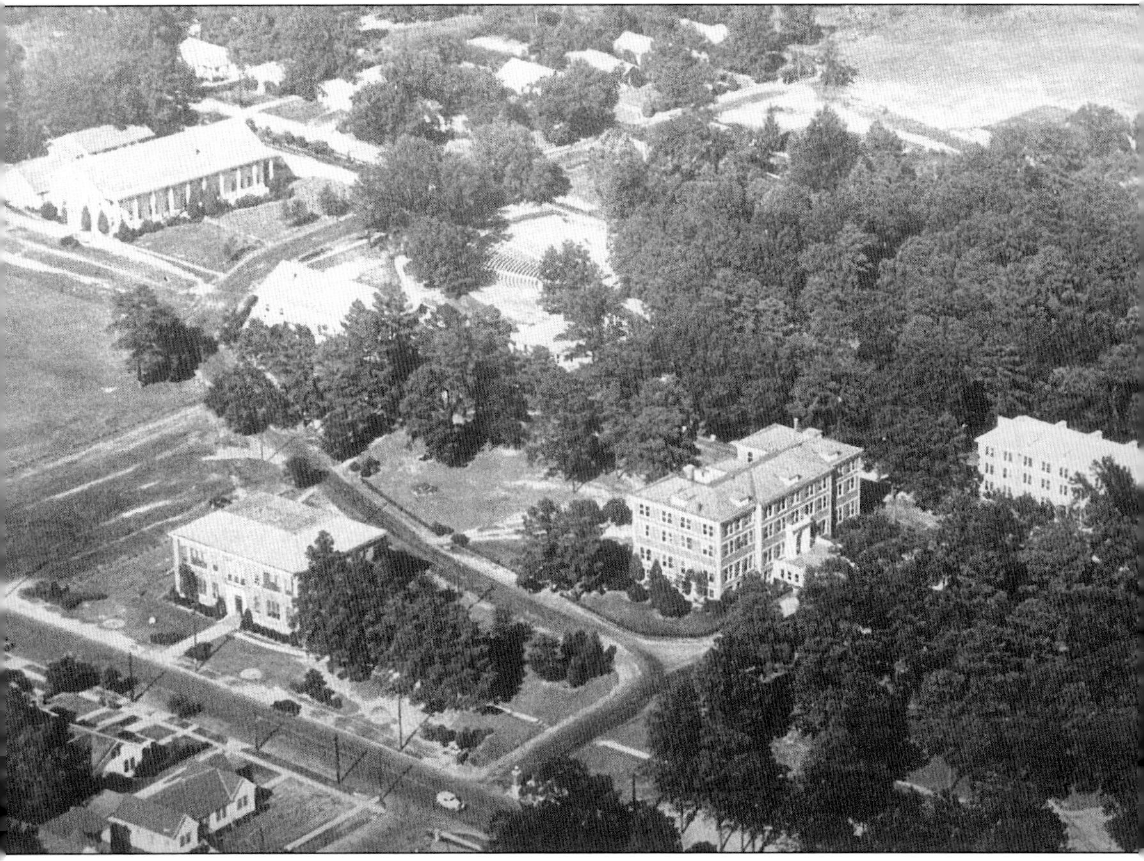

The campus is seen here in 1938, from above the intersection of Kings Highway and Centenary Boulevard, which runs diagonally across the lower left-hand quarter of the photograph. The old Arts Building, which had become the library, faces Centenary Boulevard in the lower left-hand quadrant. Behind it and to its right is Jackson Hall, with Rotary Hall at right center. Colonial Hall is in the upper left-hand quadrant of the image and the dramatics building/chapel and amphitheater are seen between it and Jackson Hall. The baseball field is at upper right with Faculty Row in between it and Colonial Hall. Haynes Gym, which had only recently been opened, is outside the scope of the photograph but would be just to the right of Rotary Hall from this angle.

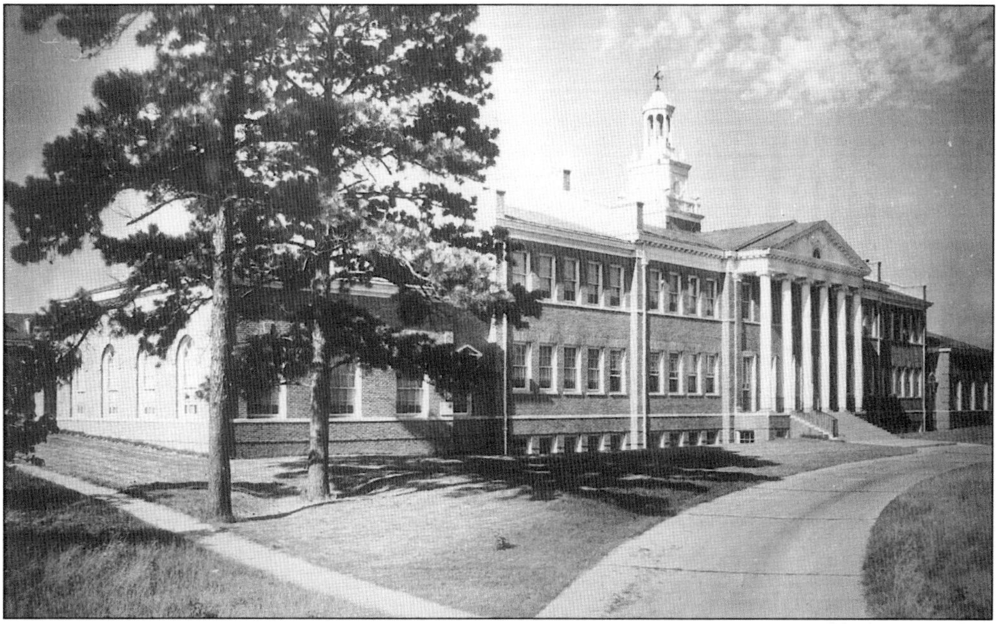

In 1943, the Haynes family purchased the former campus of Dodd College and donated it to Centenary. Dodd College was a short-lived Baptist junior college for girls which operated from 1927 to 1942. The campus was located just a little over a mile south of Centenary's campus and contained two fine college buildings designed by architect Clarence W. King of Shreveport. The former "Shreveport Hall" was renamed Annie Haynes Hall (above), and the former "Residence Hall" was renamed "Shreveport Hall" (below). The site was used for the Aviation Cadet Pre-Flight Program during World War II and afterward as an auxiliary campus for Centenary. In the late 1950s it was sold to the First Baptist Church of Shreveport, which then moved to the site from downtown. Both buildings still stand, though now incorporated into the church complex.

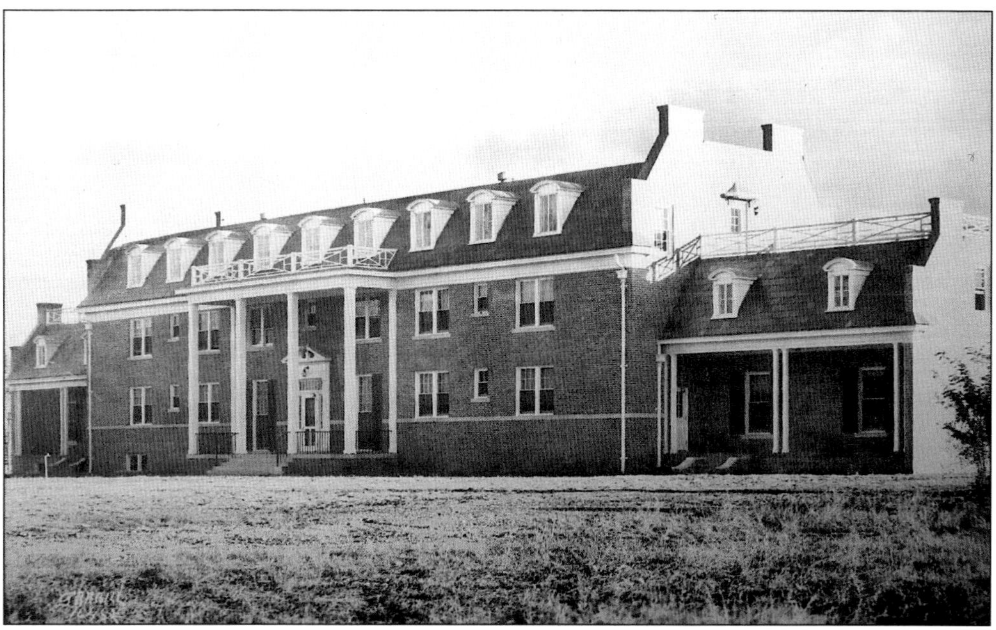

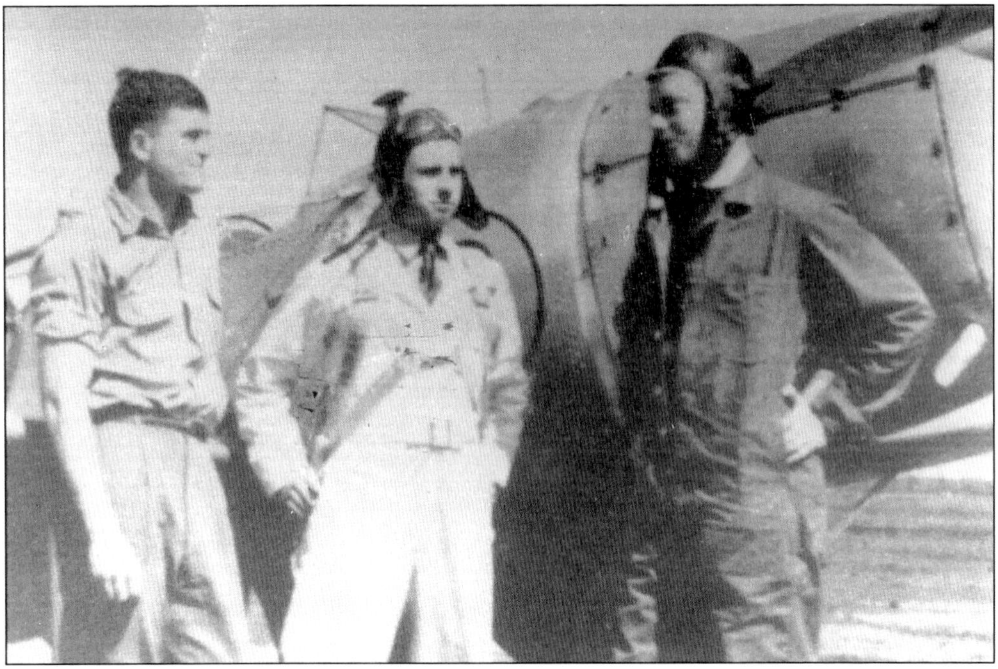

The Aviation Cadet Pre-Flight Program was an important function of Centenary's mission during World War II. The program was operated in cooperation with Barksdale Army Air Field across the Red River in Bossier Parish, and was responsible for preparing future aviators for more sophisticated training at the Air Field. Here, three Centenary cadets confer before a training plane. One such plane remained on the campus site as a prominent landmark until 1960, when the main sanctuary of the First Baptist Church took its place.

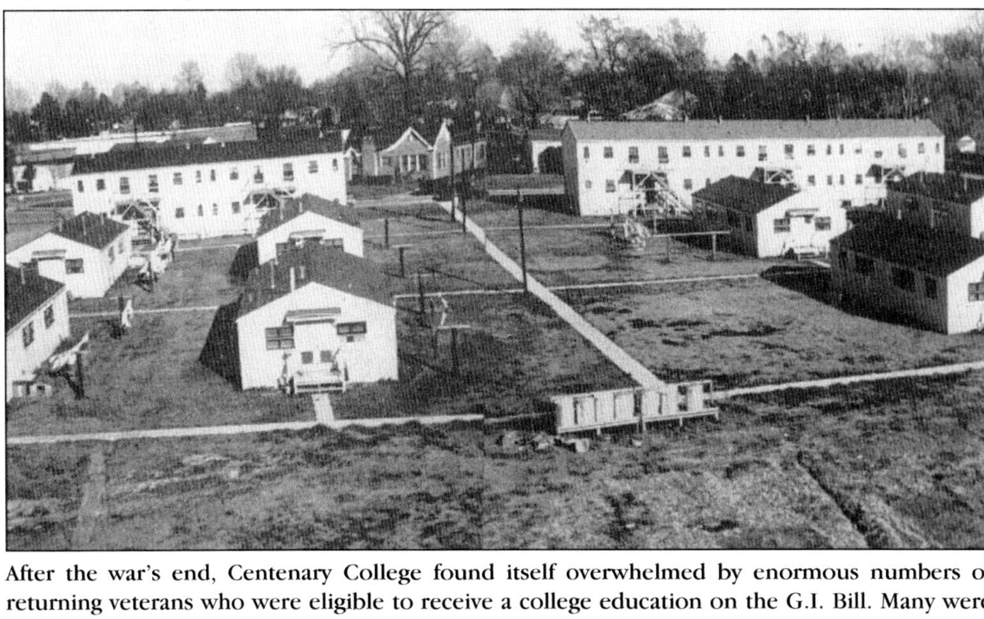

After the war's end, Centenary College found itself overwhelmed by enormous numbers of returning veterans who were eligible to receive a college education on the G.I. Bill. Many were married, and the need for suitable housing became an immediate priority for the school. The answer was "Vet's Villa," a complex of Army surplus frame buildings moved to the campus and constructed on and around the site of the stadium, which was demolished.

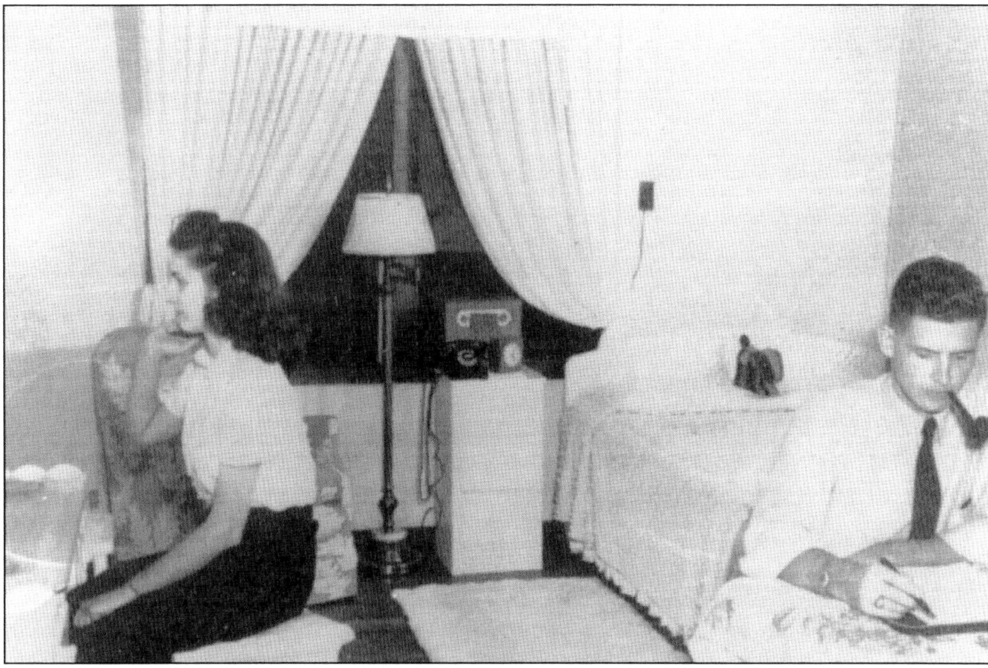

Vet's Villa was the first married housing provided by Centenary College since a building called "The Shack" was used by the school's few married students at the old Jackson campus decades before. For many young couples after the war it was their first home together. In numerous instances both husband and wife were Centenary students (above). In many more instances the husband was the student, the wife a baby-boom mother (below).

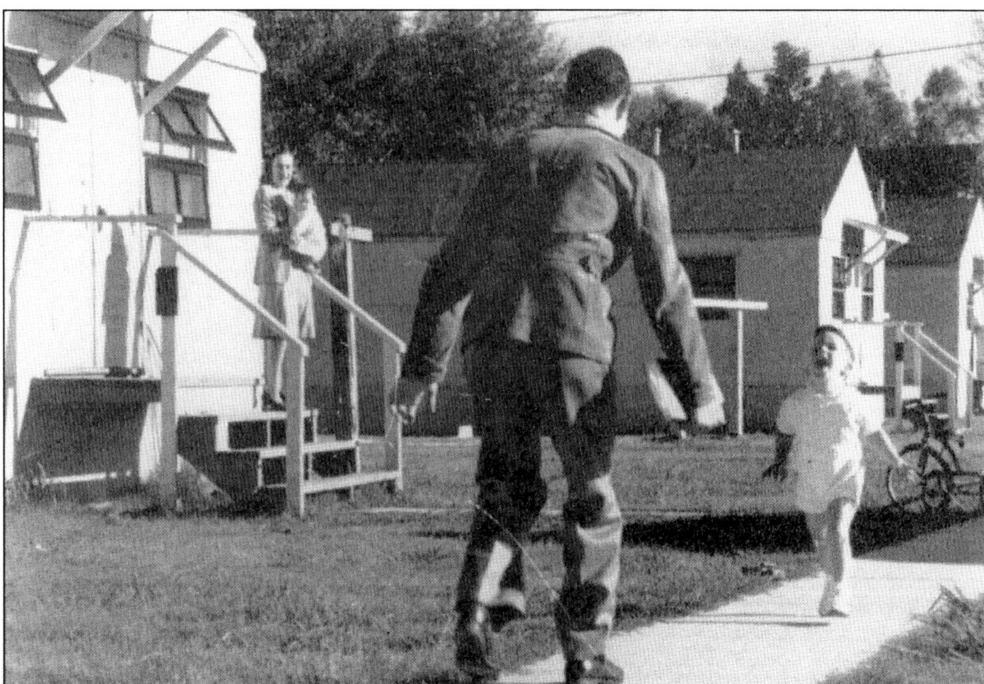

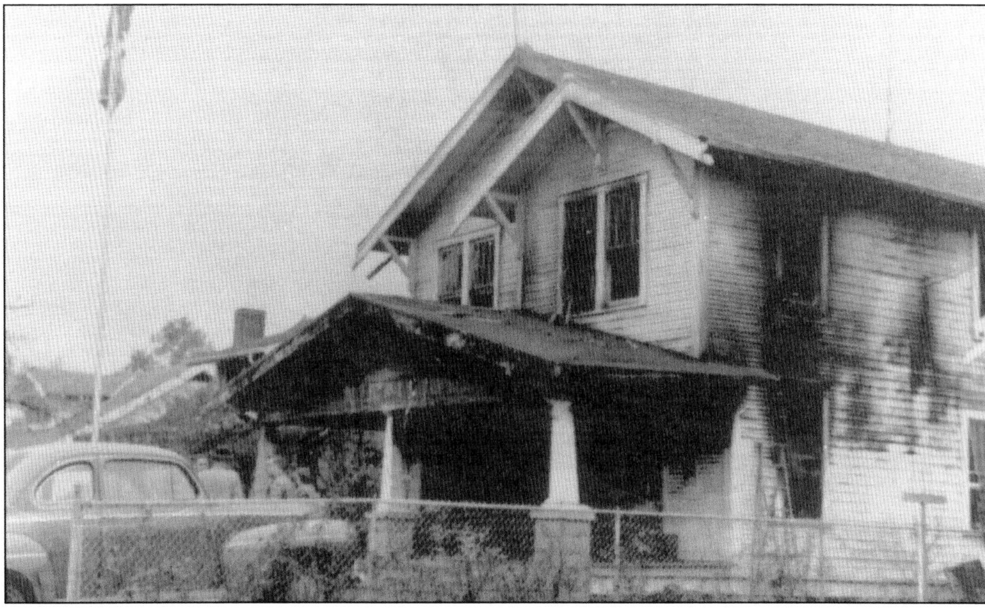

The post-war period brought many changes to student life at Centenary. For instance, the number of fraternities dwindled markedly after the war, and their base of operations rapidly shifted from "fraternity row" along the west side of the campus to new quarters on the east side. Even before the war some fraternities and sororities had considered building anew. Kappa Alpha, for example, had begun raising funds for a new house as early as 1943 but a 1950 fire (above) finally forced the move to its present East Washington Street house (below, left), next door to Kappa Sigma's new home. Two new fraternities did come into being in the 1940s, however—the short-lived Delta Chi Alpha and Pi Kappa Alpha.

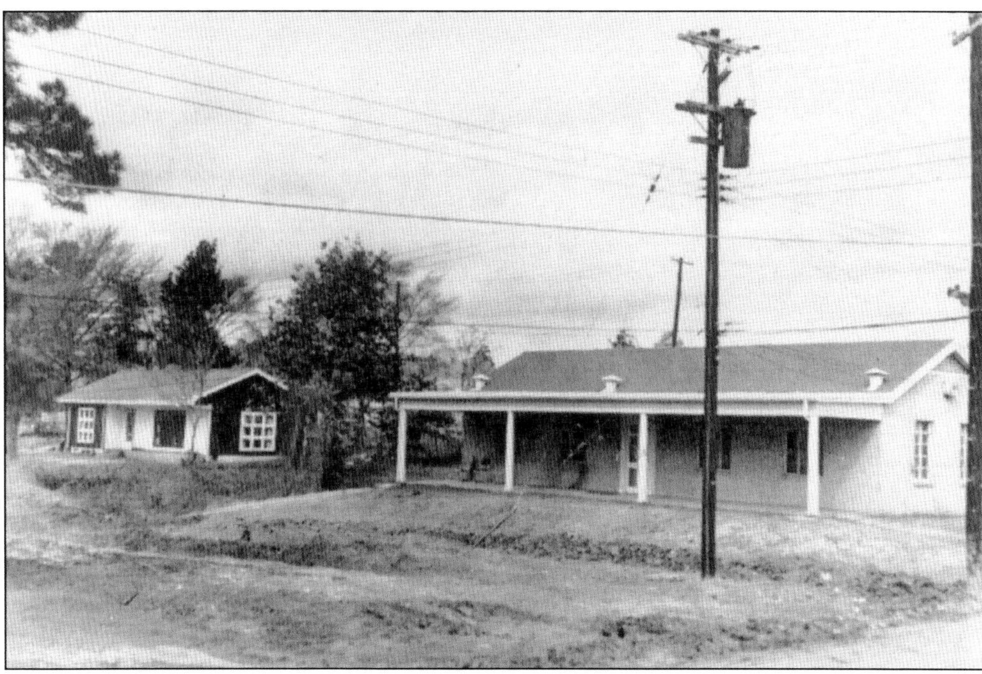

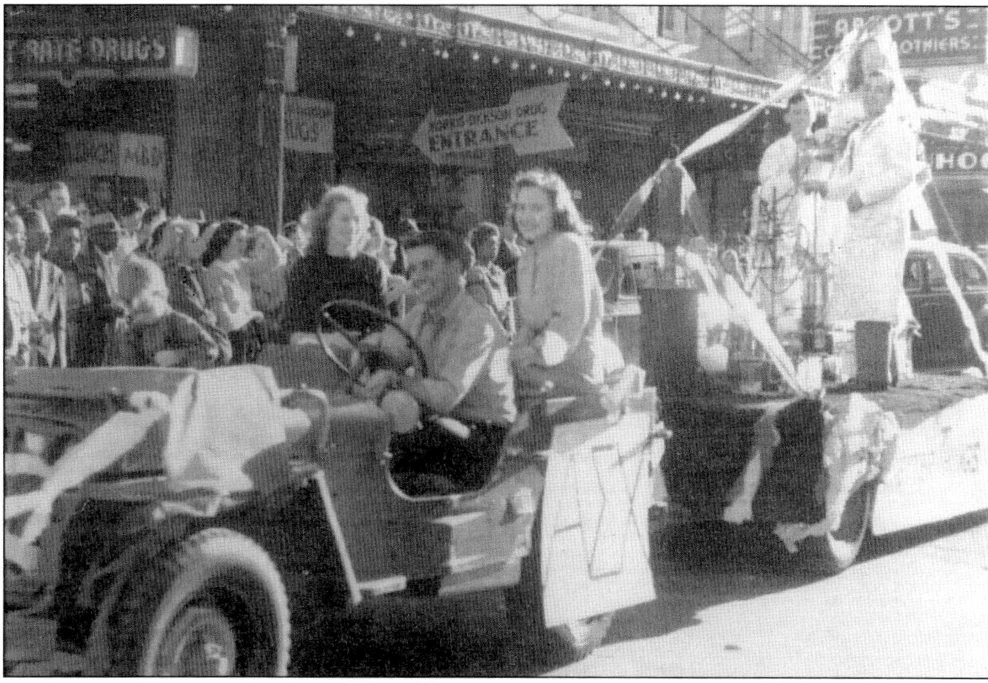

Sports, too, continued to be popular at Centenary after the war, though football came to an end in 1948. Numerous factors led to its demise, including higher costs and lack of a stadium as well as an older, often married, crop of male students less interested in playing the game than they might have been a decade earlier. Nevertheless, the 1948 homecoming parade, seen above on Milam Street in downtown Shreveport, was a big event. Other sports such as baseball and basketball continued unabated, however, and with football's exit grew to unprecedented levels of support and popularity. Below is an early 1950s baseball game on the new diamond next to Vet's Villa.

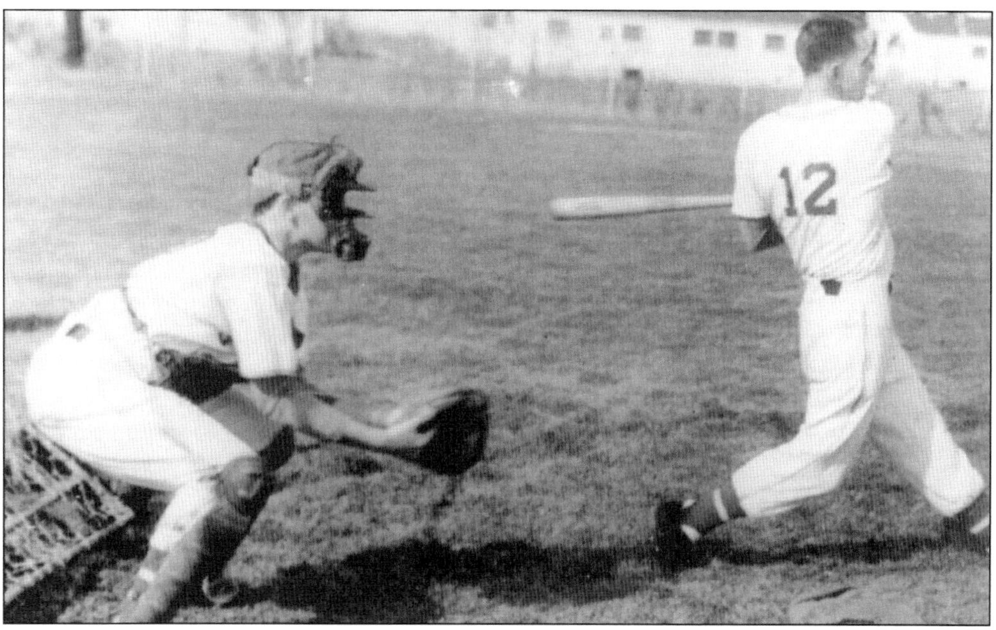

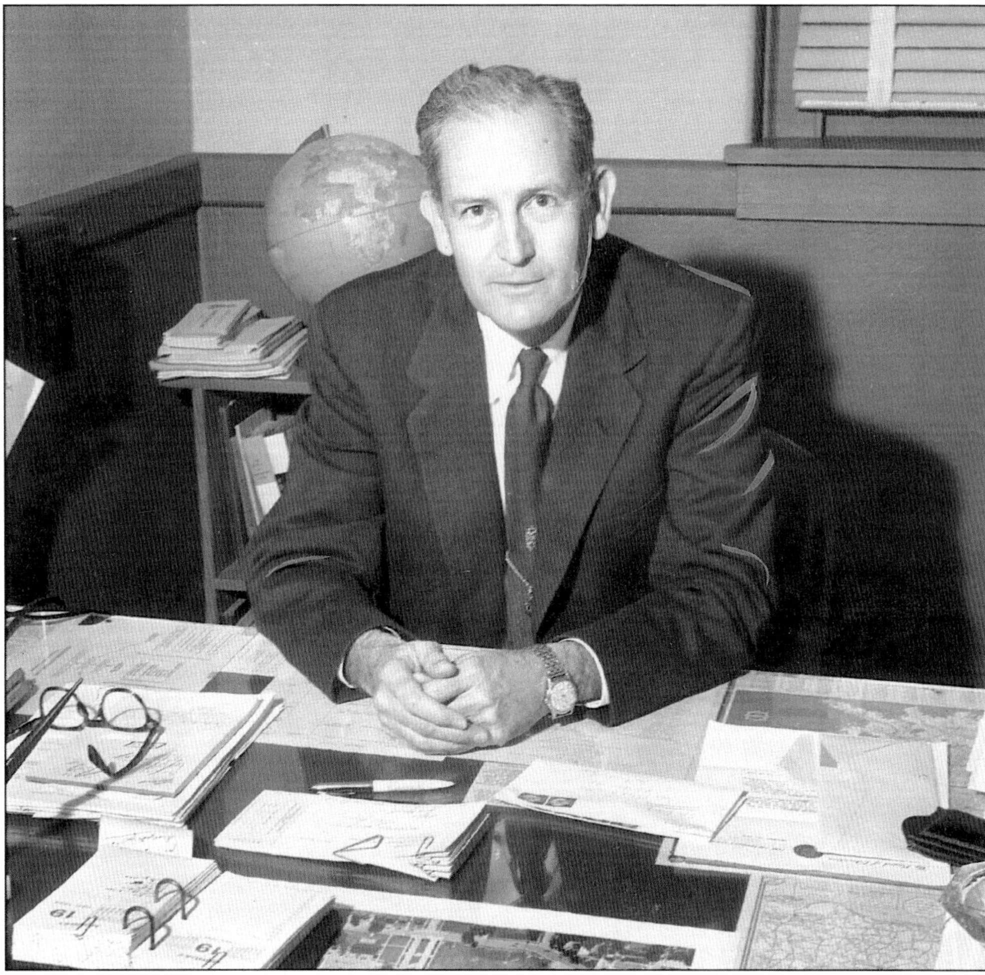

Dr. Joseph J. Mickle, Pierce Cline's successor as president of Centenary, came to the college in 1945 and led its growth for the next 19 years, longer than any other president in the school's history. It was under Dr. Mickle's presidency that Centenary saw its greatest building boom before or since, with the construction of 11 major buildings and the reconstruction of the amphitheater. Paul Brown was Chairman of the Board during this same period (see page 56). The Mickle presidency also saw the largest number of graduates in Centenary's history up to that time.

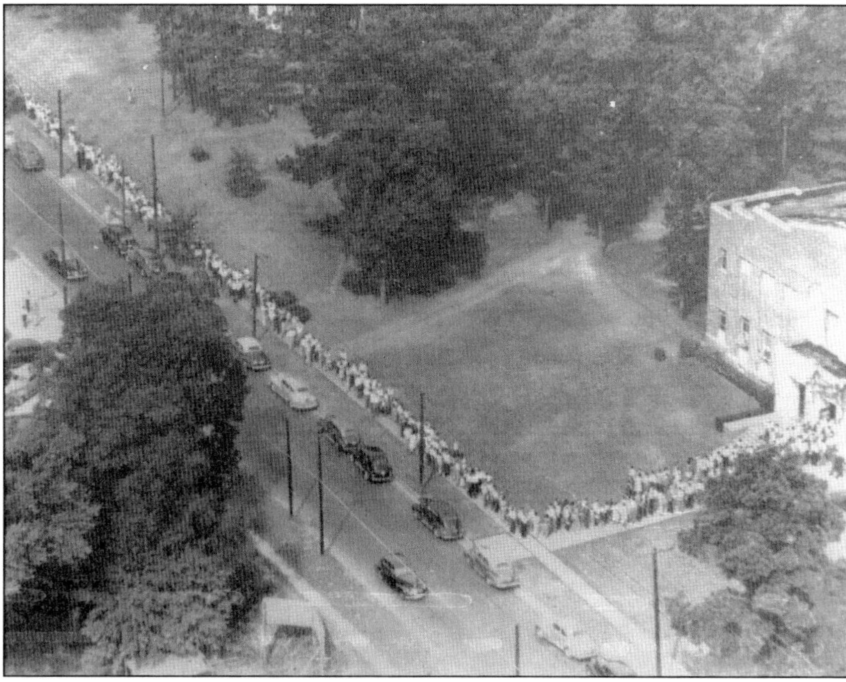

The enormous number of students at Centenary in the late 1940s is reflected in the aerial photograph above, showing the long registration day line extending from the front doors of Haynes Gym out to Kings Highway and westward down the street. The houses of Sorority Row are hidden among the dense canopy of streets seen in the upper part of the photo.

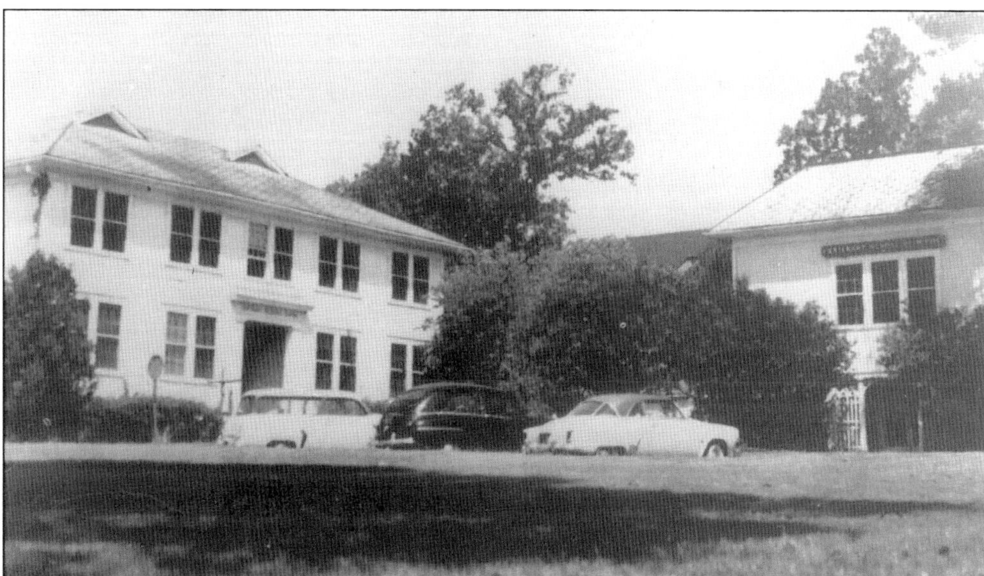

In the southeast part of the campus stood the Religious Center and the Music Building. These were destined to be replaced by more modern facilities under Dr. Mickle's building program during the 1950s and '60s. In the end, they would be the last two frame buildings constructed in the Sexton era to be left standing. Both were removed in the 1960s.

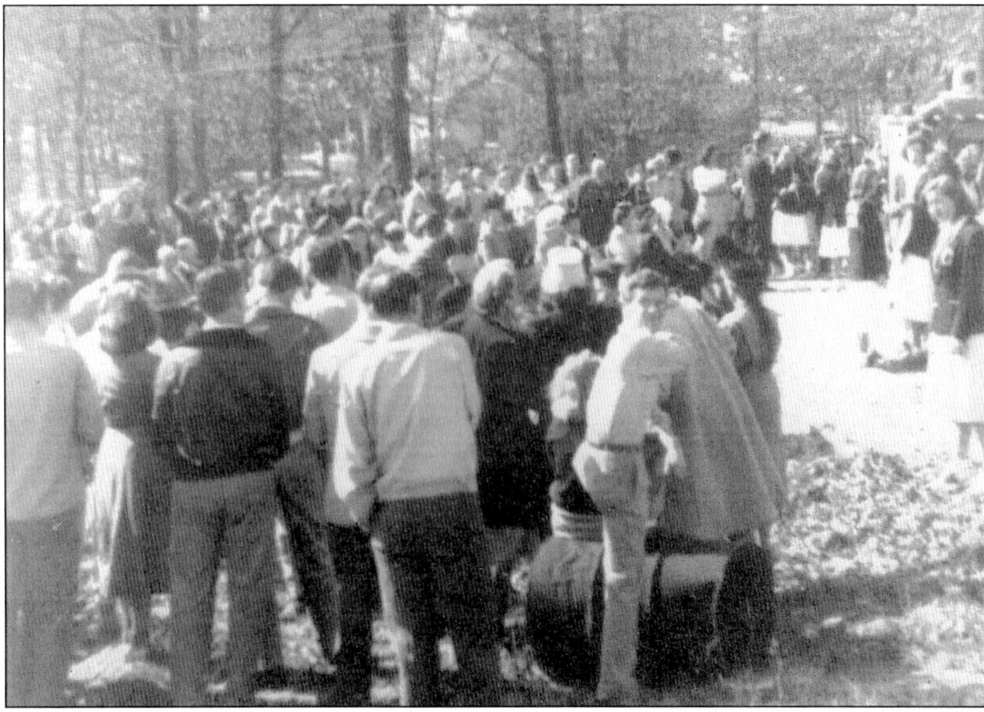

The Science Building was to be the first, and largest, building constructed in the Mickle era. On Tuesday, February 17, 1948, the groundbreaking ceremony took place on the spot where the old wooden gymnasium had stood (above). Over the next year the massive structure would rise atop the hill overlooking Woodlawn Avenue (below).

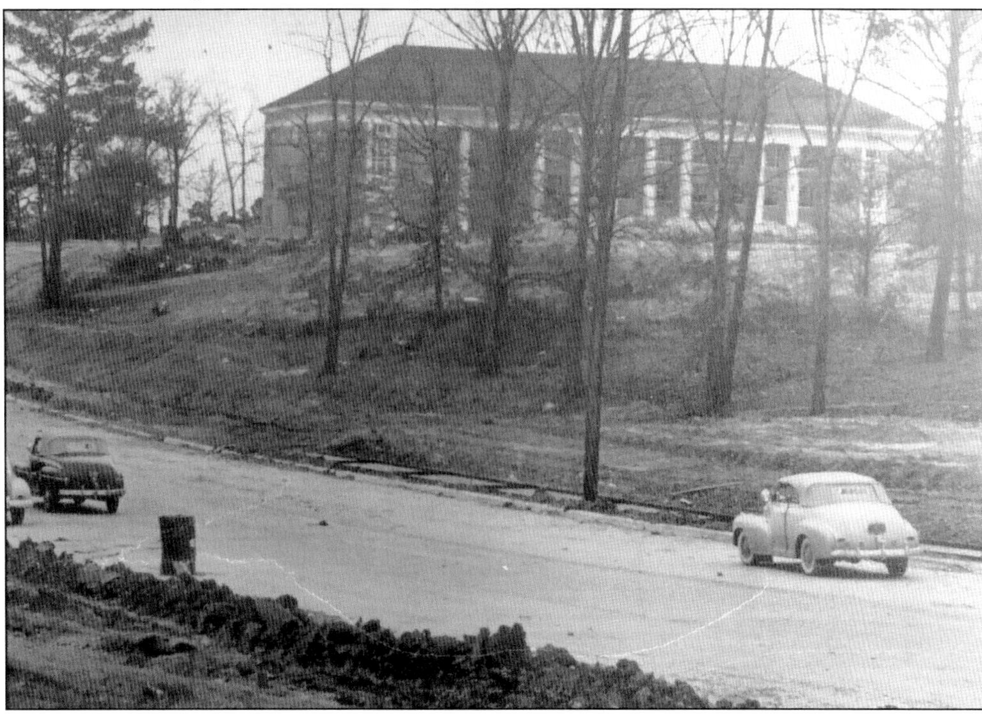

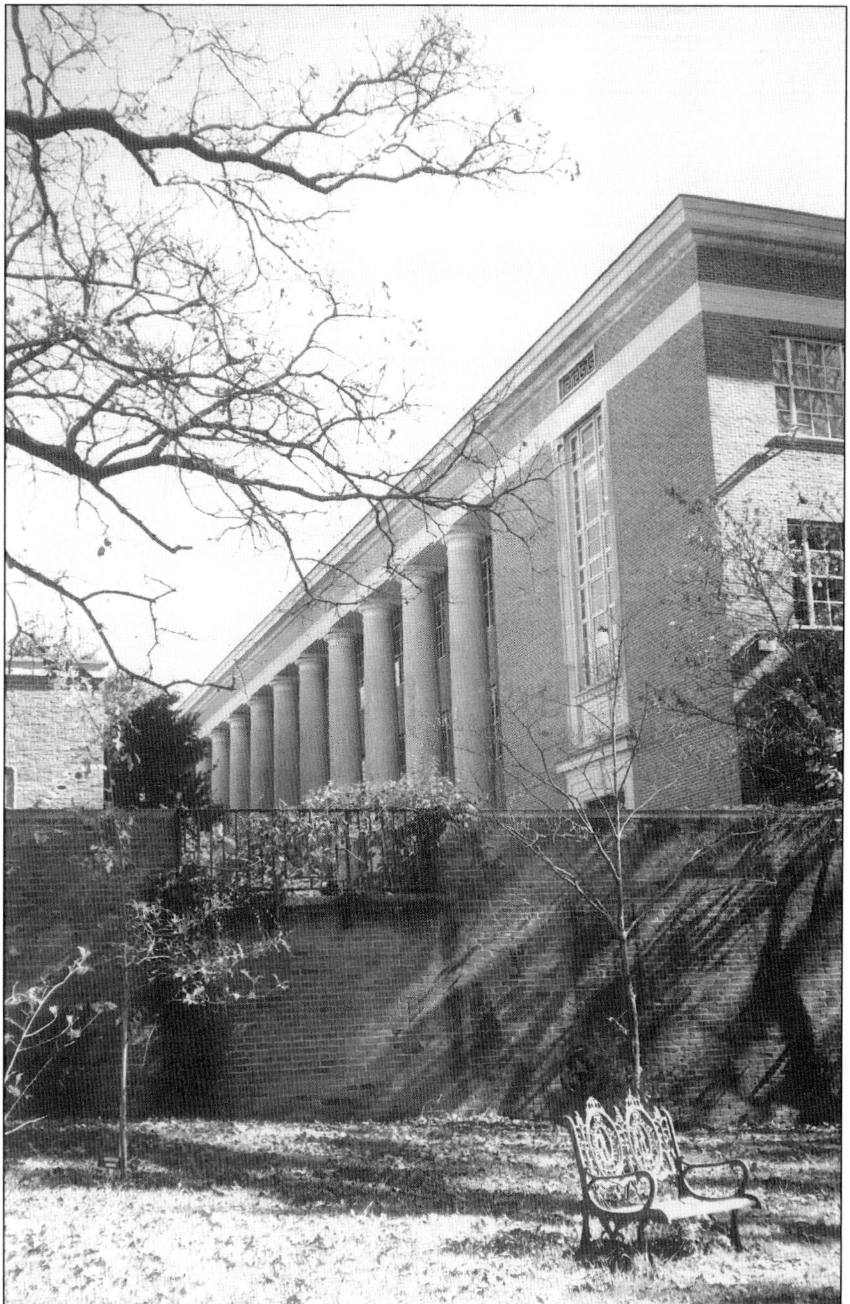

After President Mickle's retirement in 1964, the Science Building was renamed Mickle Hall, as it is known today. Its four floors and basement contain over 100,000 square feet of floorspace, making it the largest structure on the campus. It is a fitting tribute to Dr. Mickle, whose vision made it and many of the buildings around it a reality. In the view above, Mickle Hall is seen from the garden to its west. This garden contains only plants native to Louisiana, and was established in 1985 as an arboretum and wild bird sanctuary.

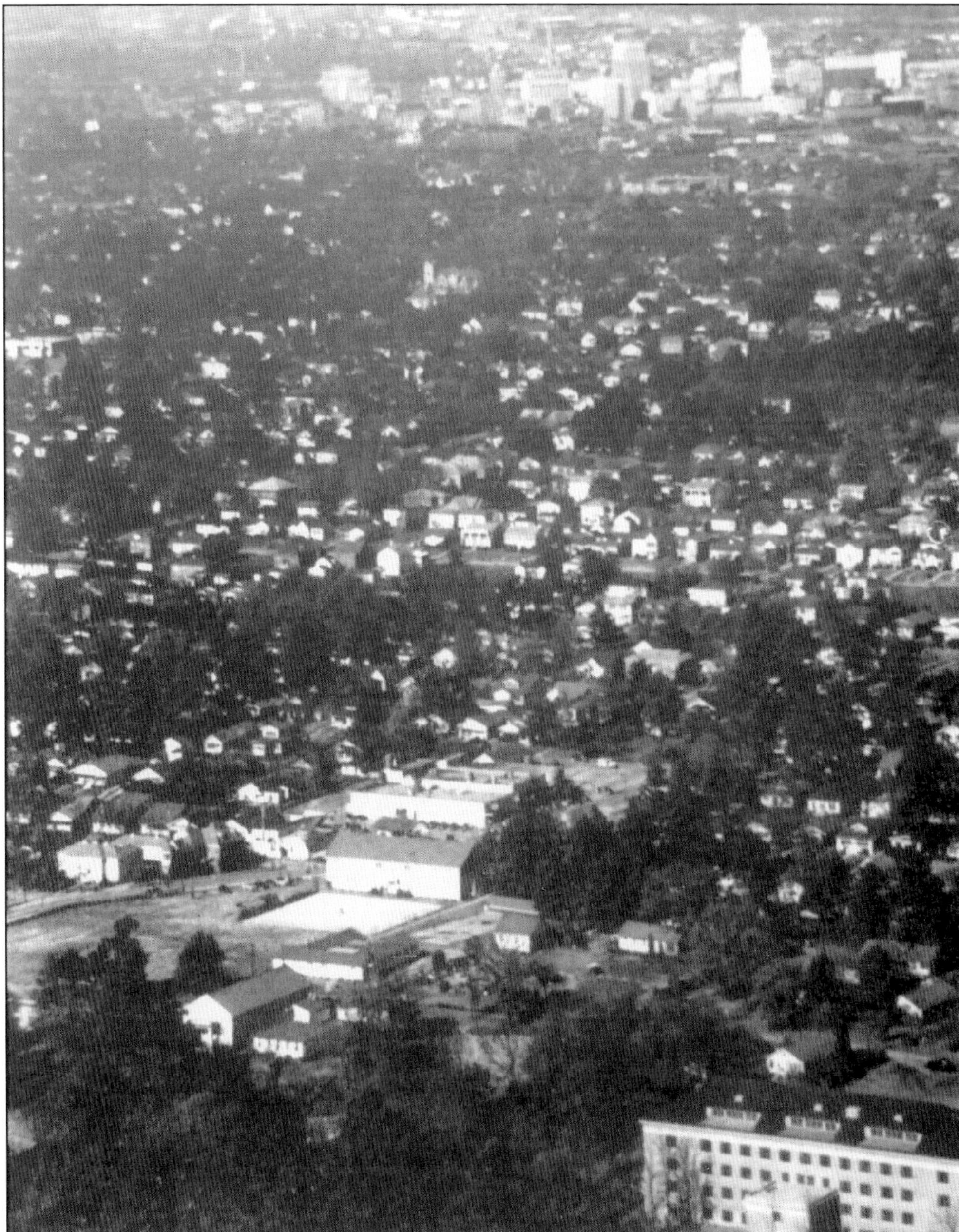

A spectacular aerial view was taken over the Centenary College campus in 1950. Mickle Hall, seen from the back, dominates the campus at lower right. Colonial Hall, now minus its columned gallery, and several of the frame buildings of the Sexton era can be seen at lower center, just above and to the left of Mickle Hall. At top right rise the buildings of Shreveport's central business district. In between them and the campus lies Shreveport's Highland neighborhood, in the center of which the Neo-Gothic Noel Memorial Methodist Church can just be made out about two-thirds of the distance between Centenary and the tall buildings downtown.

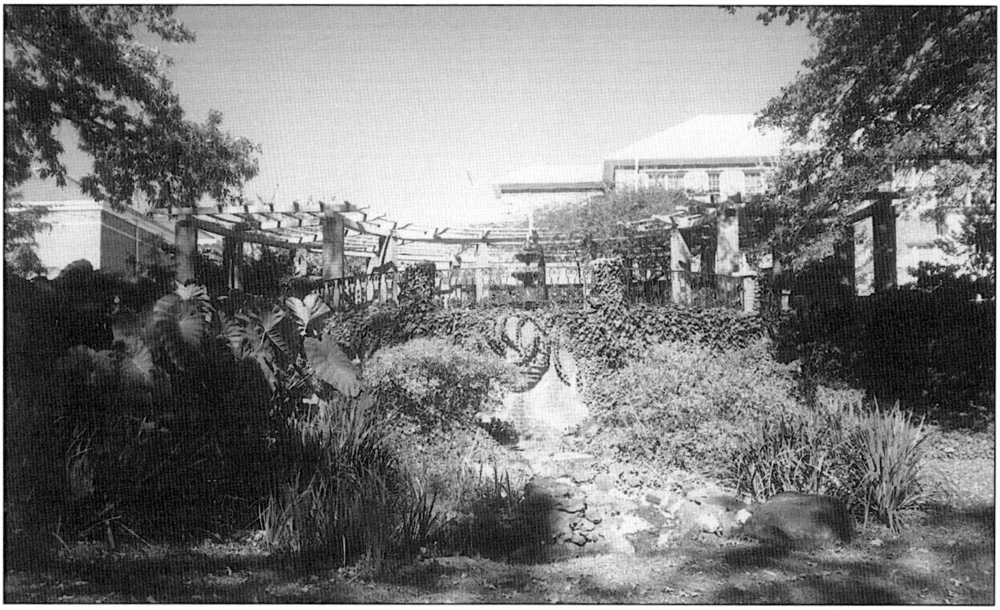

The 1950s brought many changes to the appearance of the Centenary campus. Among these was the dedication of the Crumley Gardens, with their bubbling fountain and beautiful loggia (above). The gardens were dedicated in memory of David Howard Crumley by his parents in 1954. Crumley would have graduated in 1946 had he lived. Today, it is one of the campus's most peaceful places to study and reflect. Another memorial dedicated at this same time was the Frost Garden with its Neo-Classical fountain, located in front of the north entrance to the Student Union Building. It was given in memory of longtime board member Edwin Ambrose Frost by his grandchildren.

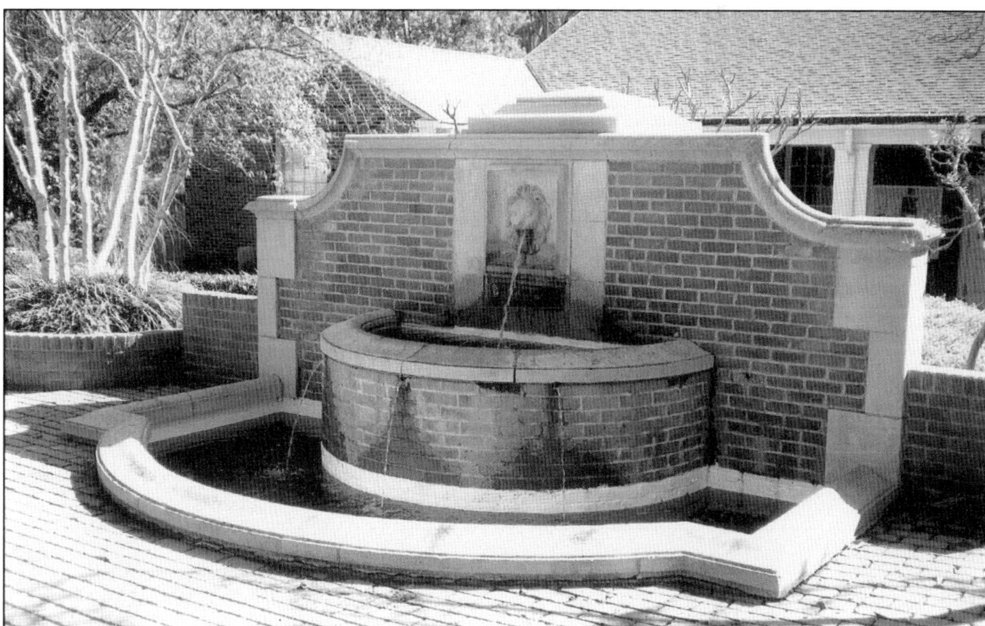

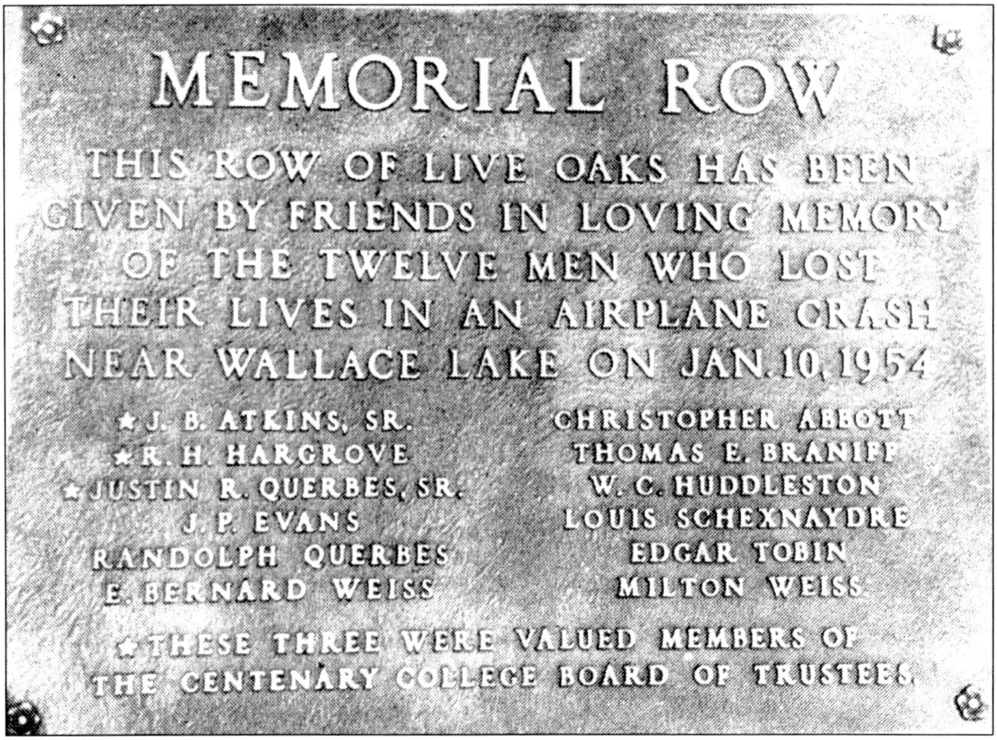

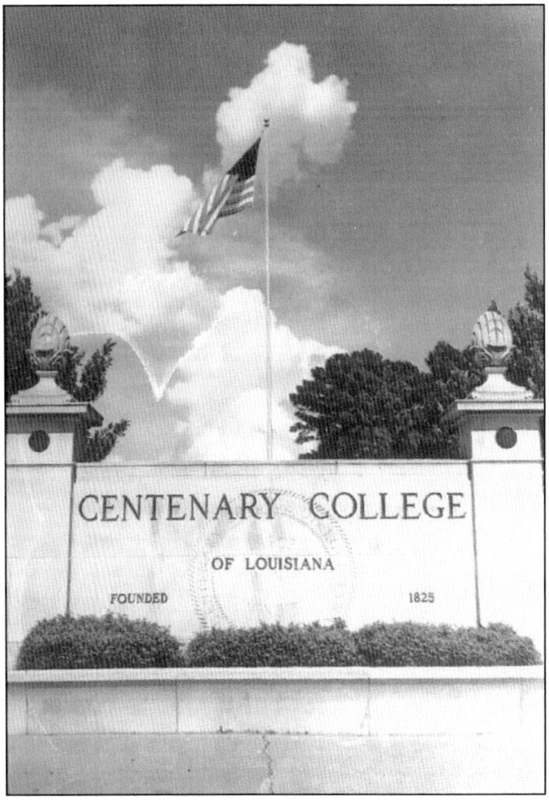

On January 10, 1954, Centenary and Shreveport were struck by tragedy when a dozen lives were lost in a plane crash over Wallace Lake, south of the city. Ten of the dead were prominent businessmen, and three of these were members of the college's board of trustees—J.B. Atkins, R.H. Hargrove, and J. R. Querbes, Also killed was Thomas E. Braniff, founder of Braniff Airlines. A row of 12 live oak trees was planted in front of the Administration Building (formerly the Arts Building) and a monument placed as well (above). Just yards away, the new main entrance to the campus was dedicated five years earlier in 1949 (below). Located on Centenary Boulevard at the head of Columbia Street, it was the gift of J. B. Atkins in memory of his father, John Baxter Atkins, who helped bring the college to Shreveport. The elder Mr. Atkins had died in 1923.

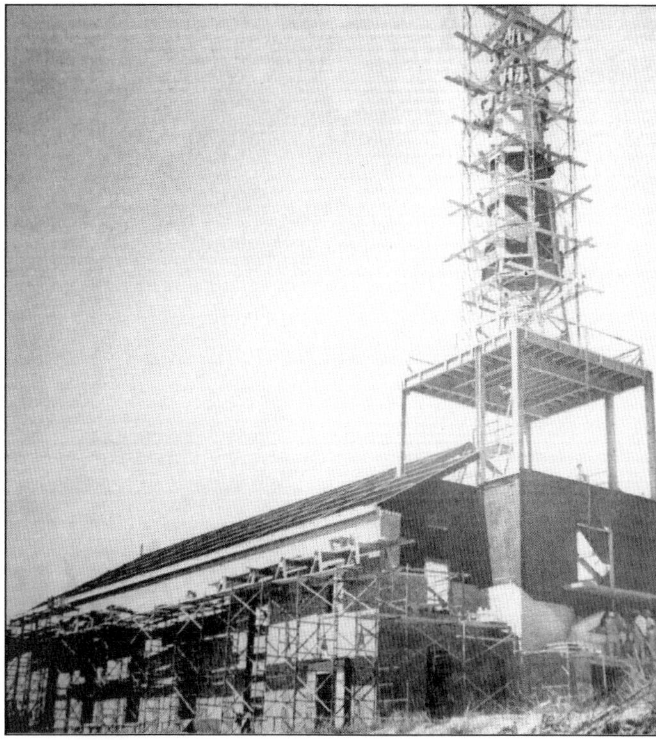

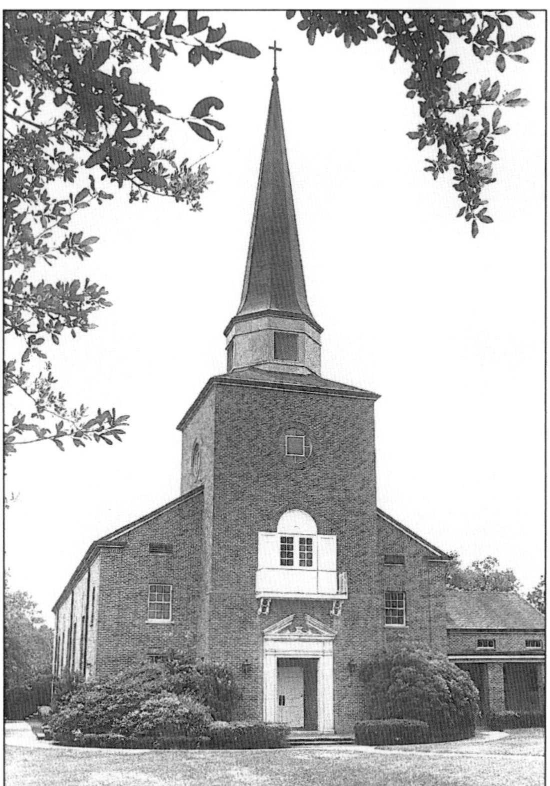

In 1954, Brown Chapel was constructed on the east side of the campus. Designed by J. Cheshire Peyton, its simple architecture, reminiscent of the work of Sir Christopher Wren, belies its large size. Methodist services are regularly held here for Centenary's students, and the chapel is also frequently the venue for convocations, choir and orchestral performances, and other assemblies. Numerous Centenary alumni have been married here as well. Above is a view of Brown Chapel under construction; below is a view of the finished structure as it appears today.

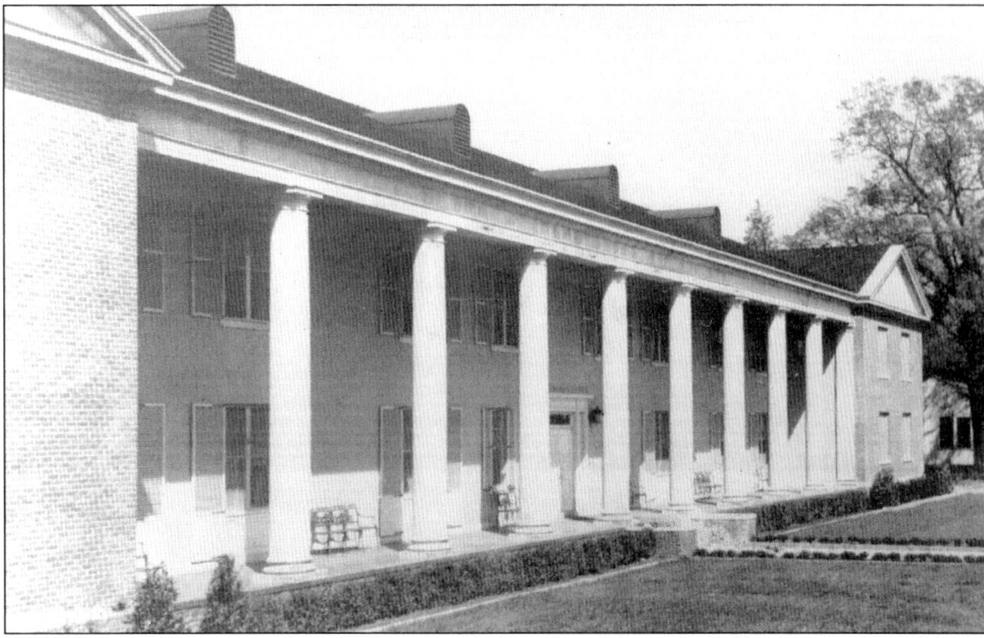

The T.L. James Memorial Dormitory, a women's residence hall built on the site of Colonial Hall, was also opened in 1954. T.L. James was a lumberman, oilman, investment banker, and building contractor from Ruston, Louisiana, who served for many years on Centenary's board of trustees and was its chairman during much of the Cline presidency. Mr. James was a noted philanthropist and a major contributor to the school's success at Shreveport, both financially and personally. A large annex was built to the dorm's rear in 1968.

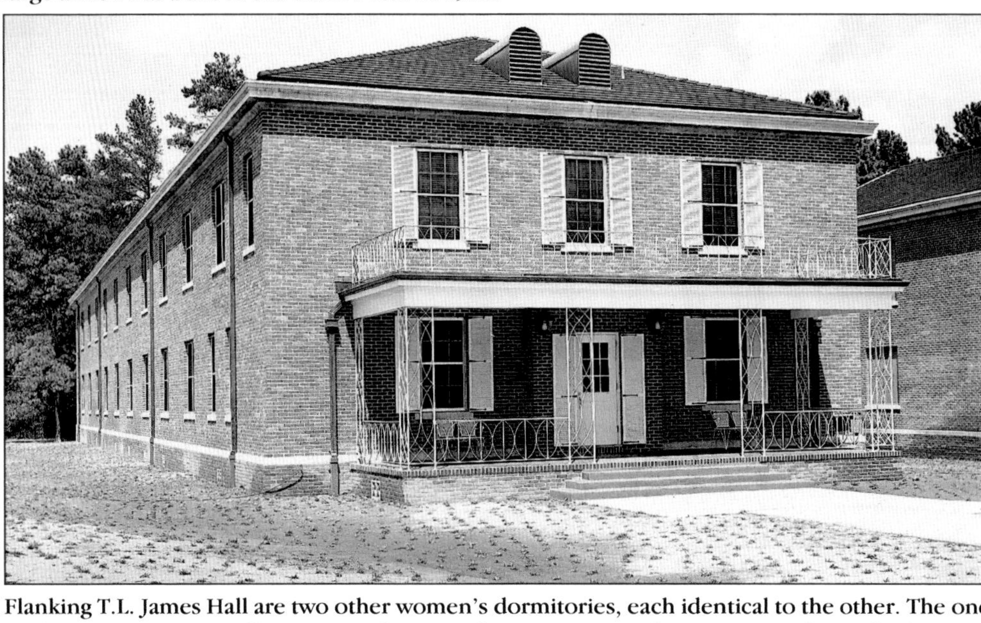

Flanking T.L. James Hall are two other women's dormitories, each identical to the other. The one to the east is Sexton Hall, a memorial to President Sexton. To the west is Hardin Hall (above), a memorial to Dr. John A. Hardin, longtime dean of the college and professor of mathematics. His wife, Anna, was college librarian and their son, John Jr., was a member of the class of 1928. Sexton and Hardin Halls were designed by J. Cheshire Peyton and built in 1957 and 1960, respectively.

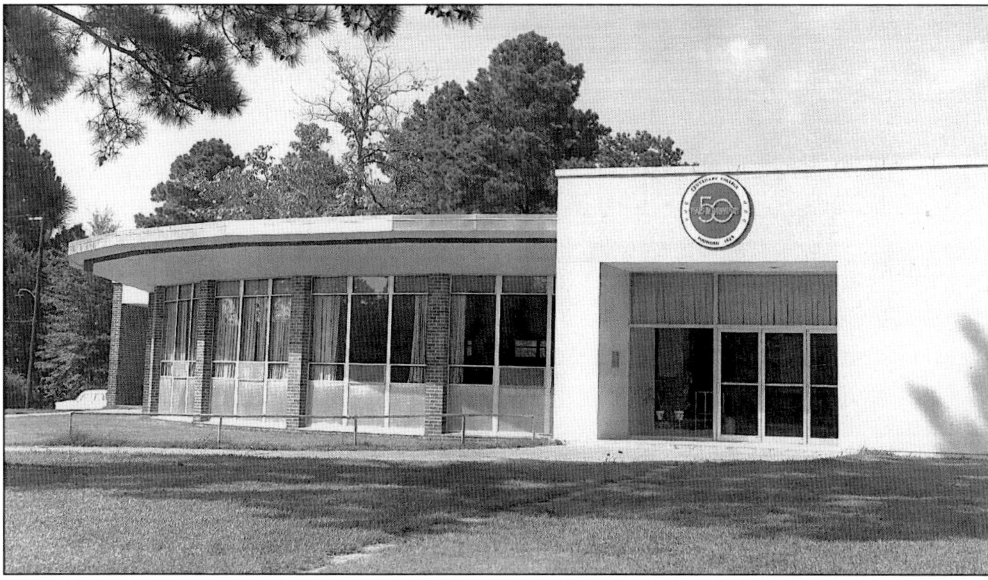

Two more Centenary buildings constructed during the building program of the 1950s were Bynum Commons (above) and the Moore Student Center (below). Bynum Commons, the college dining hall and assembly center, is a memorial to Robert Jesse Bynum, a strong supporter of the school who died in 1956, the year the building was completed on the former site of Faculty Row. The Moore Student Center was built adjacent to the old Student Union in 1958. It is a memorial to lumberman and banker Randle Thomas Moore, a board member of the college from 1921 to his death in 1957. Both were designed by architect J. Cheshire Peyton.

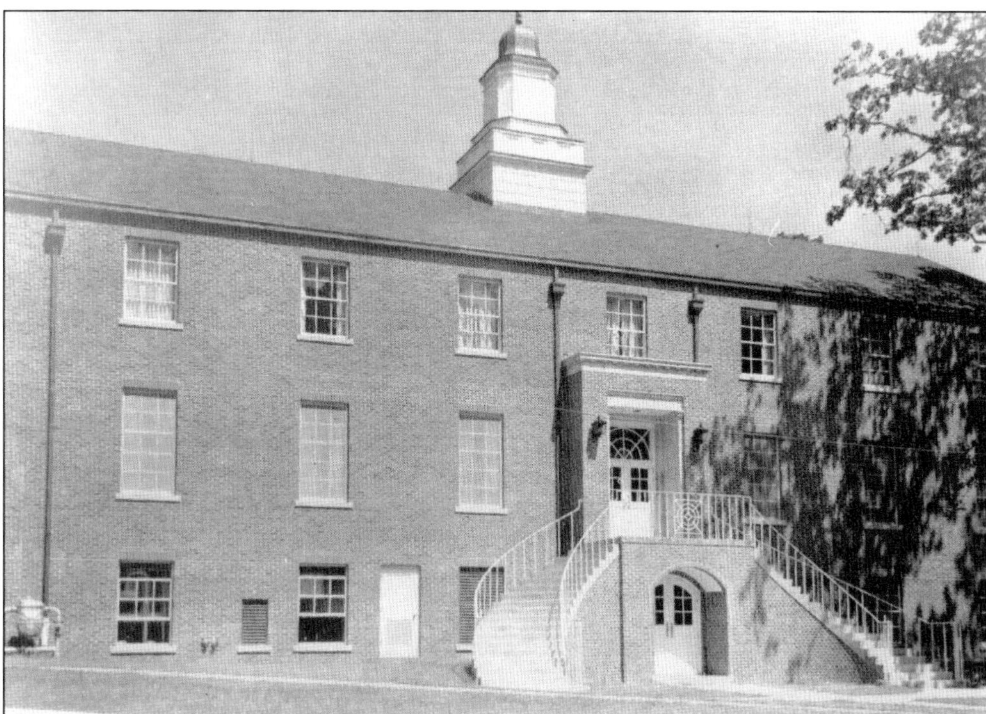

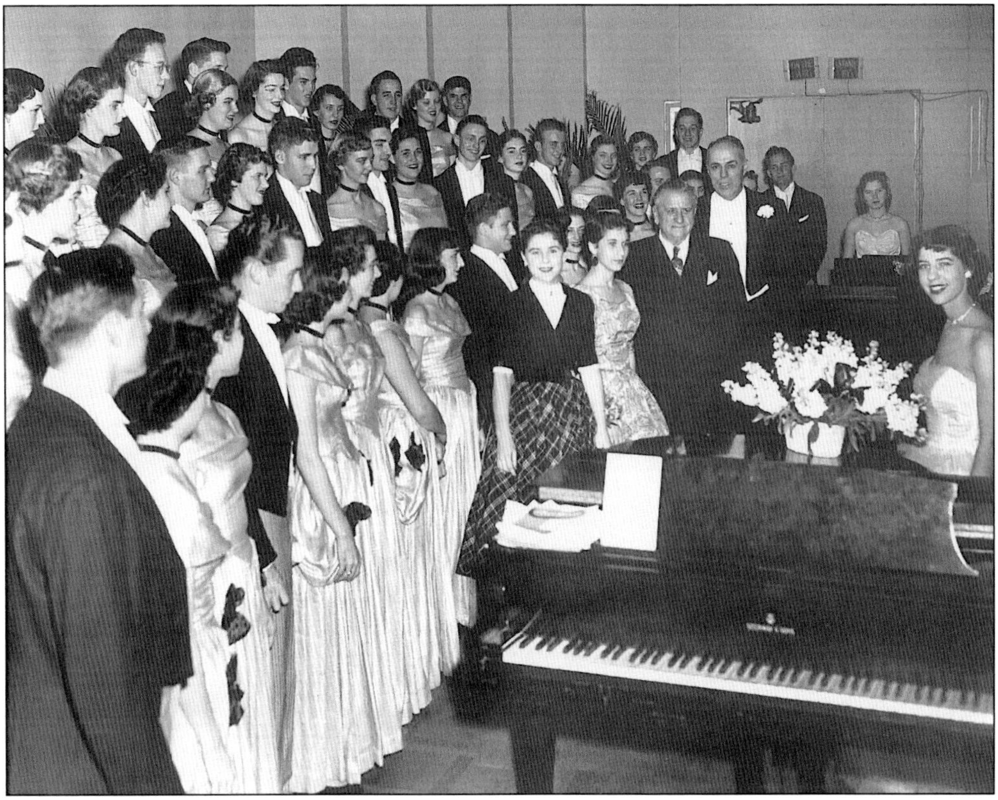

The Centenary College Choir was organized in 1942; today its members are known as Centenary's "singing ambassadors" and have brought to the college as much national and even international publicity as football did before them. The choir performs over 75 concerts annually with at least one trip abroad. They have sung numerous times at the White House and at significant national events. Longtime director A. C. "Cheesy" Voran is credited with bringing the Centenary Choir to full fruition in the 1950s. Above: The choir is pictured in New Orleans in 1957. Voran is the tall man with carnation at left side of door. Below: In 1957, the theater department moved to the new Marjorie Lyons Playhouse. Marjorie H. Lyons was a devoted supporter of Centenary and wife of prominent Shreveport lawyer and oilman Charlton Lyons.

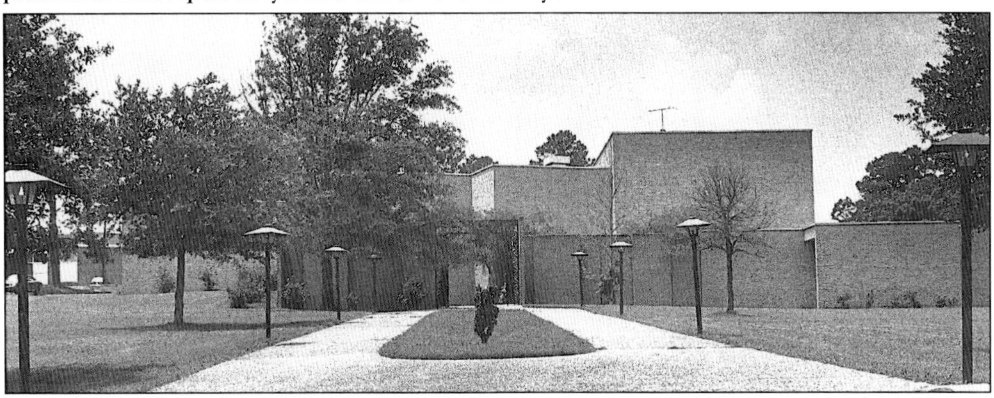

Among the numerous student organizations active on campus in the Mickle era were the Maroon Jackets—the college's official hostesses—formed in 1931 and still serving the school today (co-ed since 1979). The club is named for the maroon jackets worn by its members over white blouses—maroon and white being the school colors. Here, two members take tickets at a campus event. Other groups of the era include Aufait, a non-sorority women's club, formed in 1931; the male Masonic Fraternity (1948), and the several religious societies: Canterbury (Episcopalian, 1947), Newman (Roman Catholic, 1947), and Westminster (Presbyterian, 1954). The Baptist Student Union had been active since its founding in 1921, the Methodist Student Movement and its antecedent groups from the school's birth.

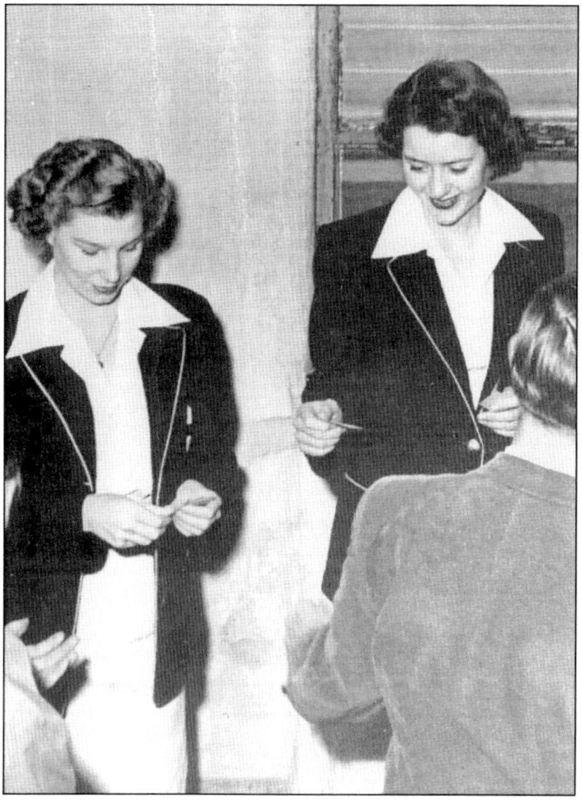

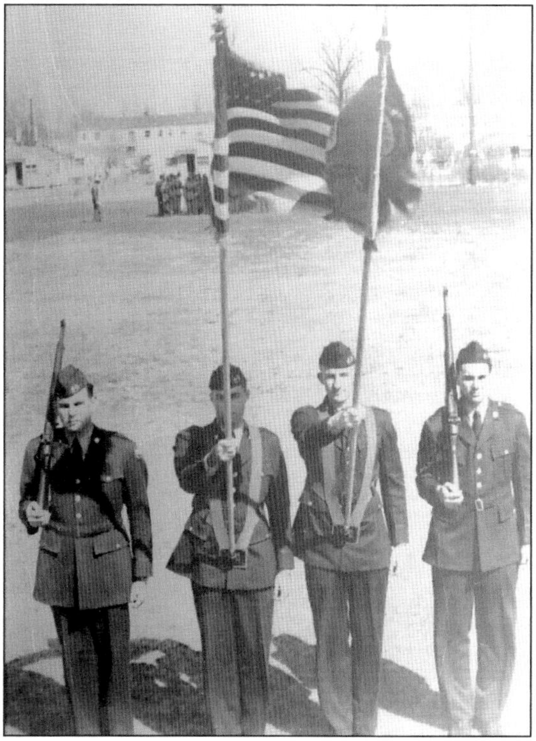

The ROTC had a brief, controversial life at Centenary during the 1950s. It returned again to the campus in the early 1980s. Below, members drill on the baseball field in 1956; Vet's Villa, still standing at the time, is seen in the background. Numerous honor societies and academic honor fraternities were active during this period as well, several of which still function on the campus today. Among these groups are Alpha Chi (scholastic, established 1925); Pi Mu Sigma (science and medicine, 1925); Alpha Sigma Chi (chemistry, 1931); Chi Sigma Nu (education, 1937); Sigma Tau Delta (English, 1948); Omicron Delta Kappa (service, 1949); Phi Beta (women's drama, speech and music, 1954); and Alpha Psi Omega (drama, 1961).

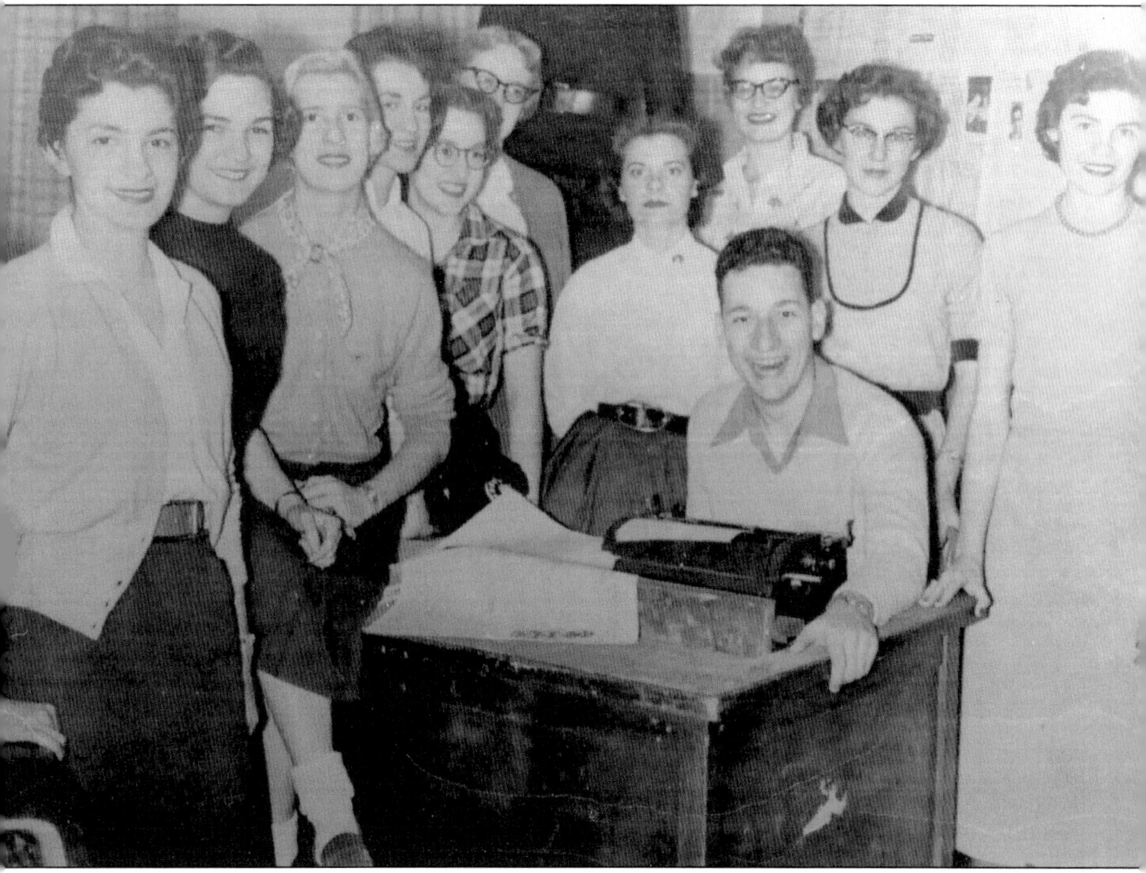

The 1957 staff of Centenary's weekly student newspaper, *The Conglomerate*, is shown above. Seated behind the typewriter, and the only male in the picture, is that year's *Conglomerate* editor Paul Greenberg. A member of the class of 1958, Greenberg went on to write for several newspapers including the *Arkansas Democrat-Gazette* of Little Rock, where he became editorial page editor. His column, which is syndicated through the *Los Angeles Times Syndicate*, is seen in newspapers throughout the United States. In 1969, while an editorial page writer for the Pine Bluff, Arkansas *Commercial*, Mr. Greenberg was awarded the coveted Pulitzer Prize for editorial writing. Among other notable Centenary graduates are television producer / writer Richard Hawkins, class of 1974; mountaineer Joby Ogwyn, class of 1997, the youngest person ever to ascend Mt. Everest; Bishop Benjamin Oliphont, class of 1943; noted cellist Charlotte Moorman, class of 1955; and numerous others.

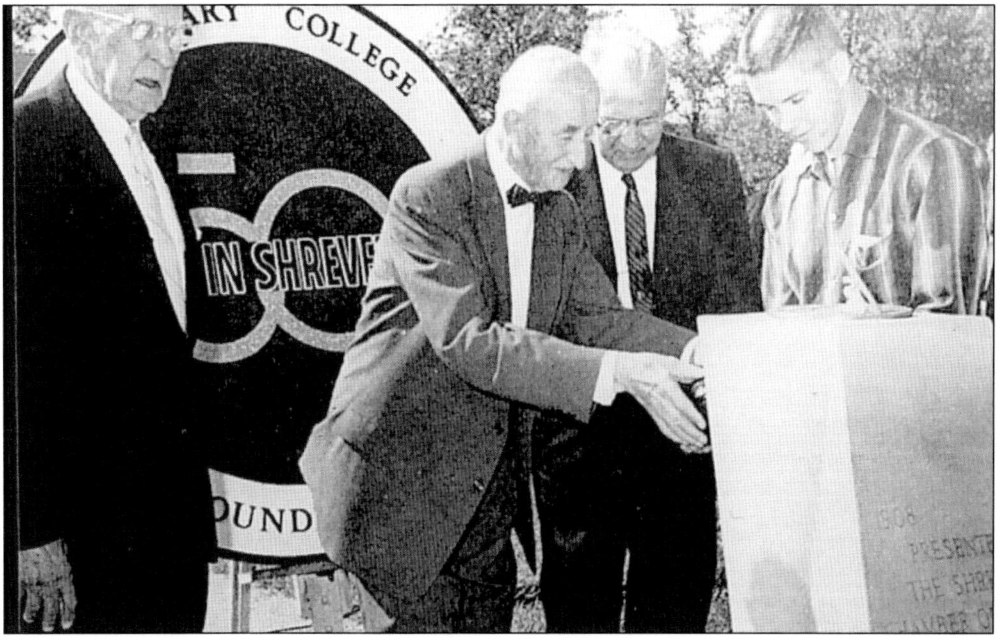

In the autumn of 1958, Centenary College of Louisiana celebrated the golden anniversary of its move to Shreveport from the original campus at Jackson, Louisiana. Numerous events, performances, and exhibits were held at the college in association with the jubilee. Among these was the placing of a time capsule, crowned by a sundial marker given to the college by the Shreveport Chamber of Commerce (above). Located near the east end of Mickle Hall along the walk connecting the chapel and the library, the time capsule is to be opened in 2008, the centennial of the move to Shreveport. Among the public attractions was the "Space Age Exhibit," featuring a rocket from nearby Barksdale Air Force Base displayed in front of Haynes Gym (below).

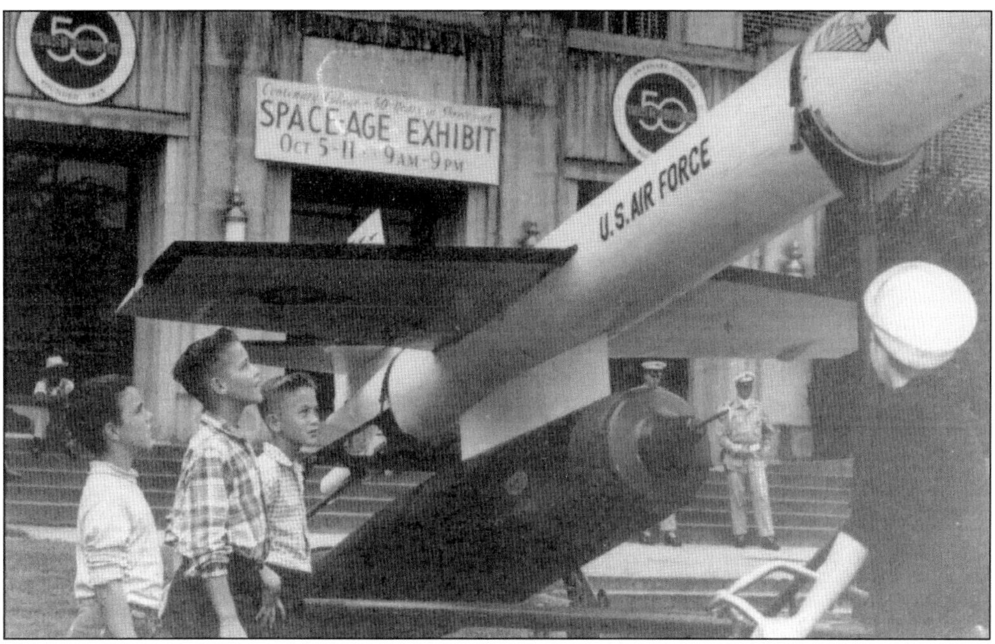

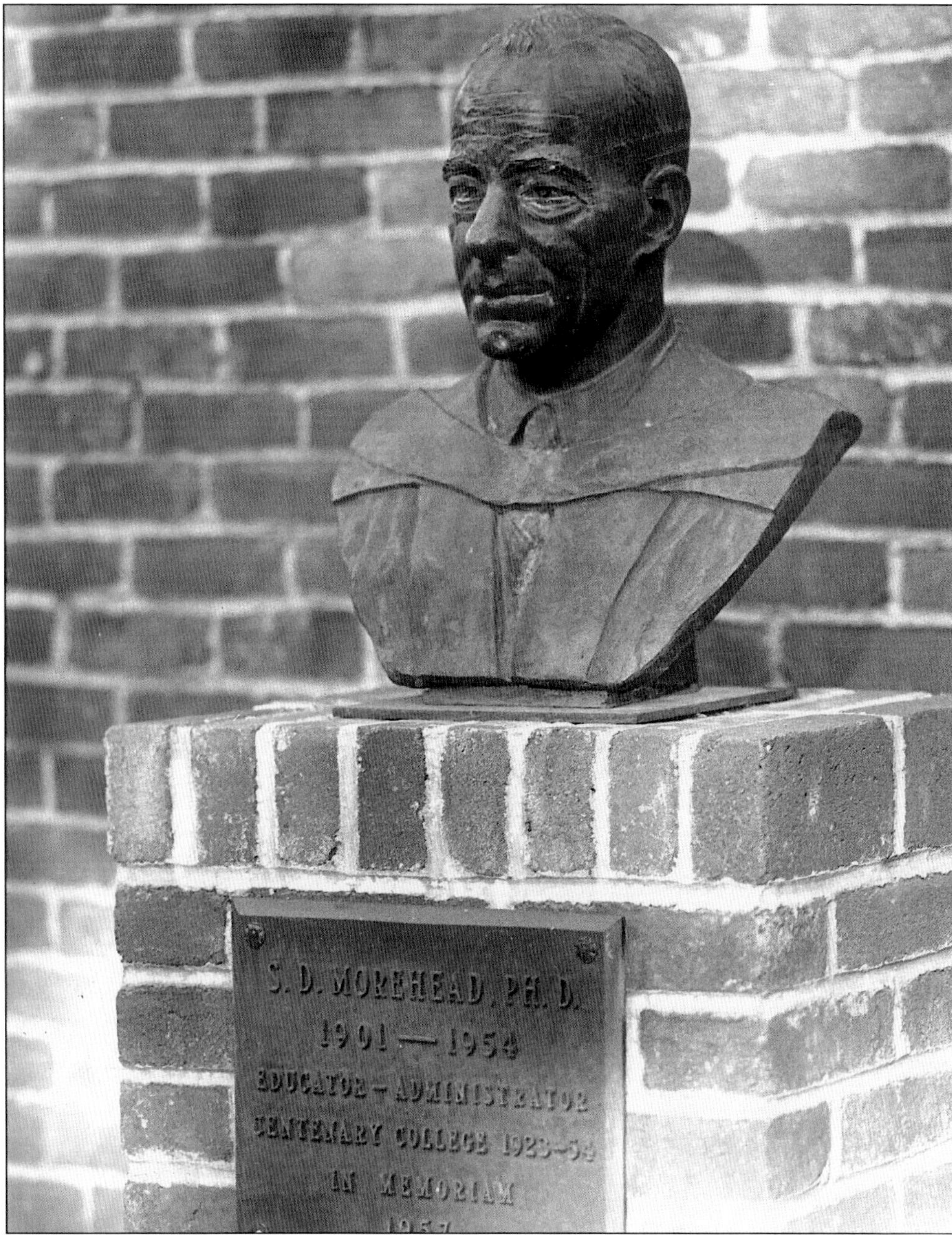

In 1957, a memorial was dedicated to Dr. S.D. Morehead, professor of economics and professor of history. Dr. Morehead came to Centenary from Columbia University in 1928, and remained at the school until his death in 1954. In addition to his teaching career, he worked as an administrator of the college and helped found the Centenary band—acting as its director for many years. One of many influential, erudite, respected, and beloved professors who have set Centenary students on their courses in life, Dr. Morehead is still a constant campus presence—thanks to this memorial which is located between the two sets of curving steps leading from the rose garden to the entrance of Hamilton Hall.

Five

Modern Centenary

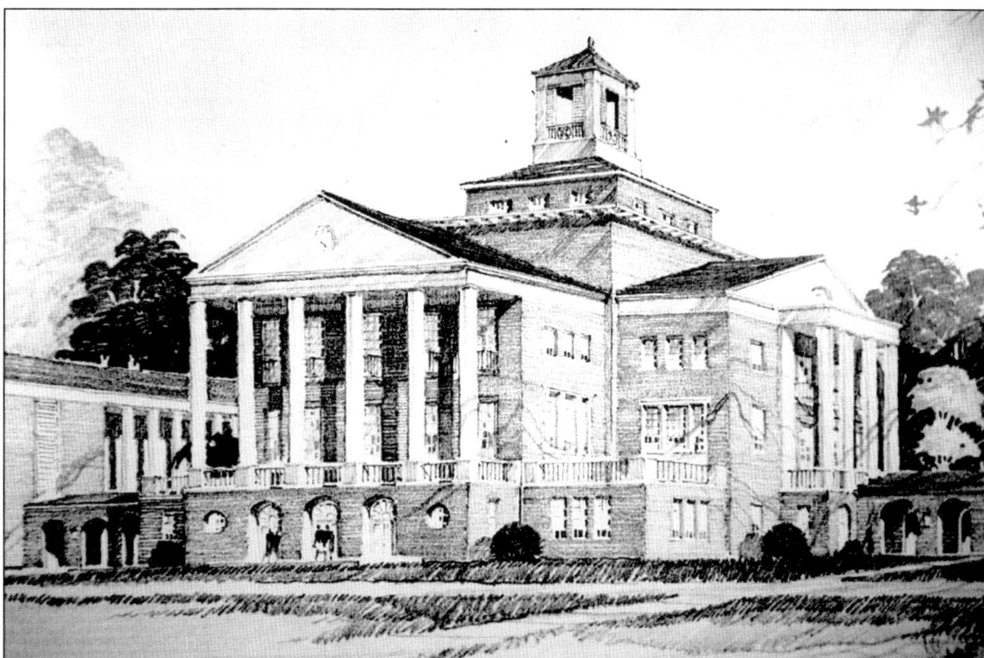

Plans for a new library for Centenary College had begun to be discussed as early as the 1940s, and part of the school's great post-war building program called for a library to be constructed between the planned twin science and liberal arts buildings. In the mid-1950s, the design shown above was approved and used in fund-raising activities on behalf of its construction. However, when it came time to actually begin construction, the building committee chose instead the design depicted in the drawing on page 71; it was that edifice, rather than the projected one pictured here, that was ultimately built. The library's cornerstone was laid in 1962.

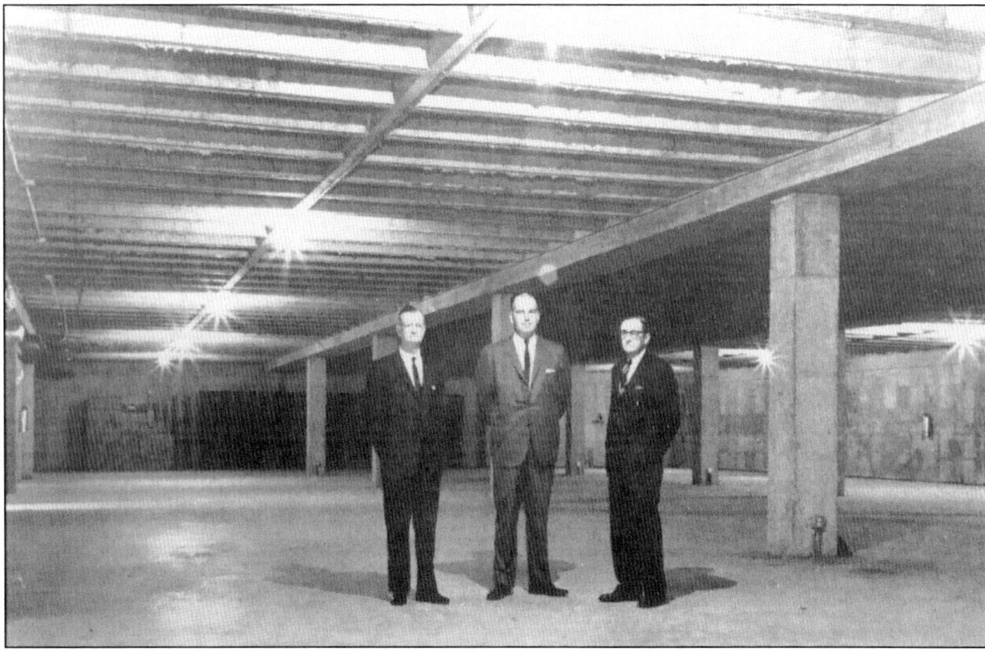

Construction of the library provided not only much-needed space for the college's books but classroom space as well. During the Cold War era—especially at the time of the Cuban Missile Crisis, which occurred just as the library neared completion—the steel and concrete basement was touted as a potential fallout shelter. Here, in March of 1964, board chairman Paul Brown and board members John B. Atkins and Edwin F. Whited stand in the library basement (above), soon to be finished as classrooms and faculty offices. Upstairs at the same time, over 120,000 volumes already filled the library with space for thousands more (below).

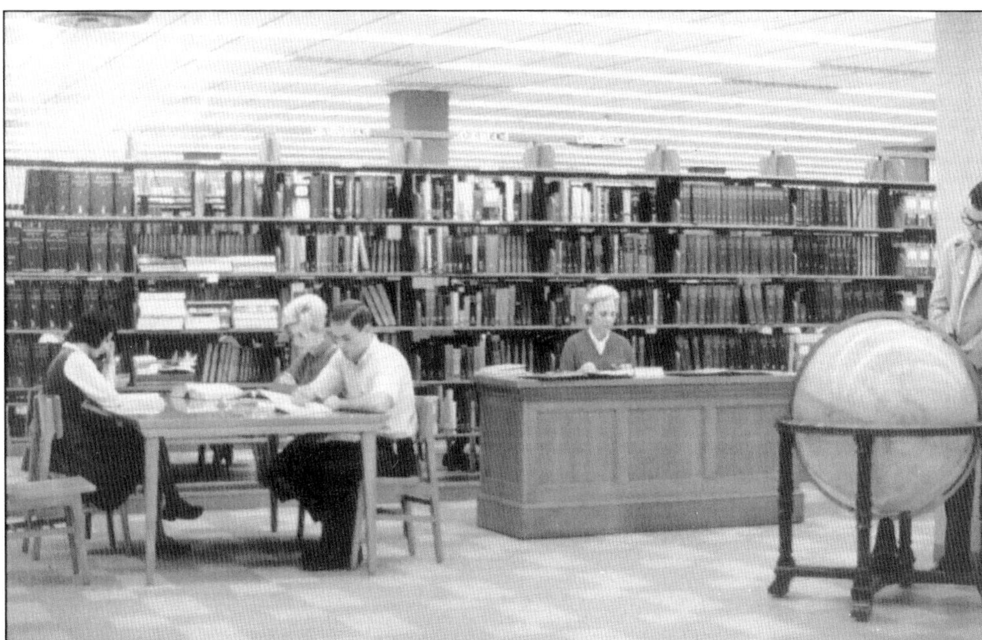

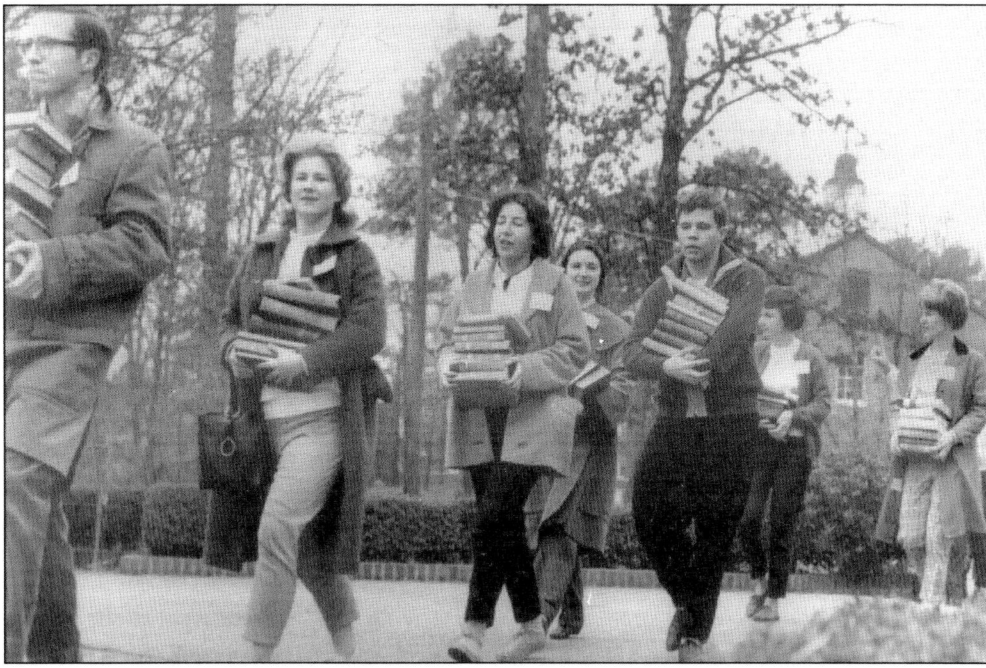

Most of the tens of thousands of books that filled the library had been brought by hand from the old library, clear across the campus. For days in 1963, long lines of students filed across the campus, carrying as many books as they could hold. Many professors were part of the human convoy as well. Above: The half-way point was marked by the rose garden next to the Student Center. Below: The books arrive in the library for the massive job of organizing and shelving.

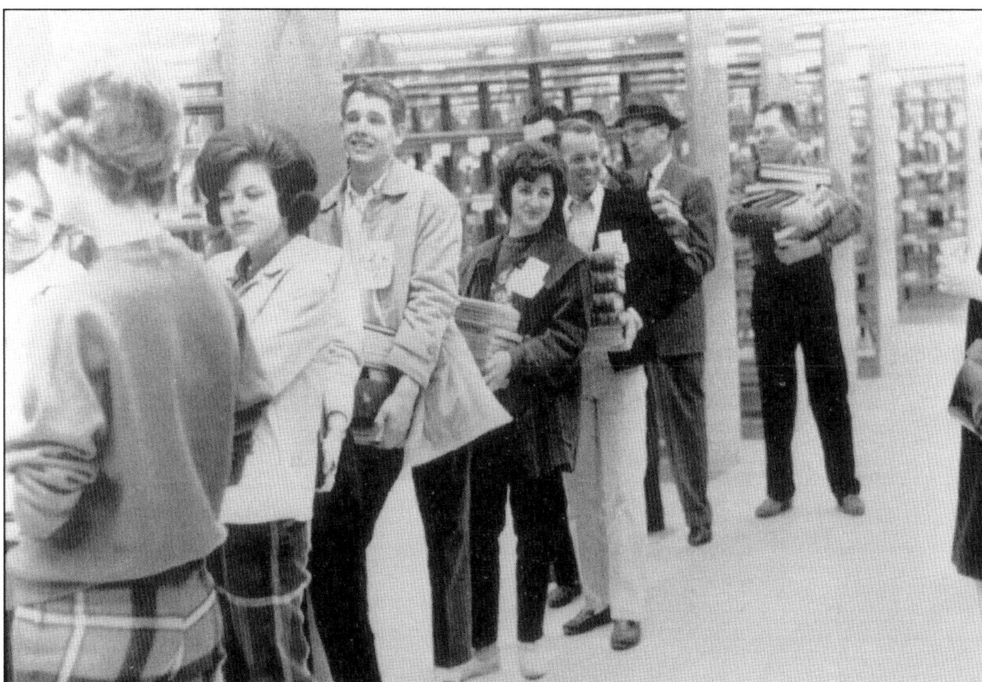

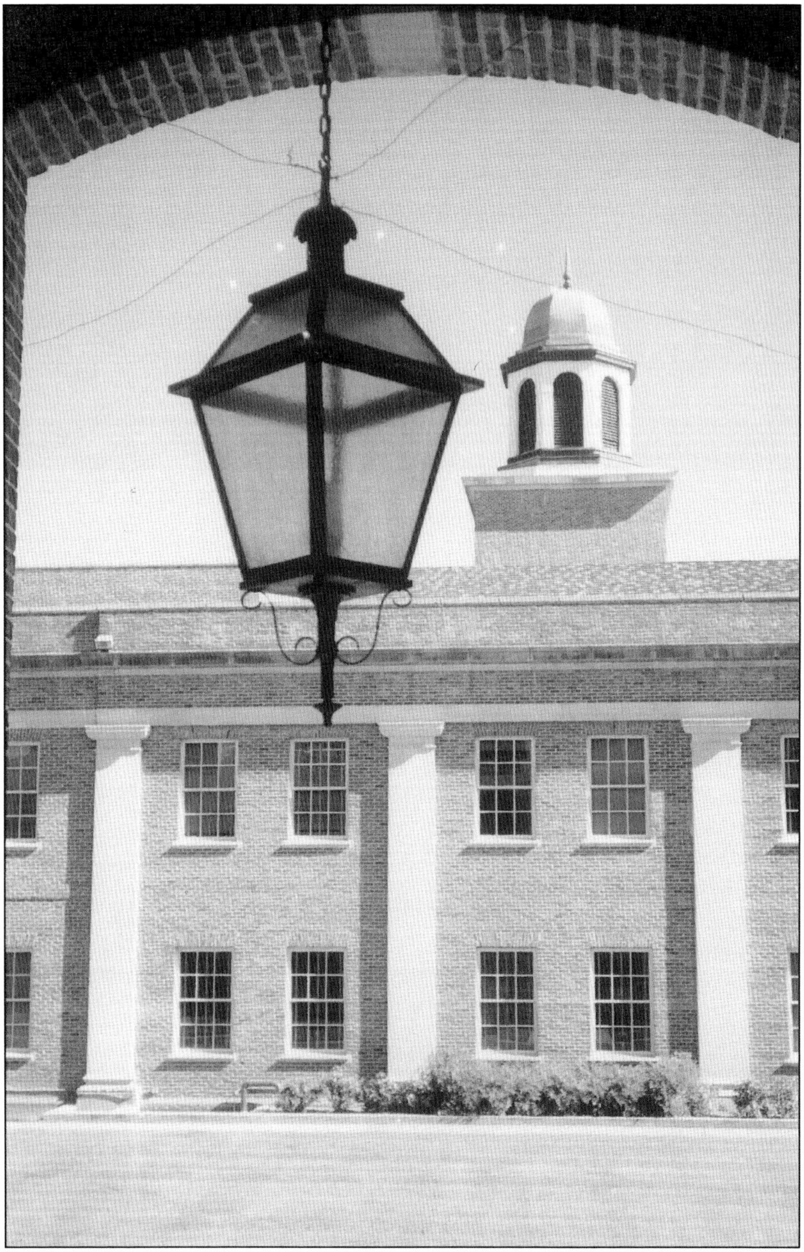

The rear of the library is seen from the east portico of Hamilton Hall, Centenary's administration building, constructed in 1971. The library was endowed by oilman John Magale and his wife Joanna, and today is known as the Magale Library and Media Center. Architects for the building were J. Cheshire Peyton, Aubrey McKelvy, and George R. Fisher. In the late 1990s, many of the books on the ground floor of the library were consolidated onto the second floor. The ground floor was extensively remodeled with computer terminals being installed where shelving had formerly been located. Thousands of other volumes, particularly periodicals, are now stored in closed stacks in the basement and attic of the library. Archival materials are housed in the Peters Building.

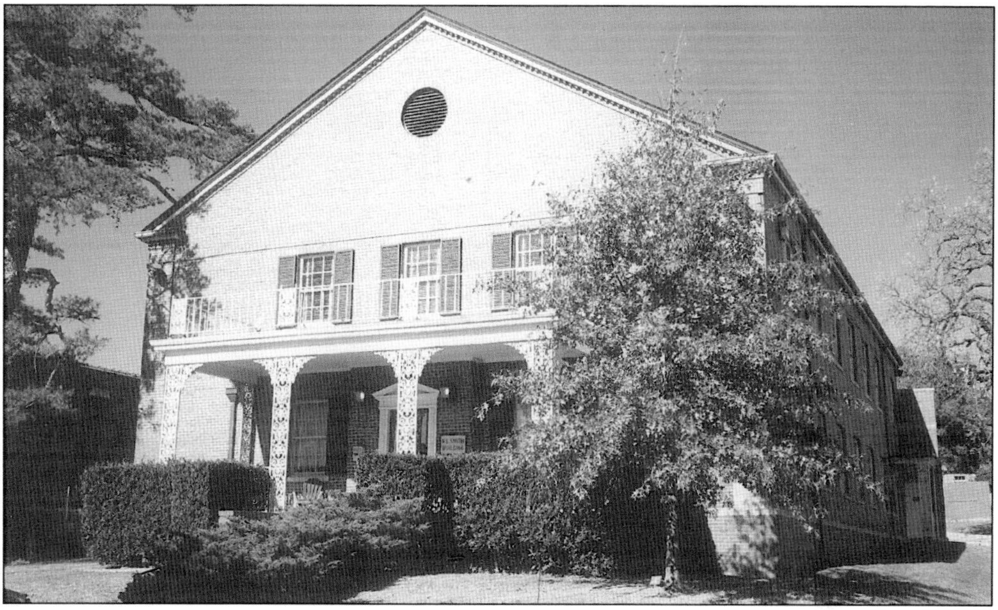

The R.E. Smith Religious Activities Building was constructed near the corner of Kings Highway and Woodlawn Avenue in 1961. Its site is close to that formerly occupied by the wooden Religion Building constructed under Dr. Sexton. Designed by architects Peyton, Fisher, and McKelvy, it is named in memory of Robert E. Smith, longtime Dean of the College and professor of religion.

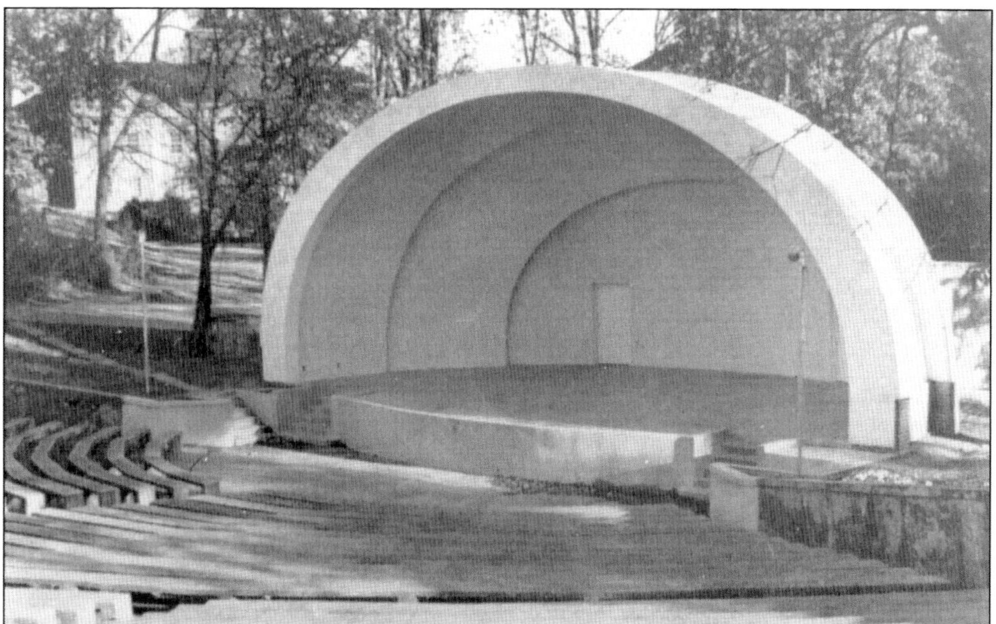

In 1963, the old wooden amphitheater was rebuilt in concrete and its frame stage replaced by an acoustic band shell. The shell was given in memory of Texas Eastern Oil Company president Reginald Henry Hargrove by his family. Hargrove, a member of the Centenary board of trustees, perished in the January 1954 airplane crash on Wallace Lake with two other trustees and nine other passengers. In 1999, the Hargrove shell was extensively renovated. This view is from 1964.

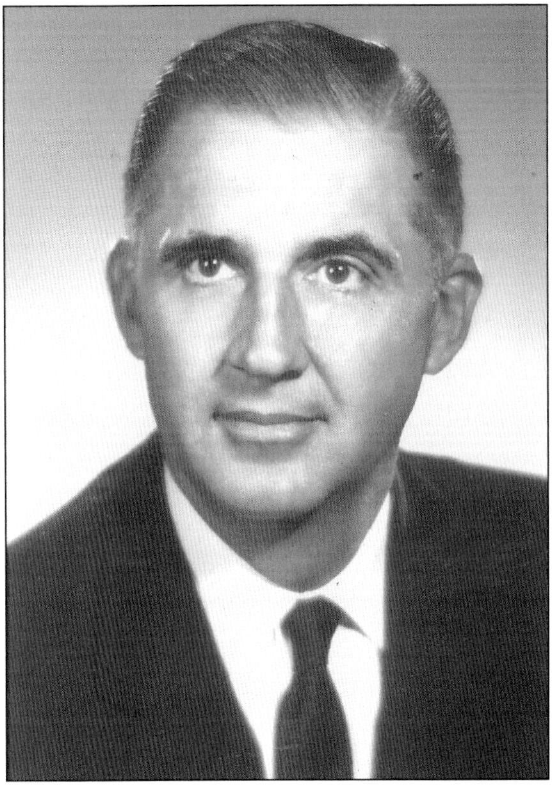

Dr. Jack Stauffer Wilkes (left) succeeded Dr. Joe Mickle as president of Centenary in 1964, serving the college for four years. Wilkes was formerly the mayor of Oklahoma City, Oklahoma. He was followed as president by Dr. John Horton Allen, who served from 1969 to 1976 (below). Both presidents, together with Board Chairman George D. Nelson (who succeeded Paul M. Brown in that position in 1964), carried on the building program begun under President Mickle. However, never again in Centenary's history would so many new buildings rise on the campus as during the Mickle era.

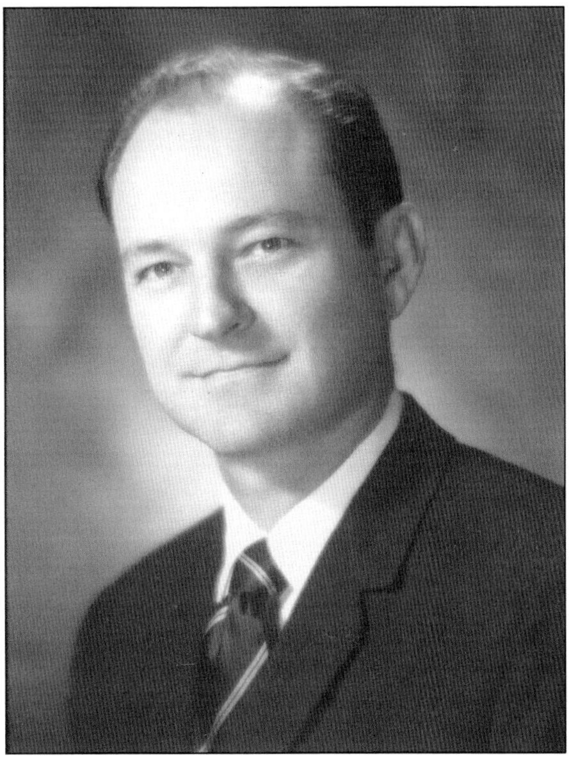

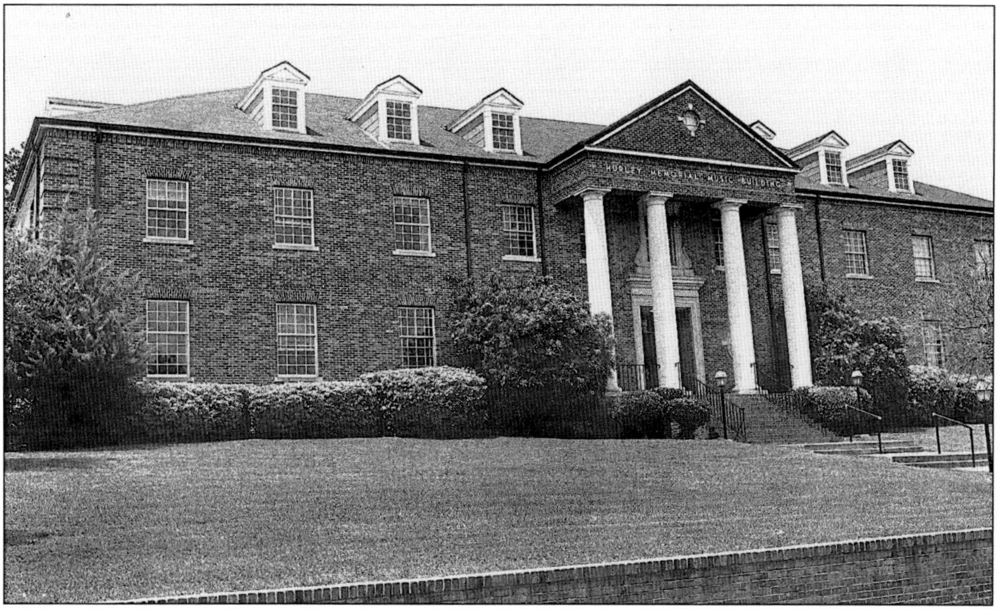

The Hurley School of Music was constructed in 1964 and marked the last move from a frame building of the Sexton era into a brick structure built for the ages. Designed by the firm of Peyton & McKelvy, it was given by Mrs. Gladys F. Hurley as a memorial to her husband, oilman Ed E. Hurley. The Hurley School of Music houses one of the college's most vibrant departments, and is also home to the opera workshop, camerata, choir, jazz band, and the annual Wideman Piano Competition, an esteemed national competition held each autumn. It is named for Nena Plant Wideman (class of 1934).

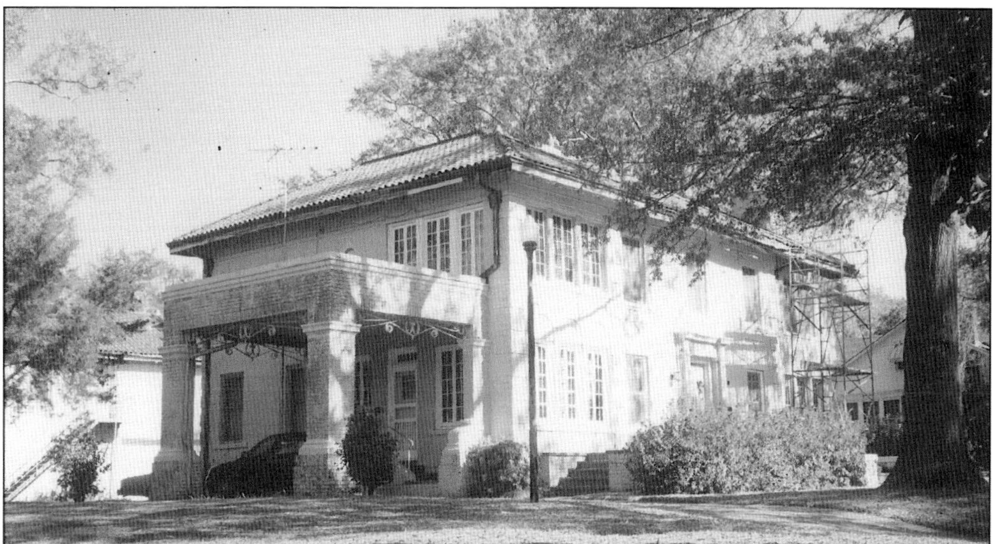

In 1964, the former Arch Haynes residence at 254 Rutherford Street, a block to the east of the Centenary campus, was given to the college for use as the president's residence. The old president's house at the corner of Centenary Boulevard and Rutherford Street was then vacated. President and Mrs. Wilkes became the first residents of the new home, a 1920s Mediterranean-style villa.

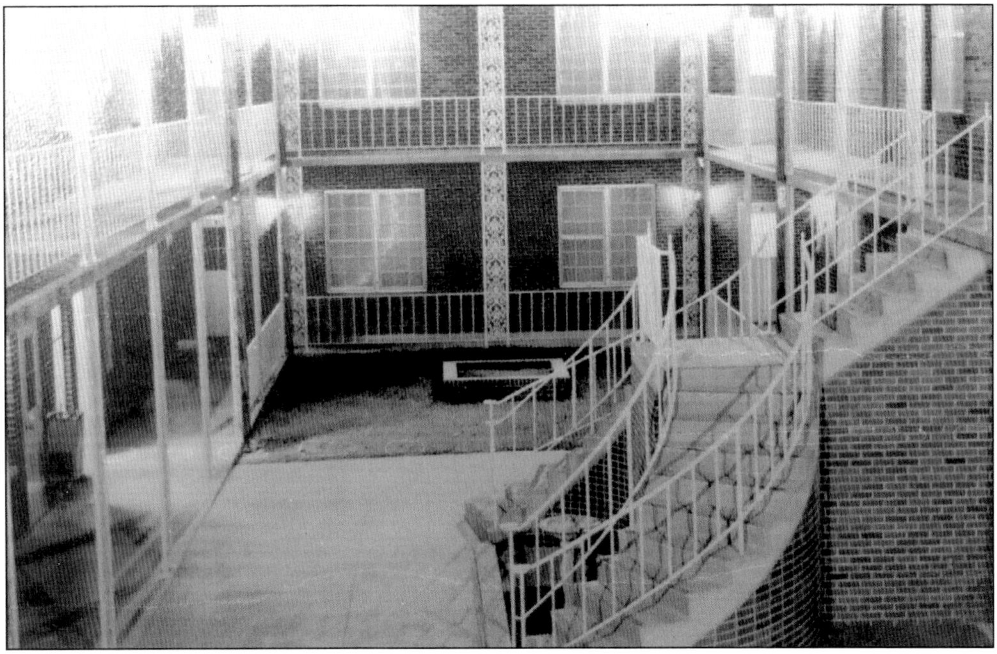

The year 1964 also saw the construction of a new men's dormitory, only the second to be built since Rotary Hall's completion in 1930. Located between Rotary Hall and Haynes Gym, on the site of old Sorority Row, the new dorm was named Cline Hall in honor of President Pierce Cline. The view above is of the courtyard of the dorm shortly after its completion. Also during the 1960s, the heavily-used Student Center, or SUB (for "Student Union Building"), was again remodeled. The picture below shows construction of the cafe in 1968.

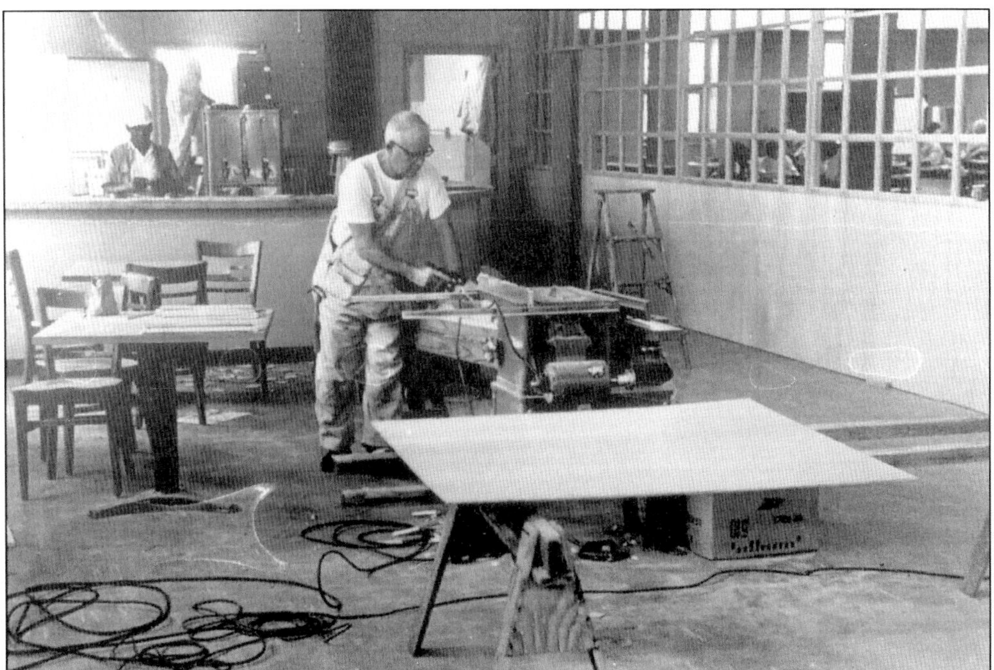

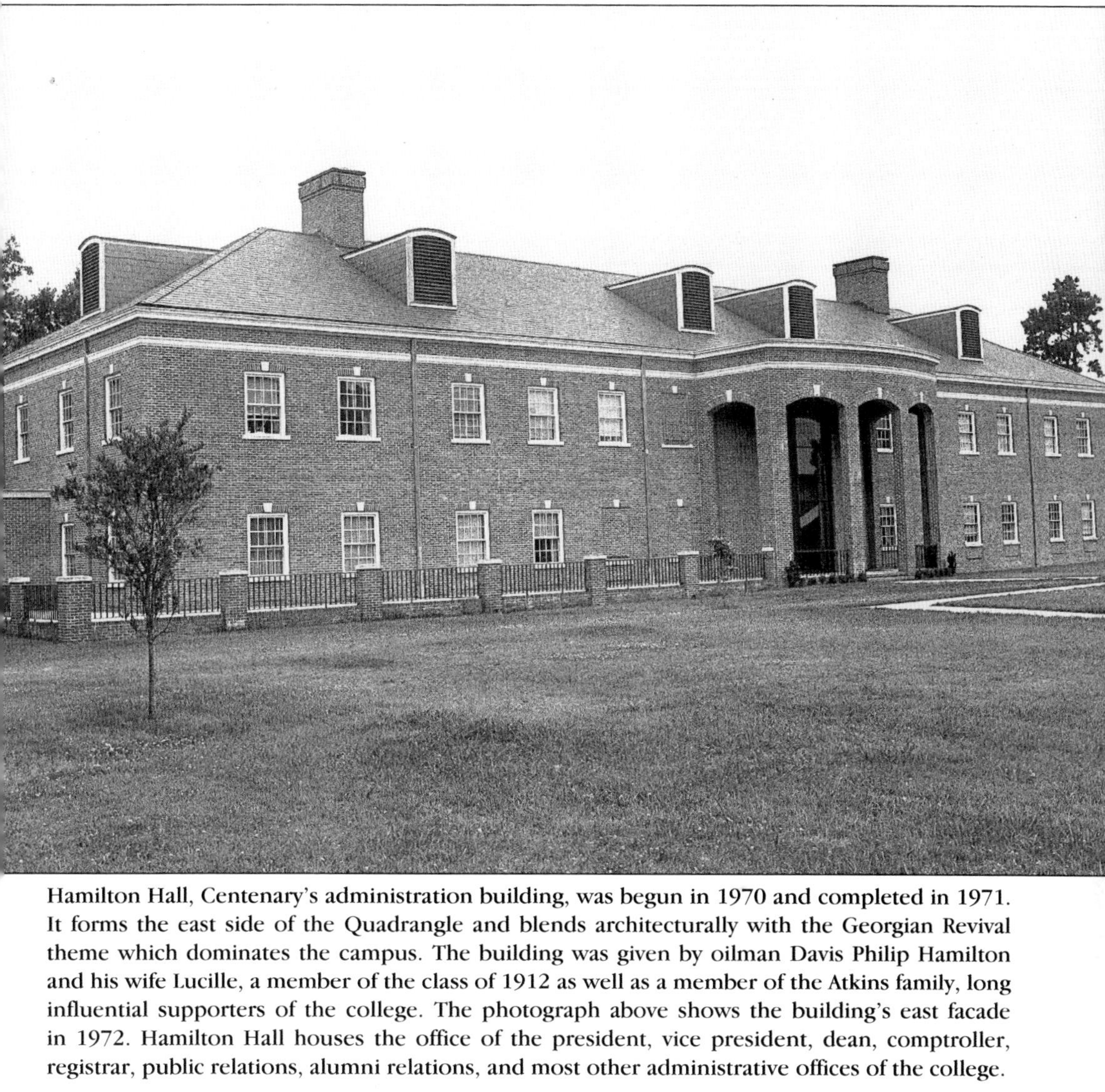

Hamilton Hall, Centenary's administration building, was begun in 1970 and completed in 1971. It forms the east side of the Quadrangle and blends architecturally with the Georgian Revival theme which dominates the campus. The building was given by oilman Davis Philip Hamilton and his wife Lucille, a member of the class of 1912 as well as a member of the Atkins family, long influential supporters of the college. The photograph above shows the building's east facade in 1972. Hamilton Hall houses the office of the president, vice president, dean, comptroller, registrar, public relations, alumni relations, and most other administrative offices of the college.

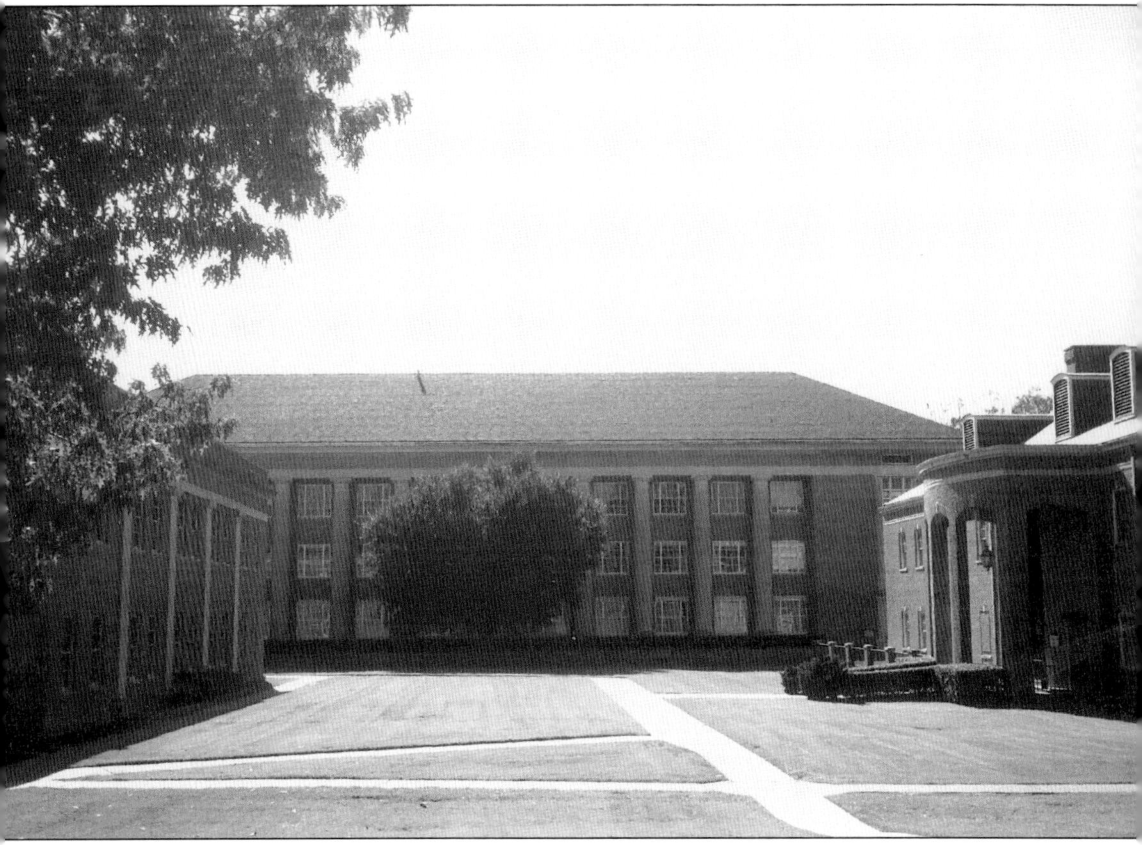

This 1999 view shows the Quadrangle looking south. The Magale Library is seen at the left, Mickle Hall at center, and Hamilton Hall at right. Note the significant growth of the oak tree at center, the same one seen over two decades earlier in the left-hand side of the photograph of Hamilton Hall on page 101. The Quadrangle's site was that of the baseball diamond early in the 20th century. The point where Mickle Hall and the library appear to meet was the site of the first wooden gymnasium. Faculty Row once stood where the photographer stood to take this picture, the site once planned for Mickle Hall's unbuilt twin.

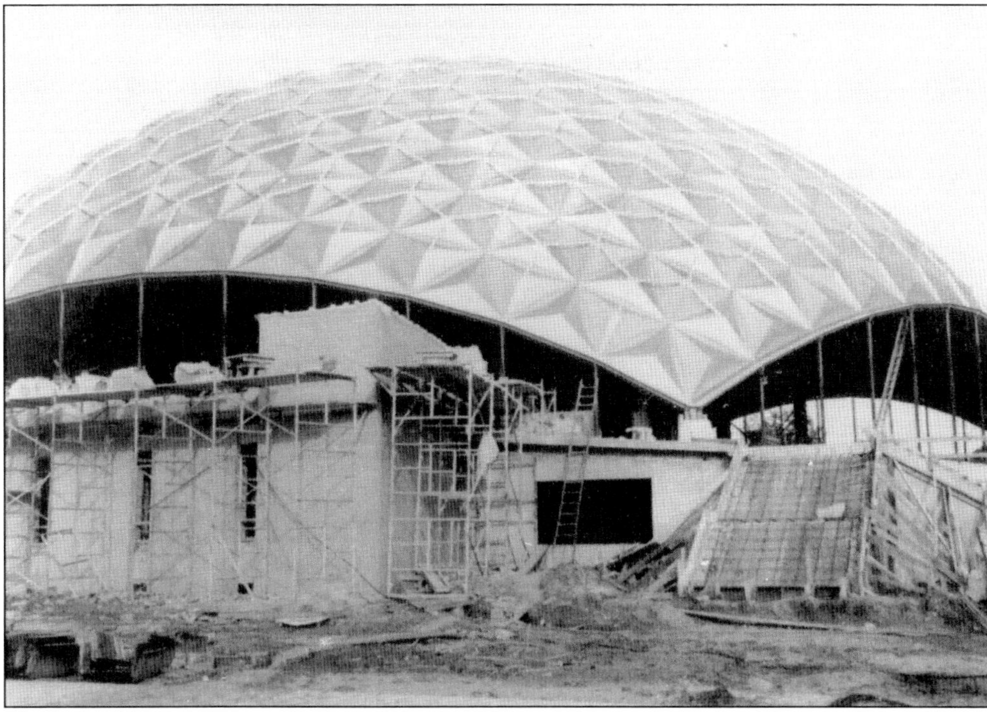

The Gold Dome, which today houses Centenary College's athletic department, was begun in 1972 and completed in 1974. The geodesic dome was designed by architect W.E. Wilson of Shreveport. It is home to the Centenary Gentlemen basketball team, the gymnastics team, and is the site each year of the college's commencement ceremonies. Above: The Gold Dome is seen under construction. Below: The completed edifice is pictured.

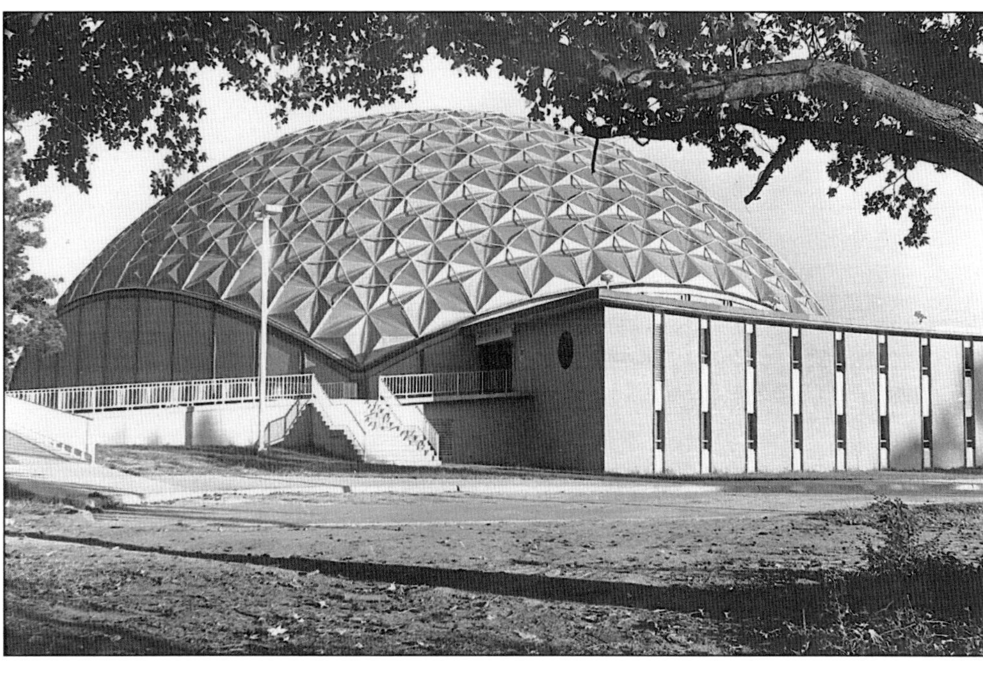

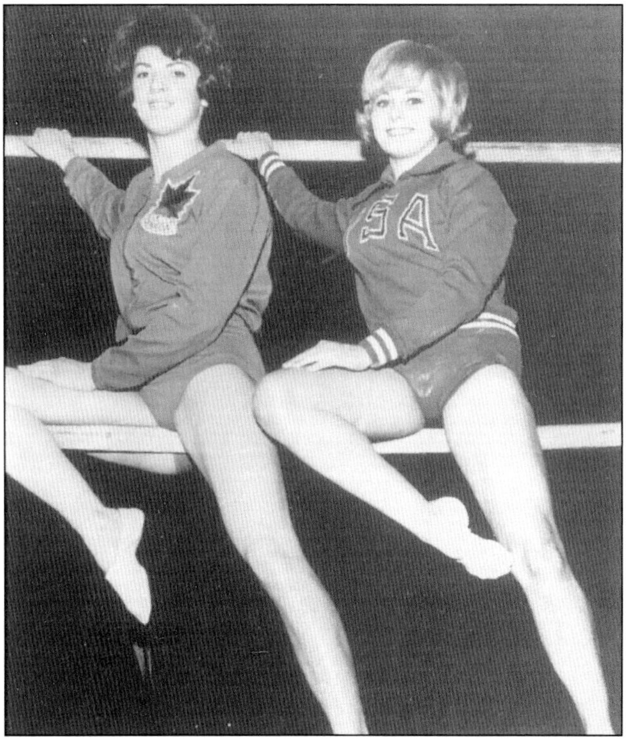

Women's gymnastics has long been one of the strongest elements of the Centenary College athletic program. Several Centenary students have ranked among the nation's top gymnasts, including Olympic medalist Kathy Johnson, a Centenary student in the late 1970s, and top ranking gymnasts Susan McDonnell and Janie Speaks, seen here in 1968. In the 1990s Centenary students Dayspring Conley and Meredith Sholars were ranked among the nation's top college gymnasts as well.

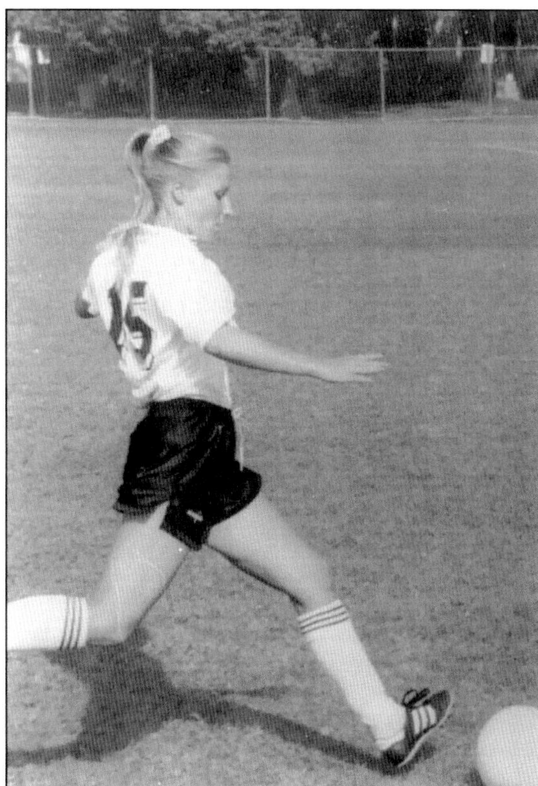

Intramural soccer was introduced at Centenary in 1981, and has since gained in popularity and significance among sports sponsored by the college. Here, Centenary Lady Wendy Eckstrom is seen on the field in 1995. Other sports at Centenary today include tennis, baseball, softball, volleyball, track and cross country, and golf. PGA star and Ryder Cup champion golfer Hal Sutton is a member of the class of 1981. In the late 1960s, there was an attempt to revive Centenary football but it failed to win support. In the past, riflery, archery, boxing, fencing, and riding have also been sponsored by Centenary.

Robert Parish, class of 1976, was one of the Centenary's Gentlemen's all-time top basketball players. He later went on to play professionally for the Boston Celtics. Parish is seen at right seated in the stands of the Gold Dome shortly after its completion in 1974. He is seen below in action in the Gold Dome that same year. He is at left, number 00.

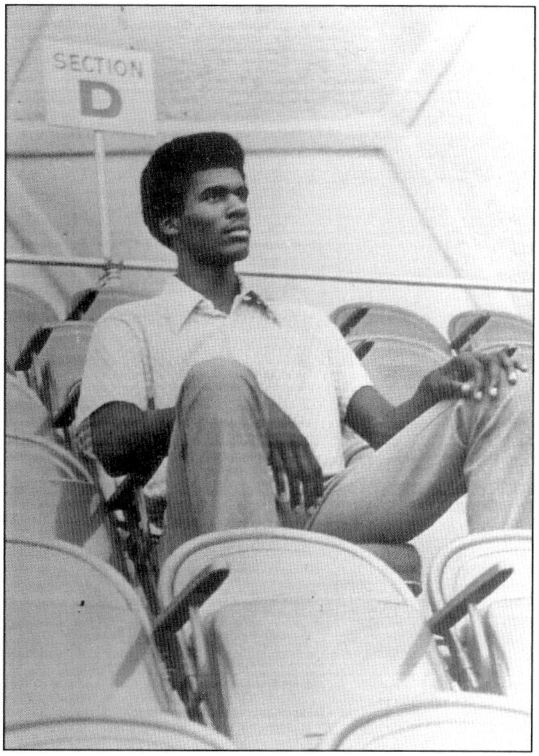

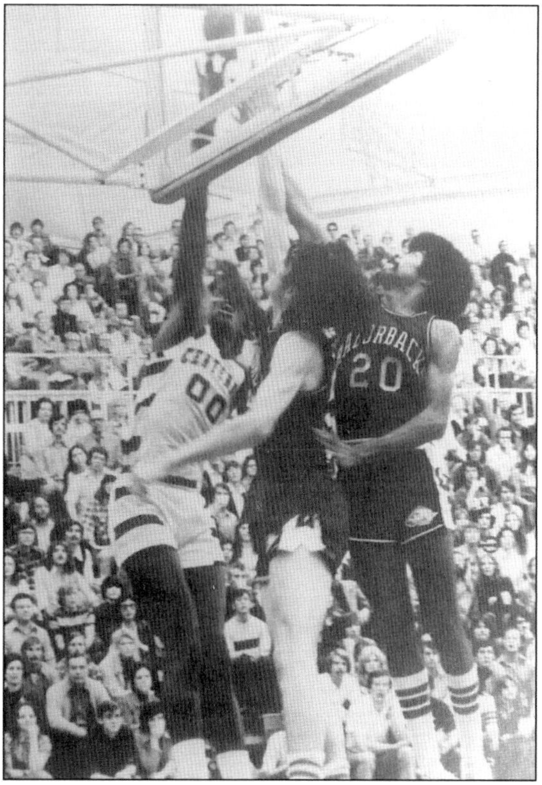

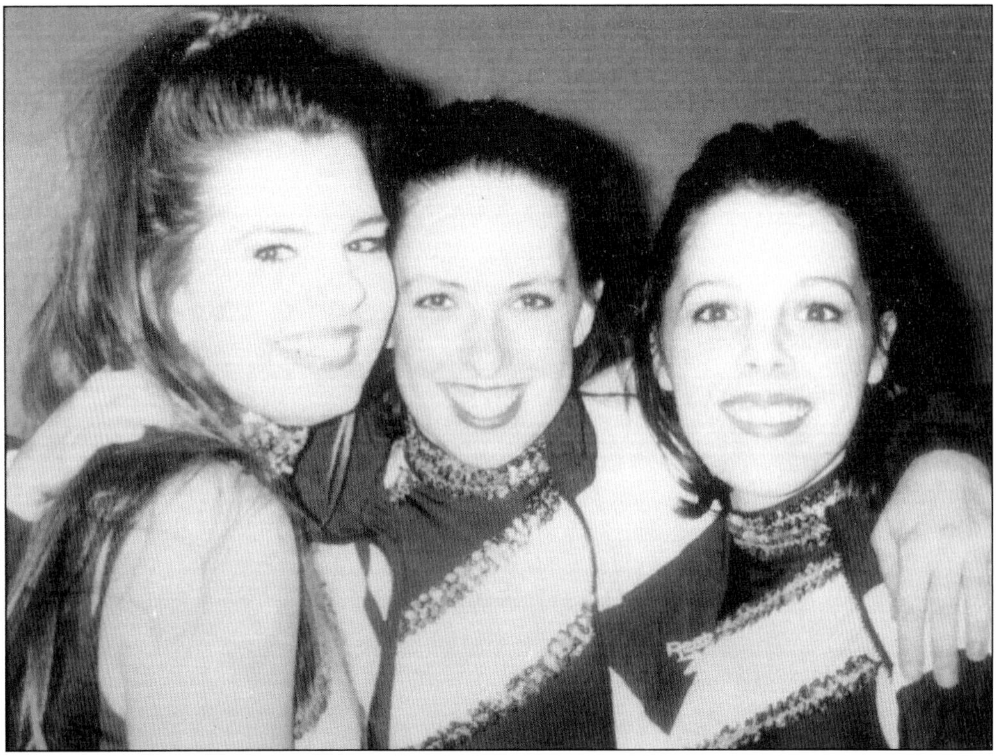

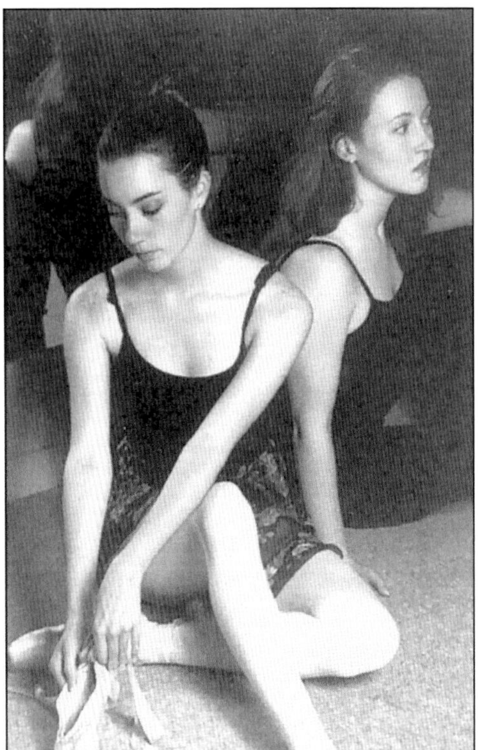

The Centenary Danceline, known as "The Leading Ladies," was established in 1993. Above: Three members of the 1995–96 danceline squad pose after a game. Pictured from left to right are Nicole McCurley, Sarah Stewart, and Renee Hough. Below: Another form of dance sponsored by Centenary is ballet. Here two student ballerinas pose in 1998.

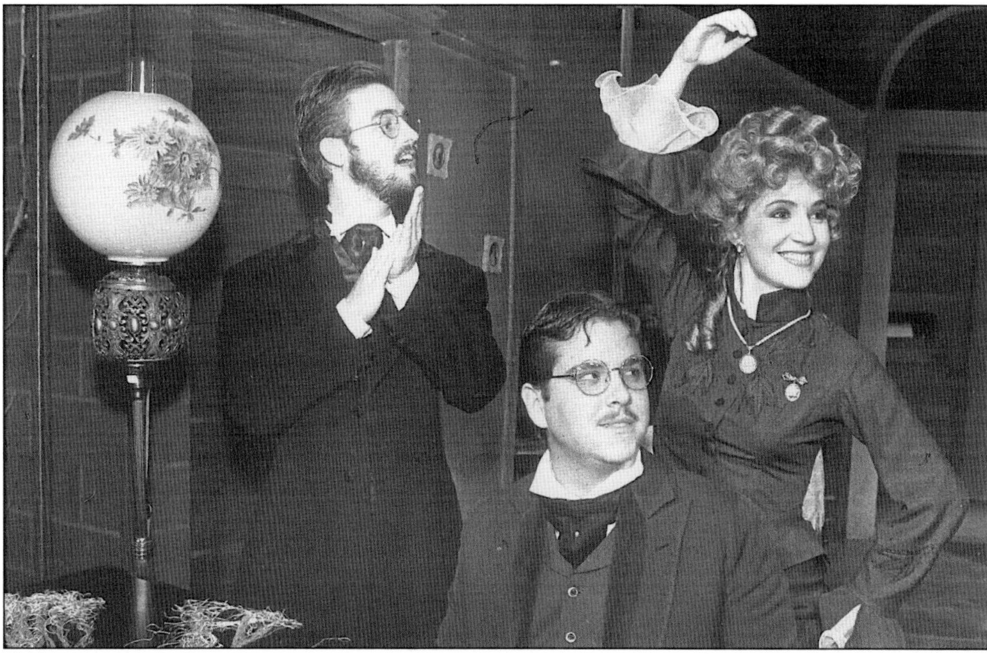

The Centenary College Choir and the dramatic performances staged by the theater department have remained among the most significant elements of the cultural life of both college and city for much of the century. Above is a scene from the Marjorie Lyons Playhouse production of Ibsen's A Doll's House, in July of 1990. Pictured from left to right are John Bundrick, Houston Chaise Waites, and Betsy Baldwin. The theater department stages at least a half-dozen plays each season. Below: Members of the choir are pictured on stage at New York's Radio City Music Hall in the 1960s.

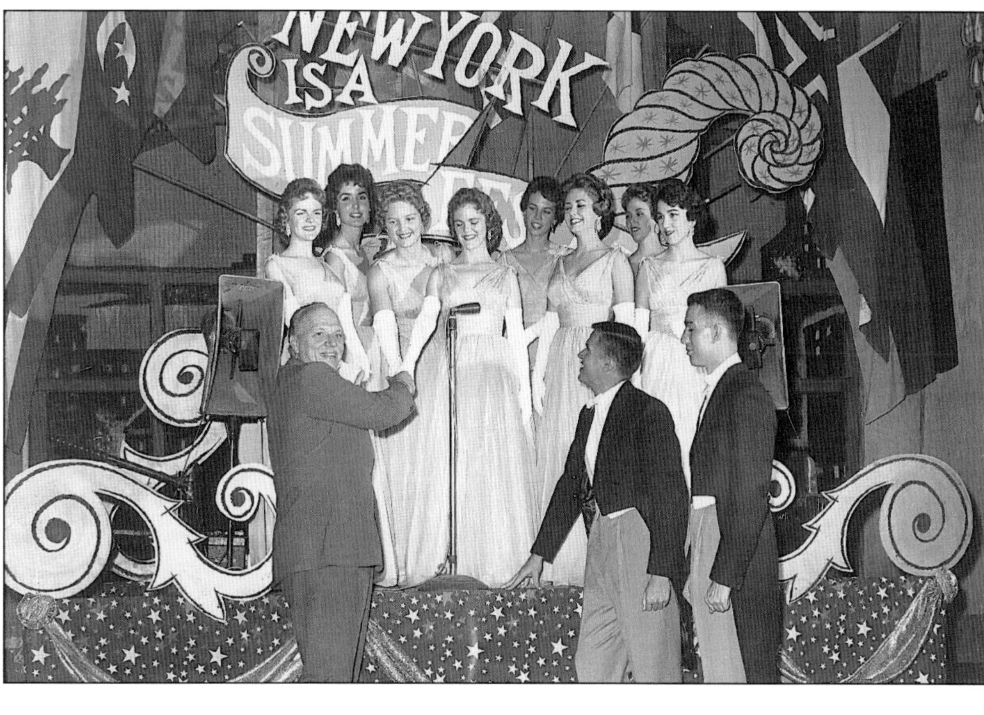

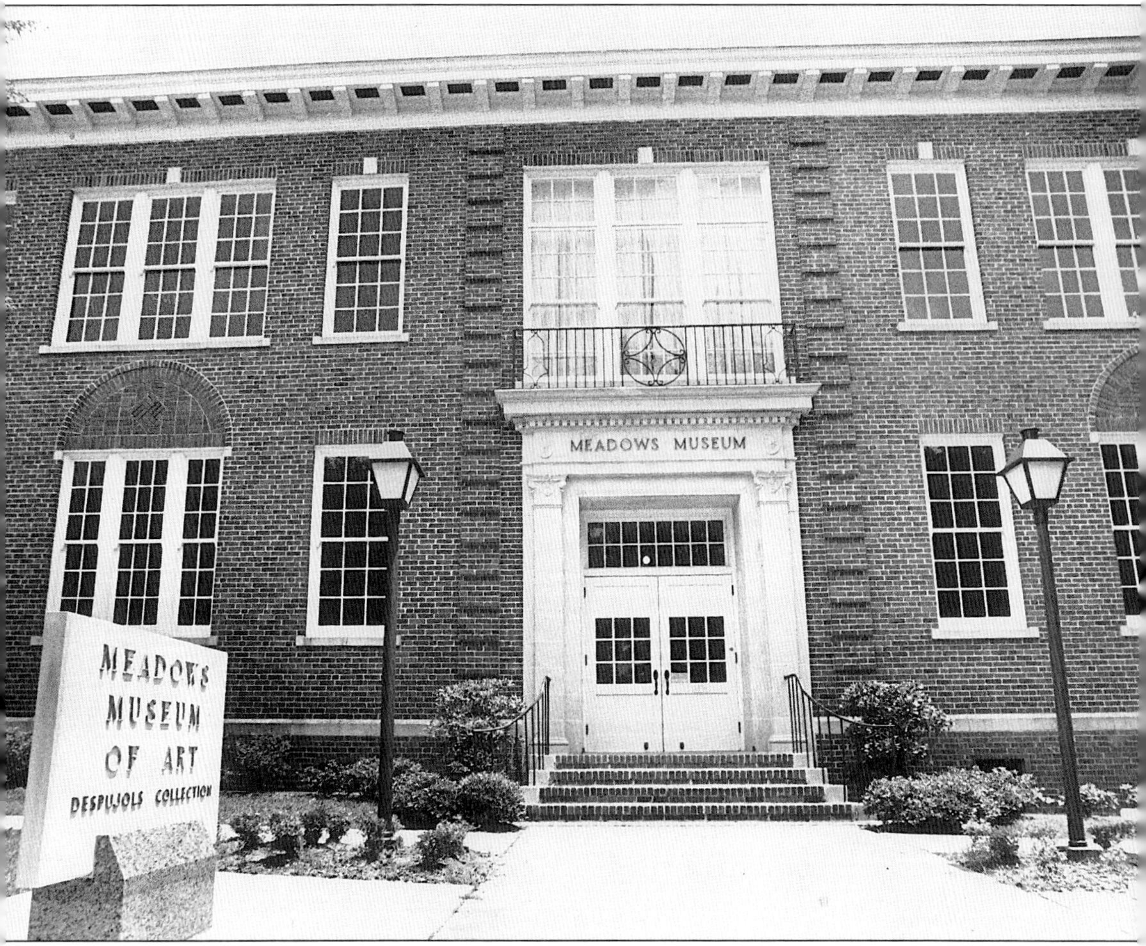

In 1975 the Meadows Museum of Art was established by Centenary College in the old Arts Building on Centenary Boulevard. The museum was made possible by a gift from Dallas, Texas oilman Algur H. Meadows, a former Centenary student. In 1969, Meadows had purchased a collection of 360 pieces by the French artist Jean Despujols, who had chronicled the culture of French Indochina in paintings and drawings before the outbreak of World War II. Meadows's Despujols collection forms the cornerstone of the museum, though its scope extends far beyond. Today, the Meadows Museum of Art is a significant cultural and educational resource not only for Centenary College, its parent institution, but for the entire Shreveport metropolitan area.

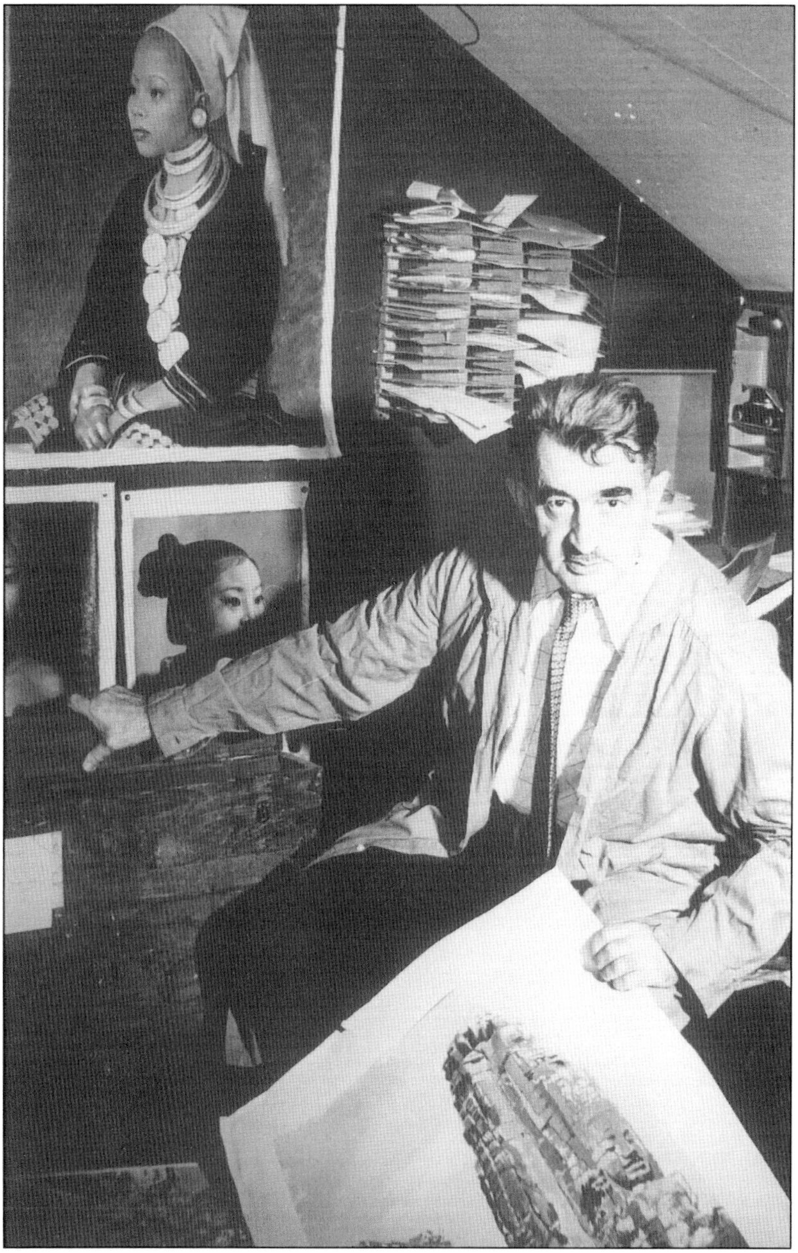

The artist Jean Despujols, whose works form the nucleus of the Meadow Museum collection, was a professor of portrait and figure painting and of mural composition at the Fontainebleau Academy in France early in the 20th century. The winner of numerous important medals of achievement from European art institutions, he traveled to Indochina in the 1930s to record the scenes of its remotest corners for the French government. Returning to France on the eve of war, the German invasion prompted him to come to the United States. Through personal connections he ended up in Shreveport, where he resided at his Broadmoor Boulevard home just blocks from the Centenary campus until his death in 1965. He is seen here in 1948 with some of the works now housed at the museum.

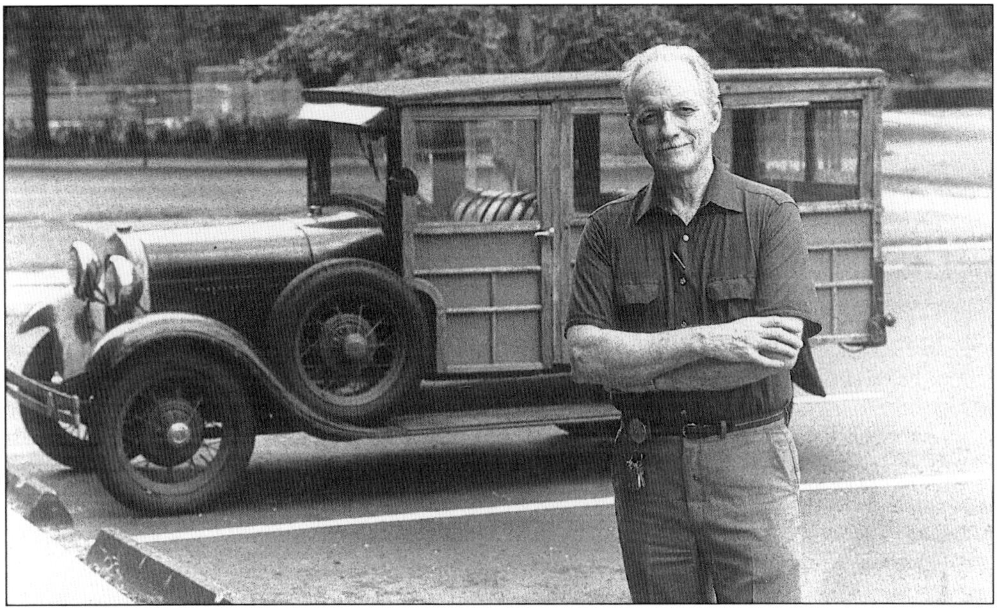

The first director of the Meadows Museum of Art was Willard Cooper, a noteworthy artist in his own right. A 1947 graduate of Centenary College, Professor Cooper returned to his Alma Mater after graduate studies in Mexico. He has served as professor of art, chairman of the art department, and now chairman emeritus of the department. Professor Cooper and his vintage Ford (above) have together been a presence on the campus since the 1940s (below). In the mid-1980s, Professor Cooper was instrumental in transforming the old President's House into Turner Art Center, named for Los Angeles art collector and former Centenary student Sidney R. Turner, who endowed the facility shortly before his death.

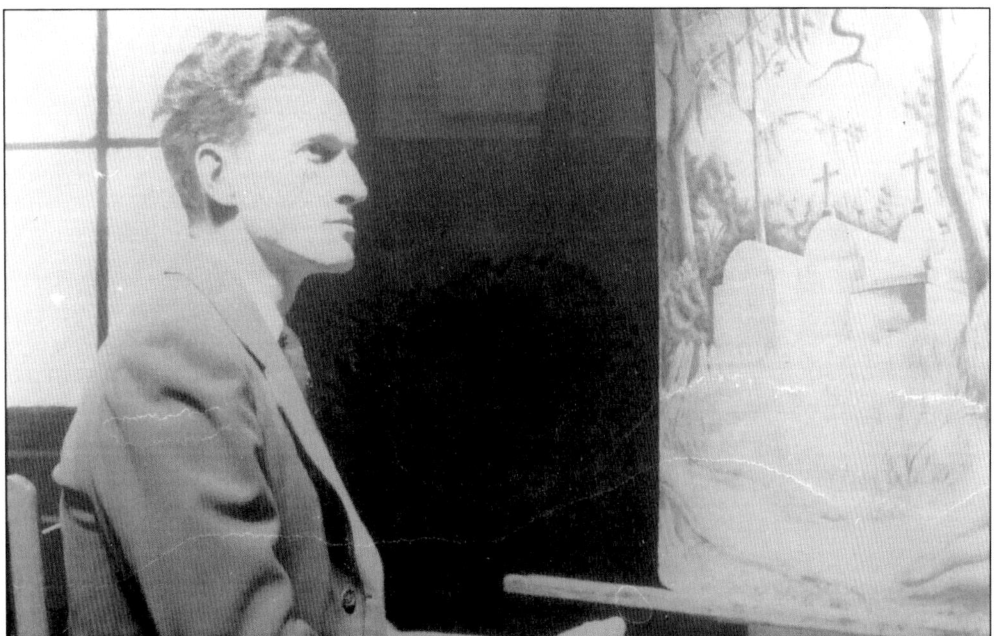

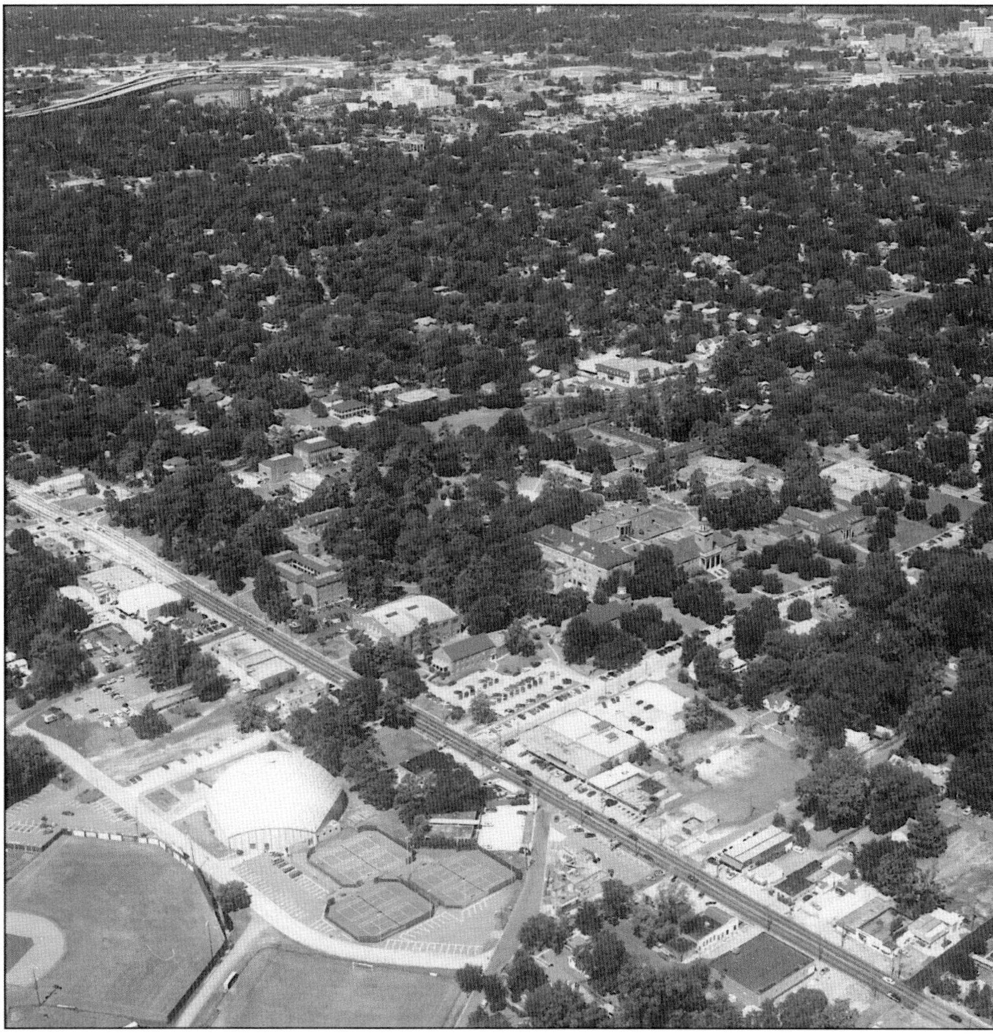

As seen from the air, this is the Centenary campus of today. The image was made from almost the same vantage point as the view of the old stadium seen on page 66. Kings Highway is seen bisecting the image's lower portion. The Gold Dome is prominent at lower left, and the main part of the campus is across Kings Highway at center.

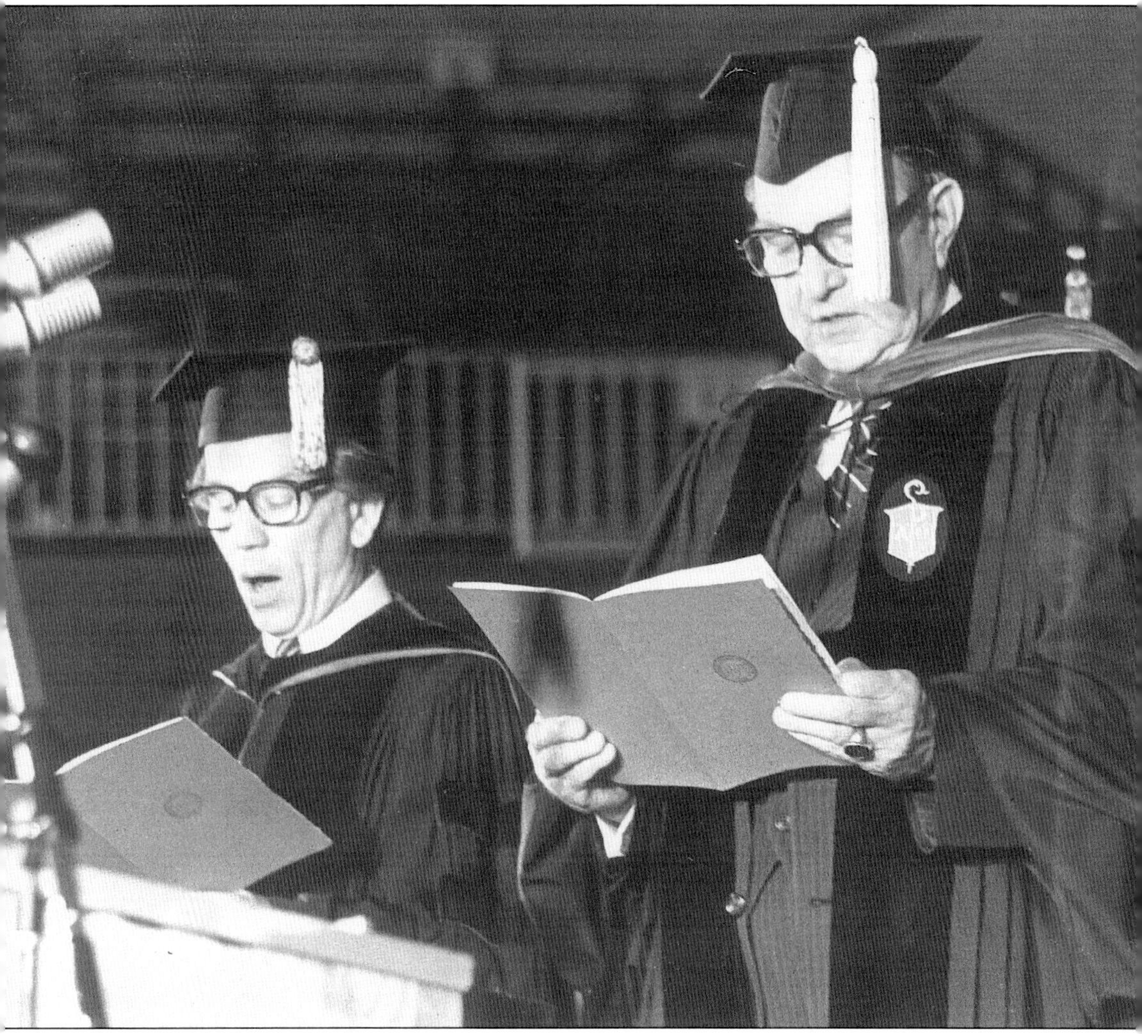

On December 1, 1977, Dr. Donald Webb was installed as president of Centenary College. He is seen at left, standing beside Methodist Bishop J. Kenneth Shamblin during the ceremony. Dr. Webb, a native of Wales and a distinguished educator and minister, served the college faithfully as president until his retirement in 1991. He and his wife Renee have remained active supporters of Centenary during the years since his retirement.

Among the many influential faculty members at Centenary during the 20th century, Dr. Bruno Strauss stands out as one of the most remarkable. Dr. Strauss was professor of German from 1939 to 1964, and also taught history and philosophy. A 1911 doctoral graduate of the University of Berlin, he was a noted authority on German language, literature, and history in his native Germany where he held several teaching posts—Heidelberg University among them. When the Nazis denied Jews teaching positions, he and his wife Bertha fled, ending up in Shreveport owing to personal connections.

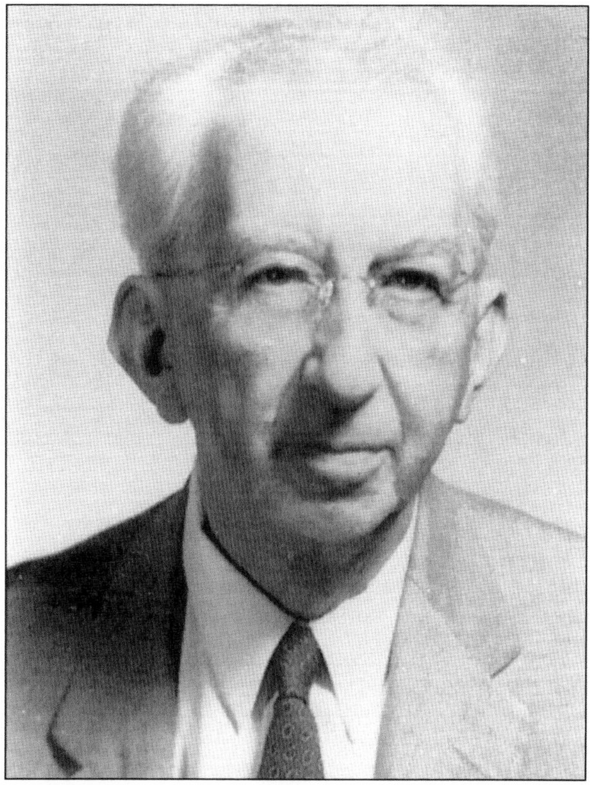

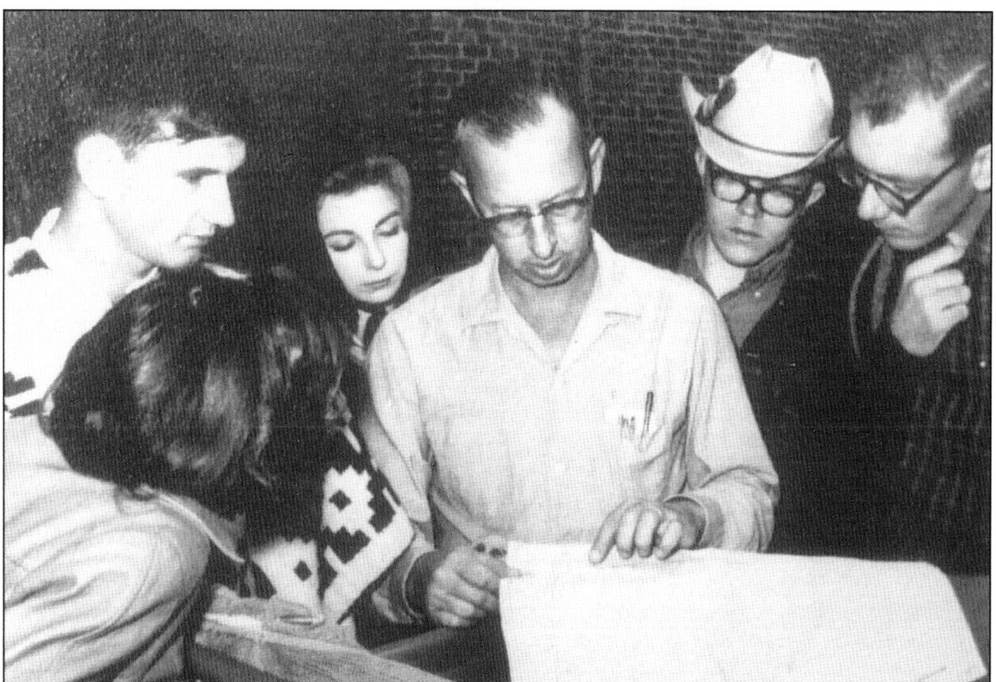

In this 1965 photograph, biology professor Dr. Richard Speairs, center, works on a problem with several of his students.

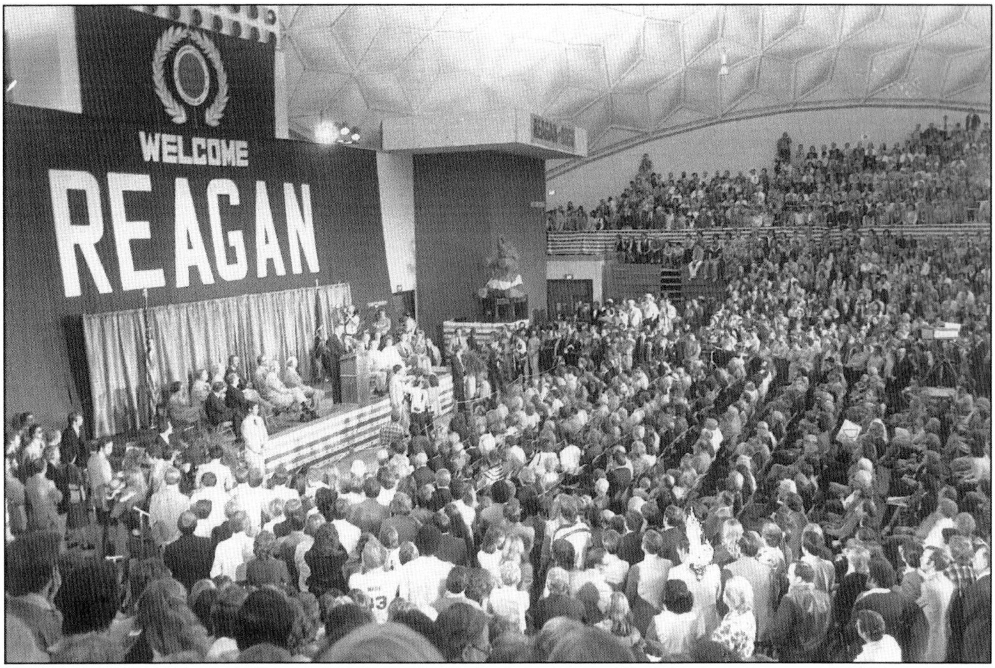

Convocations have been important events during Centenary's 175 years. Many notable persons have spoken to the student body through the years including religious and political leaders, writers, academics, celebrities of stage and screen, distinguished alumni, and others. Here presidential candidate Ronald Regan addresses a packed crowd at the Gold Dome in October 1980.

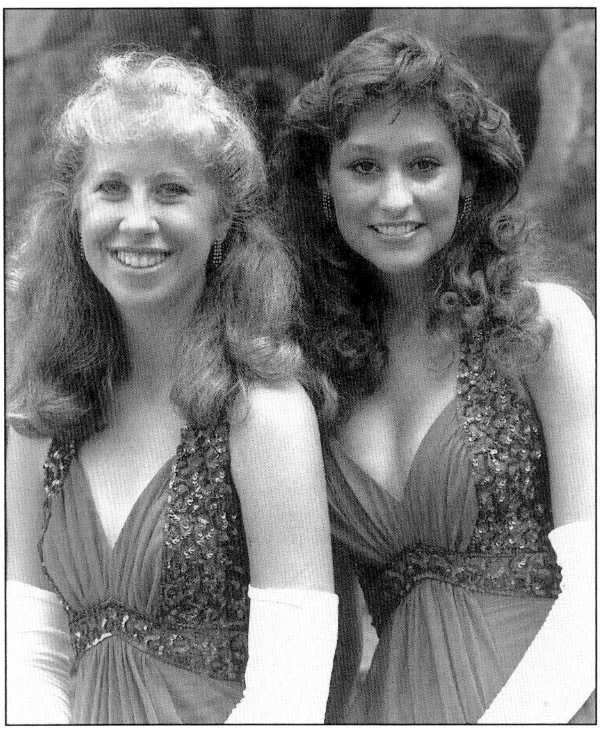

Members of the Centenary Choir are celebrities in their own right, performing at many convocations, services, commencements, and other college functions. Here Kristin Martin (left) and Pam Hardy pose before a choir performance during a convocation in October 1987.

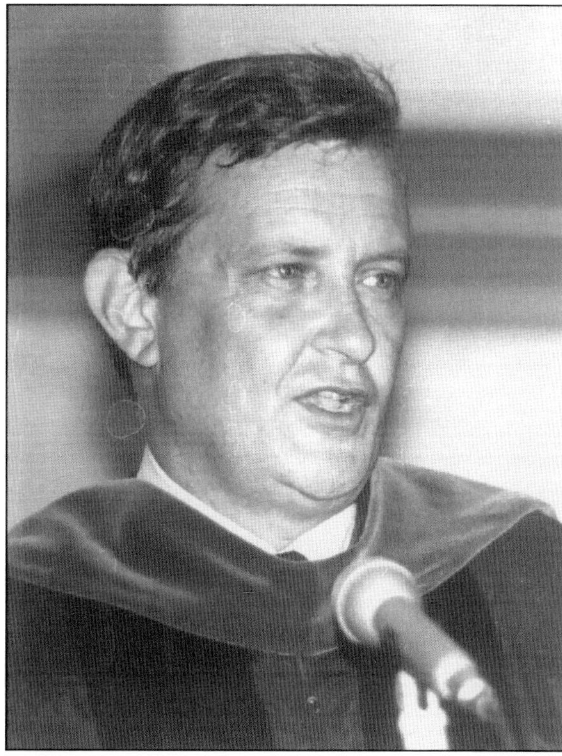

Pictured are convocation scenes from the 1980s. Right: Noted novelist and screenwriter John William Corrington addresses a new generation of Centenary students. Corrington, also a lawyer and professor of literature, was a noted Southern writer and winner of several national literary awards. He died in 1988. Below: Watergate figure and media celebrity G. Gordon Liddy (right) walks past the SUB with Centenary Republicans president Tom Ufert, class of '88, during a 1985 visit to the campus.

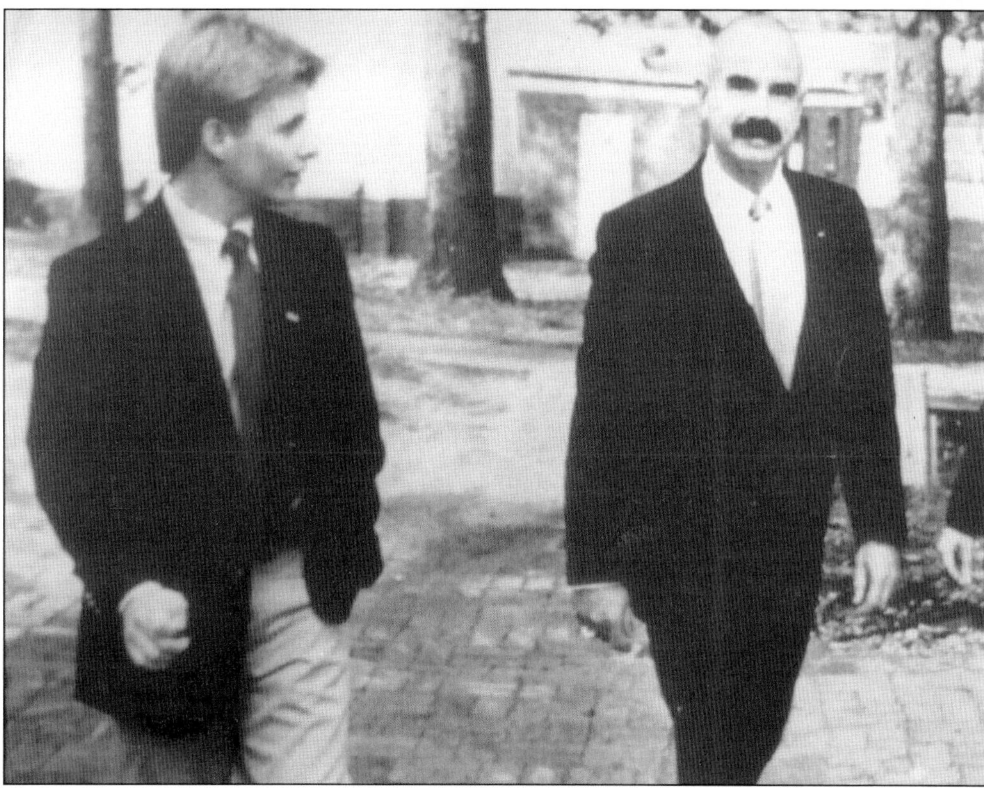

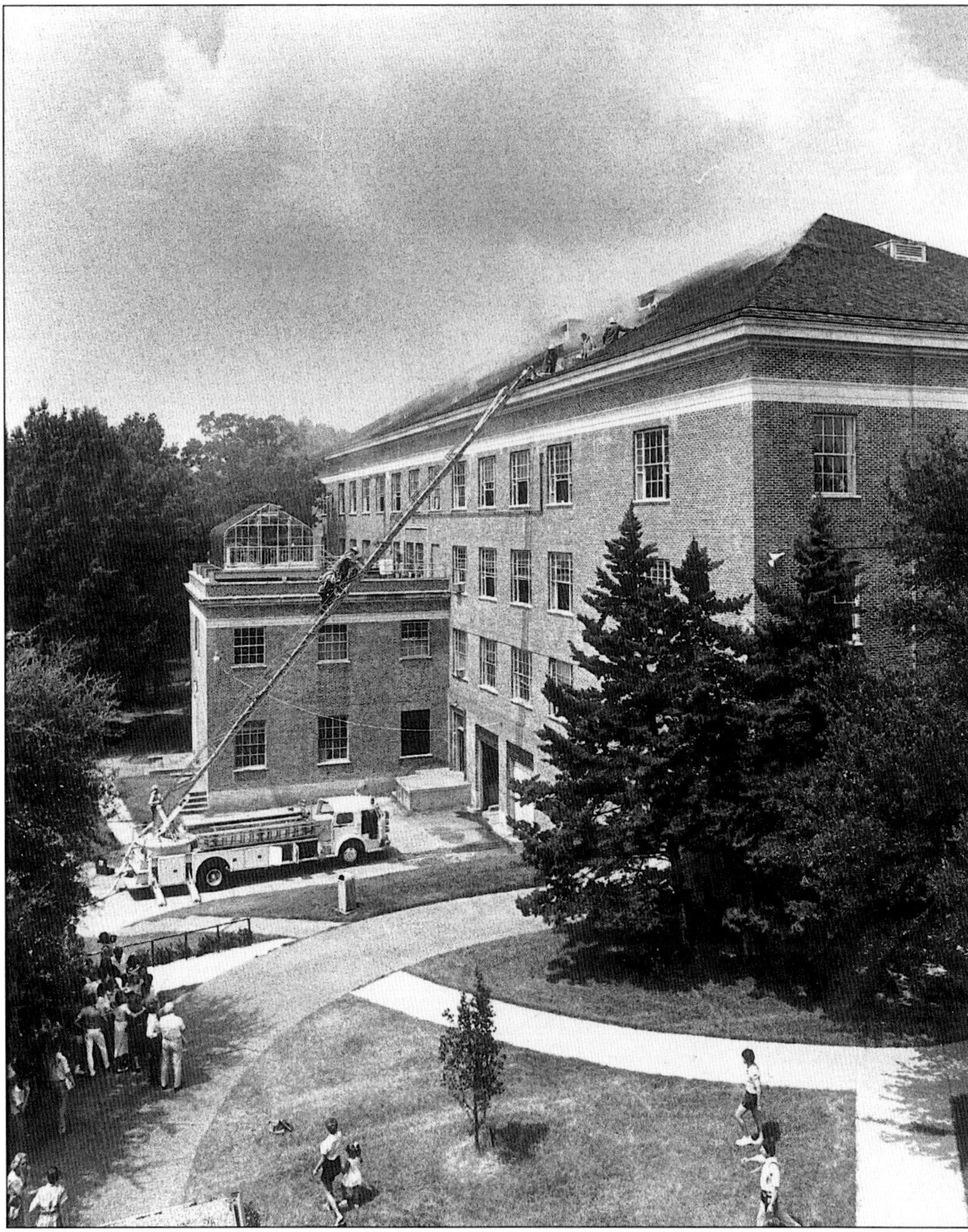

In August 1983, a major fire gutted much of the fourth floor of Mickle Hall, destroying a library of sheet music belonging to the choir, together with many costumes, archival materials, and other choir-related items kept there at the time. Although the damage to the top floor was extensive, the rest of the massive structure was unharmed. After the fire was extinguished, the fourth floor was repaired and remodeled. This photograph shows the south side of the building as firefighters battle the blaze. The wing behind the fire engine houses a theater. The bays directly in front of the fire engine lead into a wide underground tunnel which connects the basement of Mickle Hall with the basement of the Magale Library, allowing deliveries to be made to the buildings without necessitating additional roadways across the campus.

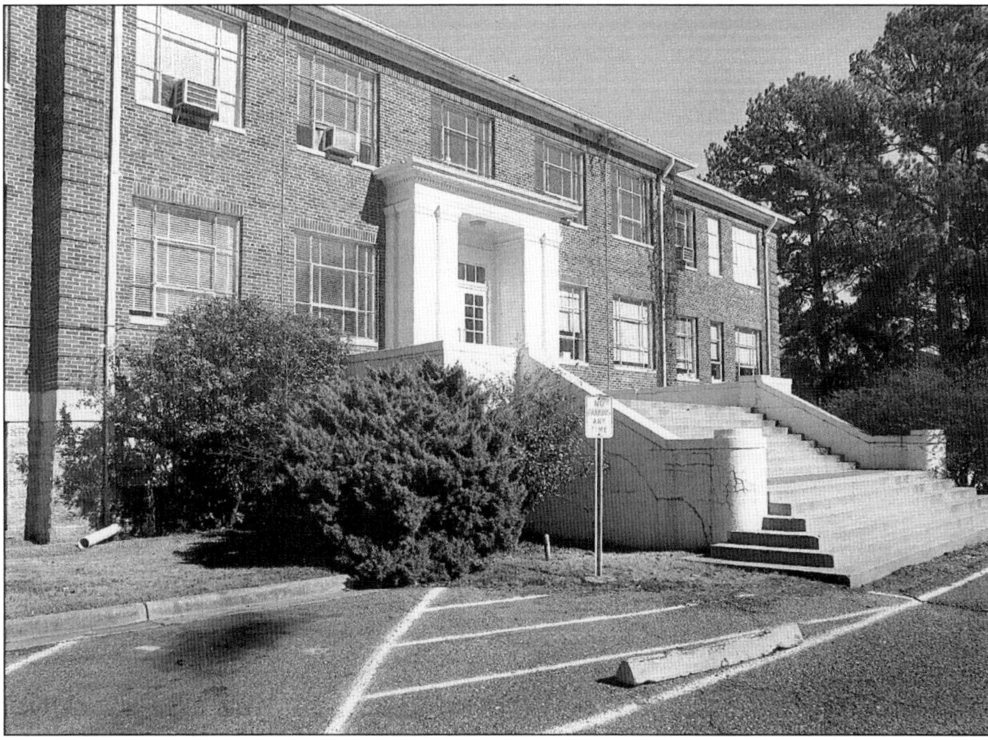

Above: By the mid-1980s, almost eight decades of wear and tear on Jackson Hall had taken its toll. The building was badly deteriorated and in need of major repairs. Students jokingly referred to it as "Jackson Hole." Since 1908, it had seen such varied uses as classroom building, dormitory, administration building, and classroom building again. By the 1980s it housed the English, art, and languages departments.

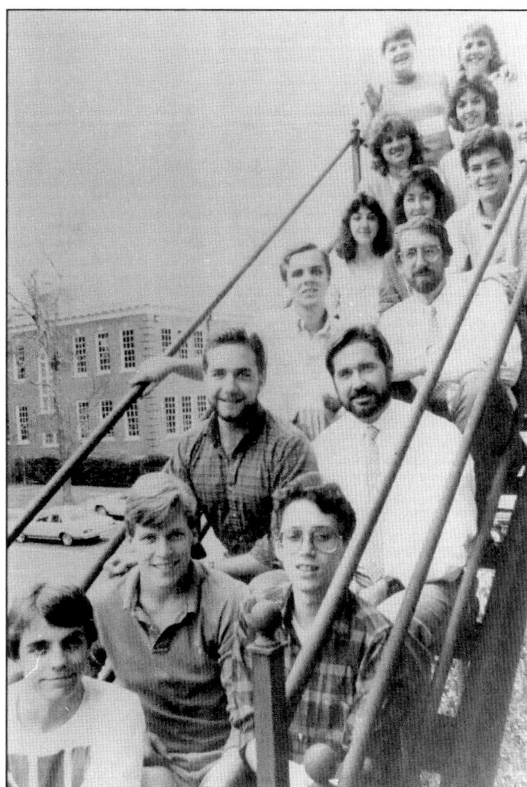

The membership of the Sigma Tau Delta English Honor Fraternity poses on the fire escape of Jackson Hall in 1985. Advisors Dr. Jeff Hendricks (right-hand row, second from bottom), class of 1975, and Dr. David Jackson (just behind Dr. Hendricks) join the group for the photo. The author of this book and Sigma Tau Delta president at the time is next to Dr. Jackson (with hand on rail). The Meadows Museum (old Arts Building) is in the background.

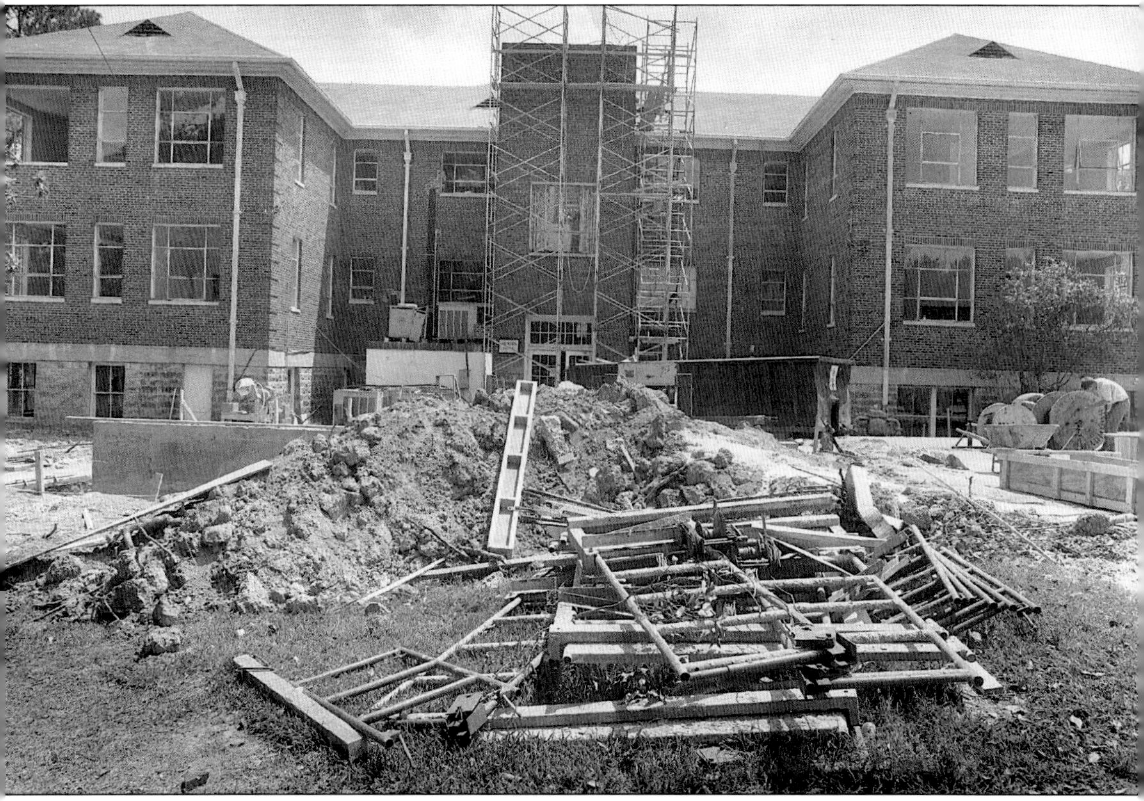

The renovation of Jackson Hall began in the spring of 1988 when this photograph was made. Here the rear (north facade) of the building is shown. As can be seen in the image above, the original plan was a U-shape with an enclosed stairwell at rear center. Renovations amounted to gutting the entire structure and filling in the space between the wings. In the 1920s, the old frame dining hall had connected to Jackson Hall via the door in the basement of the left-hand wing. The appearance of the building prior to the 1988 renovation was virtually unchanged from the time of the renovations made following the tornado damage of 1940.

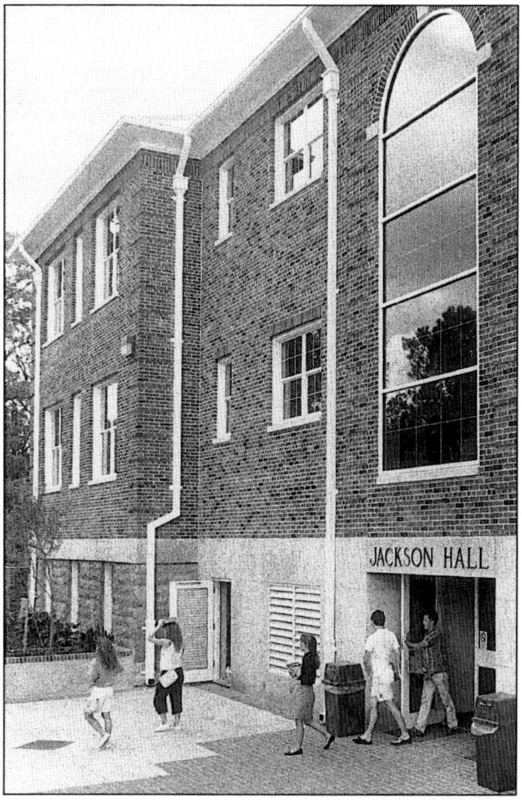

The results of the 1988 renovation of Jackson Hall are illustrated by the photographs on this page. Pictured above is the rear entrance to the building, where the stairwell formerly was located. The space between the wings has been filled entirely, adding substantially to the building's volume. Below: A 1999 view was taken near the main campus gate. A portion of the Meadows Museum is visible at right, and Jackson Hall is at center. Compare this image with the top photograph on page 35, taken three-quarters of a century earlier from exactly the same vantage point.

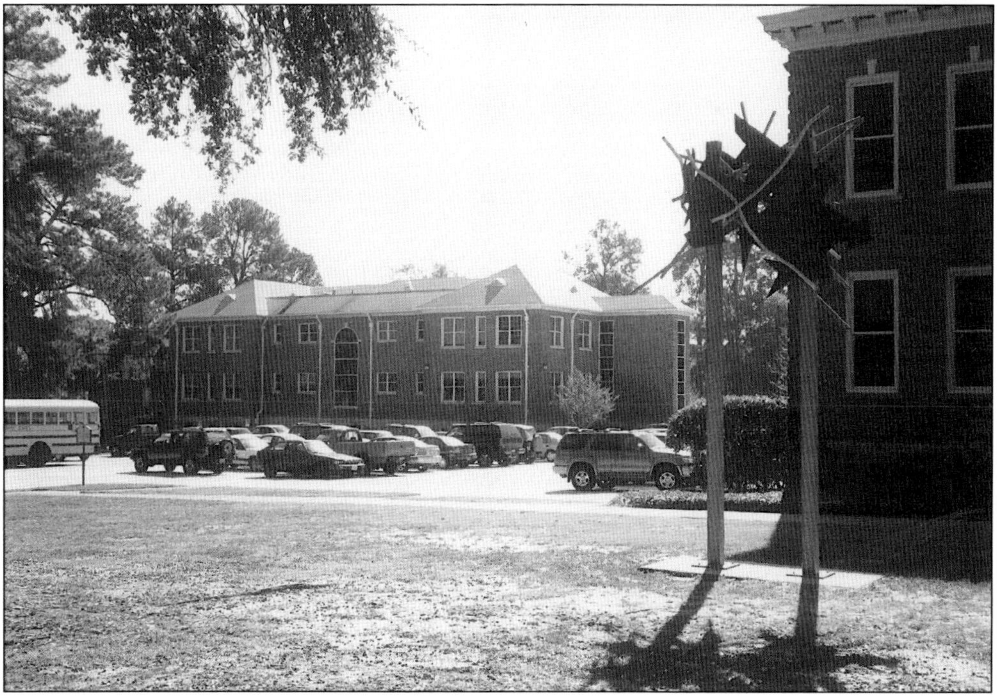

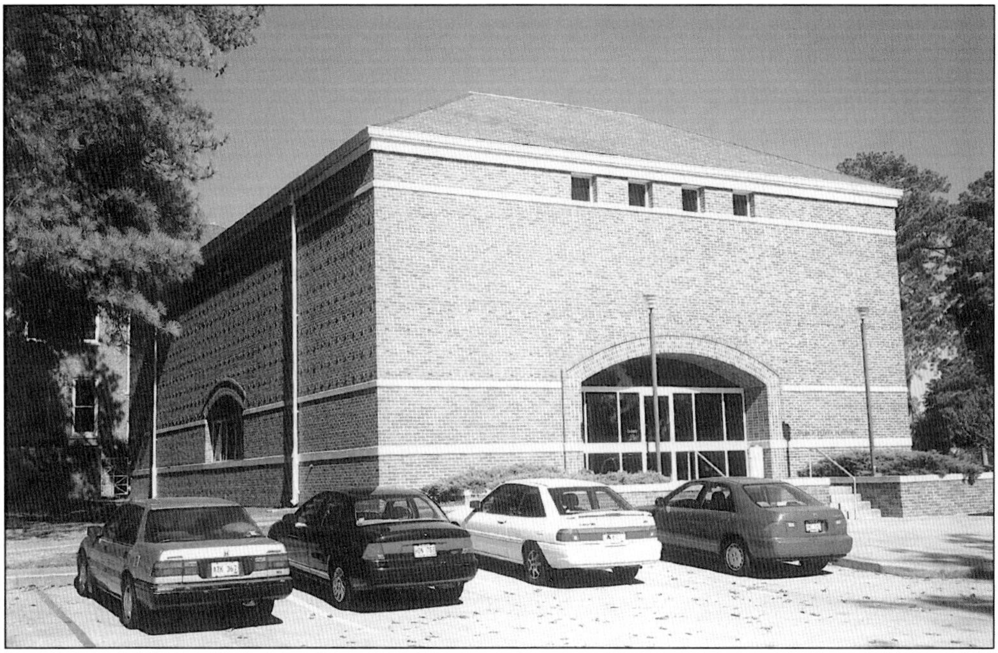

The Peters Research Center (above) was built in 1990 to the immediate south of the Meadows Museum. The building houses the college archives; the archives of the Louisiana Conference of the United Methodist Church; the papers of writer John William Corrington, class of 1956; and the Jack London and American Literature Research Center, founded by Dr. Earle Labor. It was the gift of Coca-Cola executive Samuel Paul Peters Jr., class of 1939, a member of the college's board of trustees. The Peters Center was dedicated on November 12, 1990 (below).

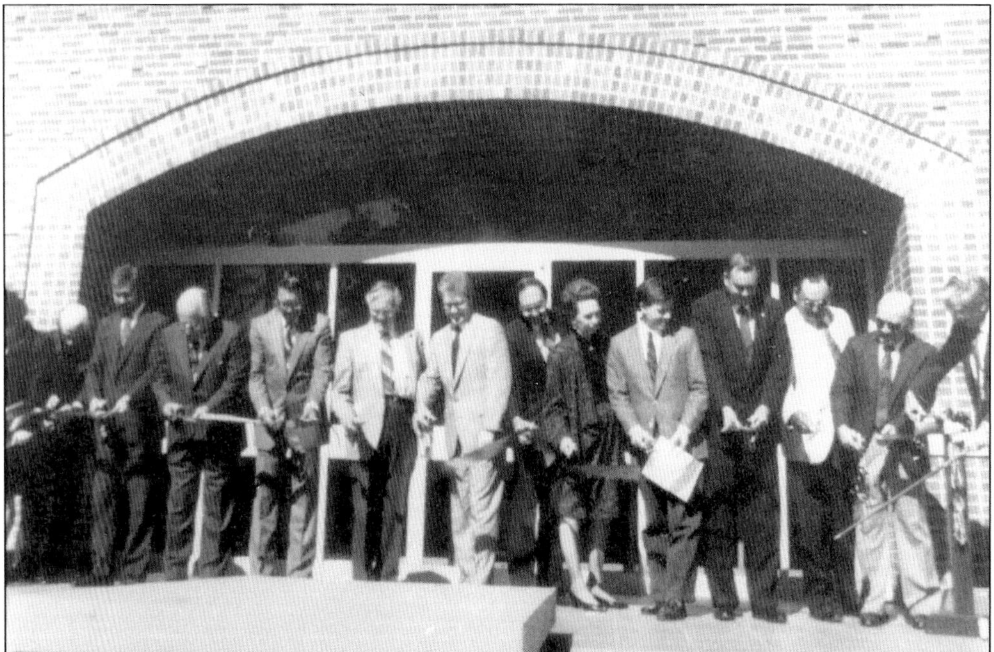

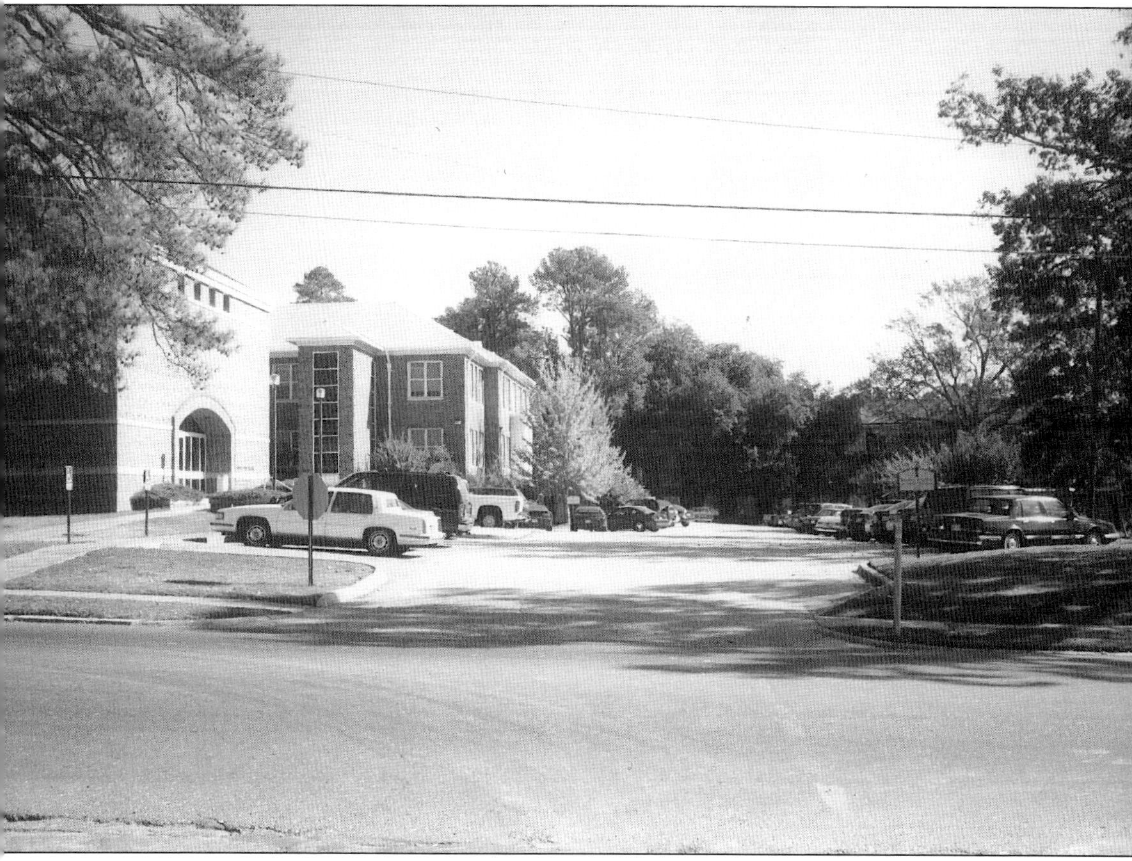

The south entrance to the campus on Centenary Boulevard is pictured in 1999. The Peters Research Center is at left, and Jackson Hall to its immediate right. Rotary Hall is to its right but is hidden by trees and shadows. Just outside the right-hand edge of the photograph are the Crumley Gardens. Compare this view with the bottom image on page 37, taken from the same perspective almost 80 years earlier.

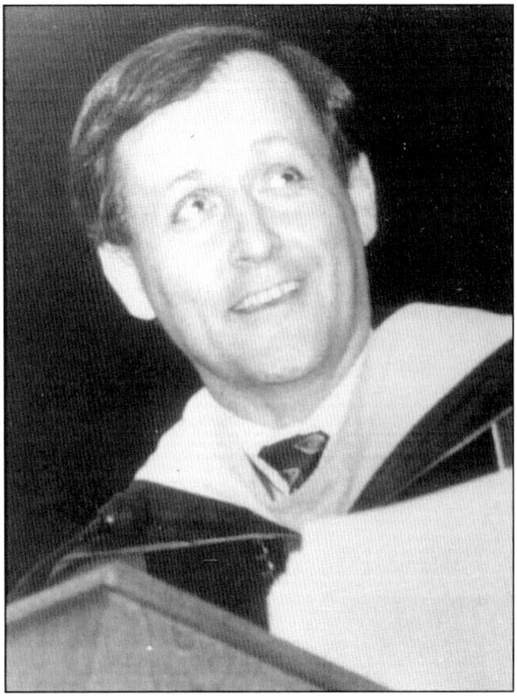

Dr. Kenneth Schwab, who became president of Centenary College of Louisiana in 1991, is seen here at his installation. Dr. Schwab, Centenary's 34th president, has the distinction of being in office during the observances of the 175th anniversary of this, the oldest college west of the Mississippi River.

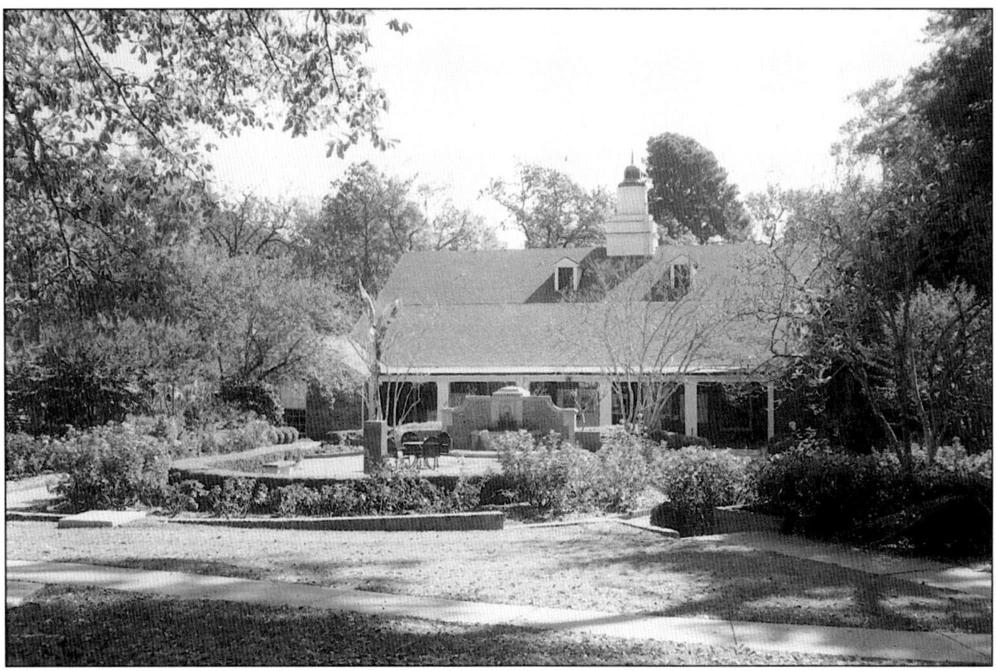

The SUB is seen from the garden to its north. The galleried front portion with the lower roofline marks the original Student Union Building; the higher-pitched roof with dormer windows and cupola marks the adjacent Moore Student Center of 1958. Two sculptures dominate the formal garden: The Frost Fountain to the right, and the tall sculpture, Grace, by John Raimondi, given by Harney Skolfield Bogen Jr. as a memorial to his parents in 1997. Several other artworks are also found here.

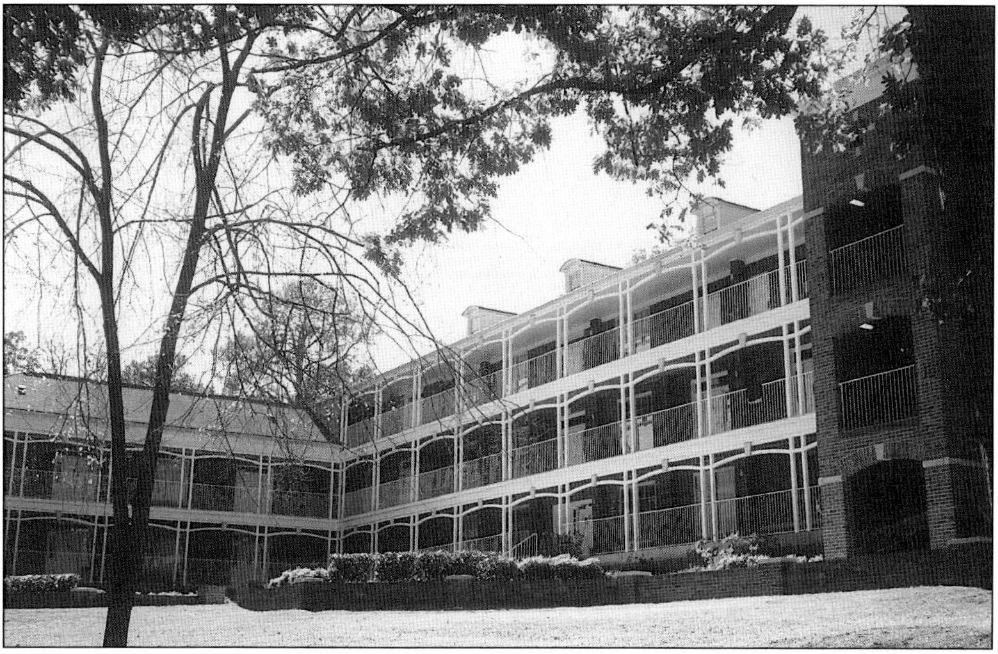

In the late 1990s, Rotary Hall underwent extensive renovations, transforming it from a building little changed since its completion in 1930 into a stunning modern facility. Nevertheless, the structure's architectural and historical integrity was maintained during the renovations. Here, Rotary Hall is seen from the northeast.

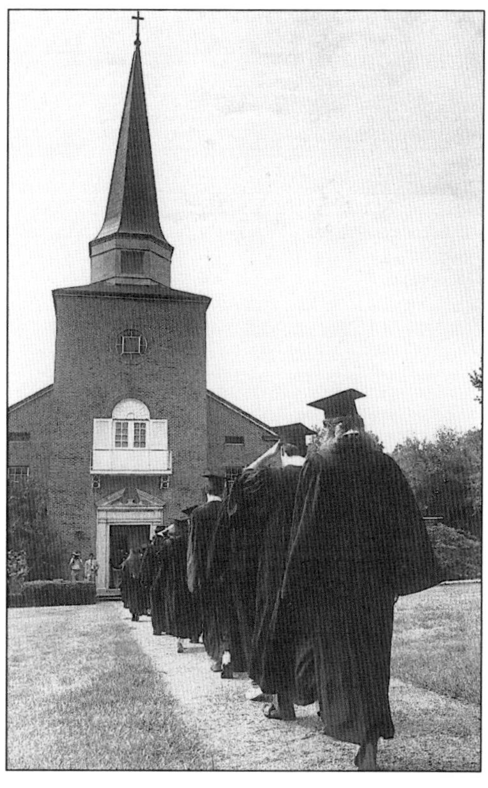

The final weeks leading up to each year's Baccalaureate services in the spring are charged with the excitement of seniors preparing to graduate. Ancient academic rituals, with all their attendant pomp, circumstance, pageantry, and historical beauty, are faithfully maintained at Centenary. Academic accoutrement is not limited to the commencement only but to convocations and many formal and official college functions.

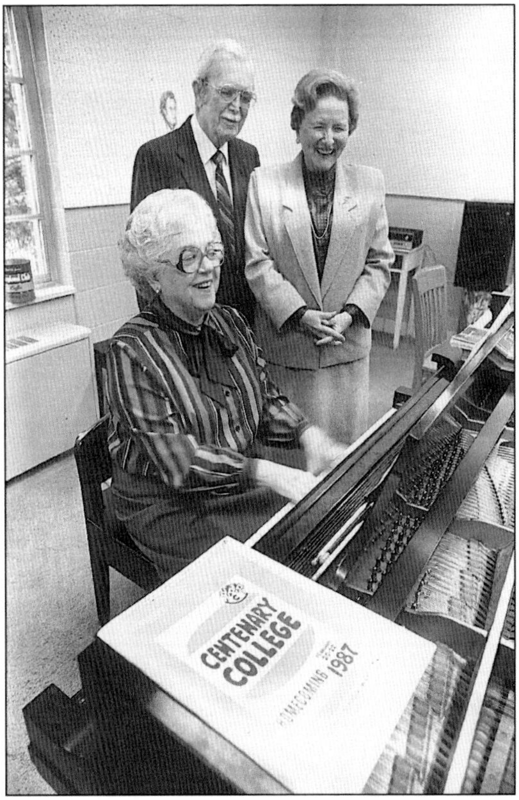

Links between the present and the past are strong at Centenary and are actively maintained. The college alumni association is a vibrant entity and many alumni remain active supporters of the college for the whole of their lives. Annual reunions bring former students together from all over the United States and beyond. At the time of its 175th anniversary, Centenary counts approximately 10,200 living alumni, with members from graduating classes dating back to the 1920s. Above: The Class of 1937 reunion committee prepares for the class's 50th anniversary gathering in 1987. Pictured from left to right are Juanita Odom, William Glassell, and Virginia Palmer Harris. Below: Centenary students visit the old campus at Jackson in 1992. The West Wing is in the background.

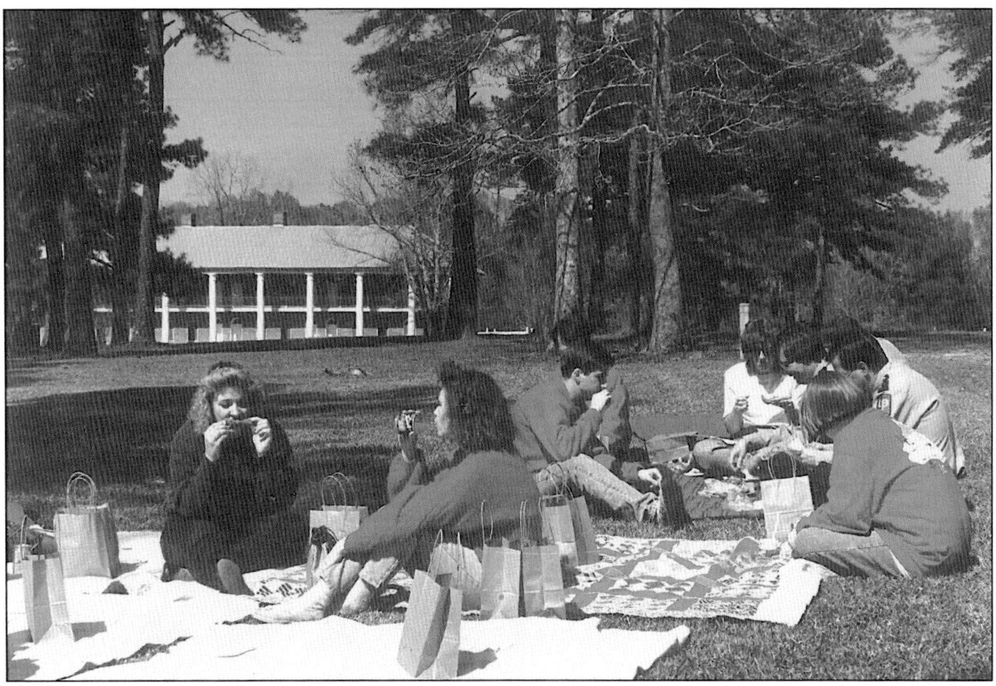

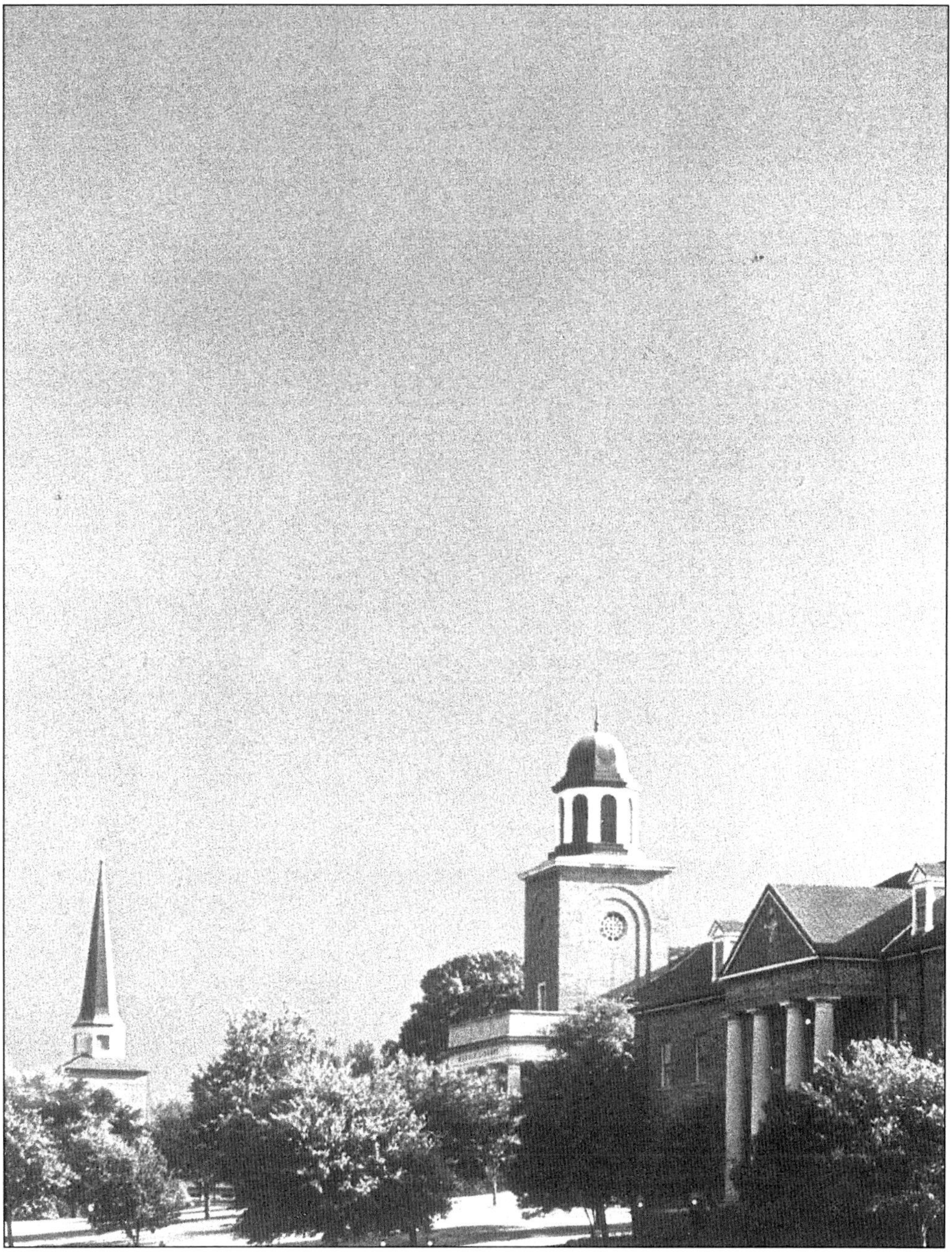

A striking image of the east side of Centenary's campus was made in the 1980s as the buildings caught the brilliant sunshine preceding an approaching thunderstorm. Pictured from left to right are Brown Chapel, the Magale Library, and the Hurley School of Music. The wide oak-filled lawn in front of the buildings sweeps down towards Woodlawn Avenue.

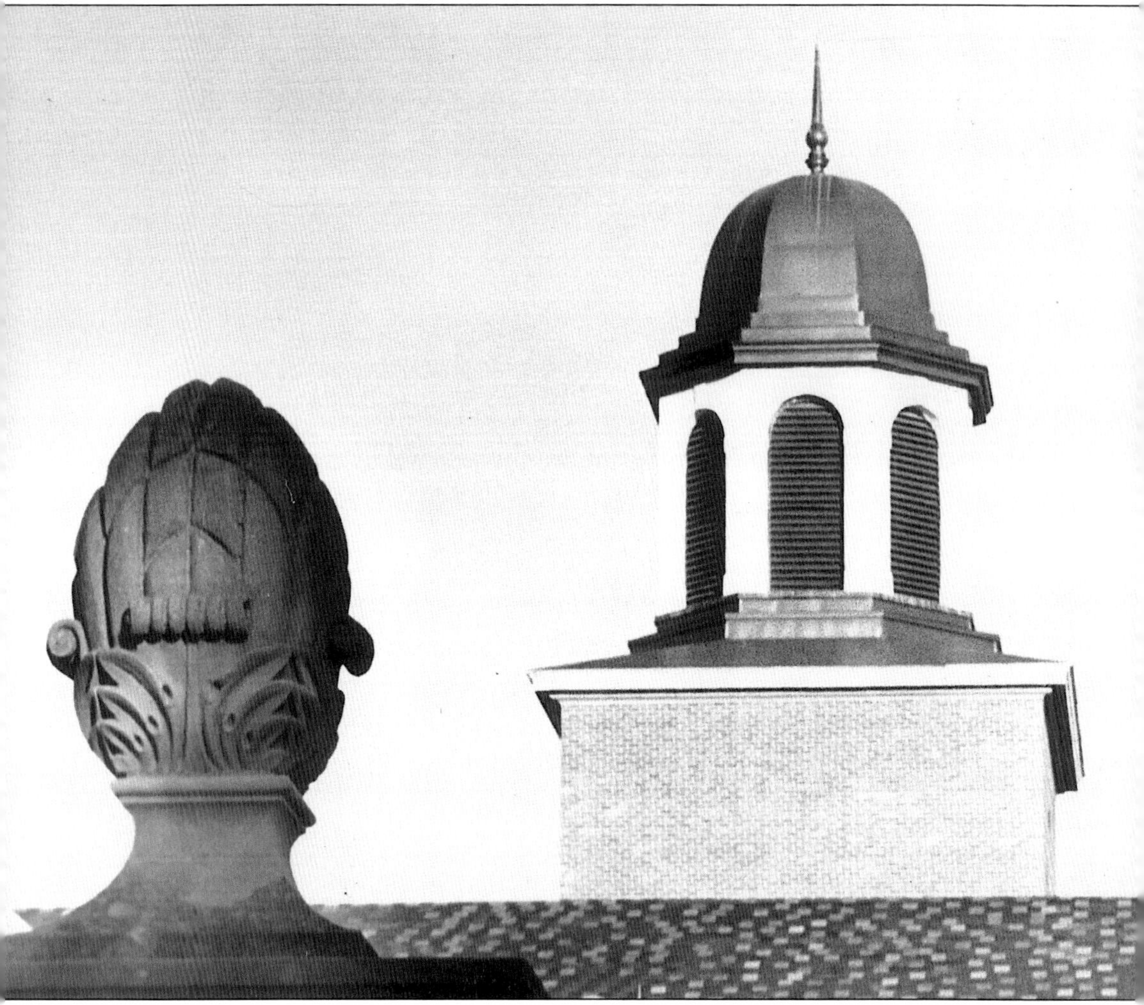

Since its construction in 1962, the cupola of the Magale Library has been a symbol of Centenary College of Louisiana. A more ancient symbol of the school is the stylized pineapple, an old Southern emblem of hospitality and generosity. The two are juxtaposed in this 1964 image of the library's rooftop looking over the rose garden wall. The view today would be impossible to replicate, Hamilton Hall having since been built between the two sites.

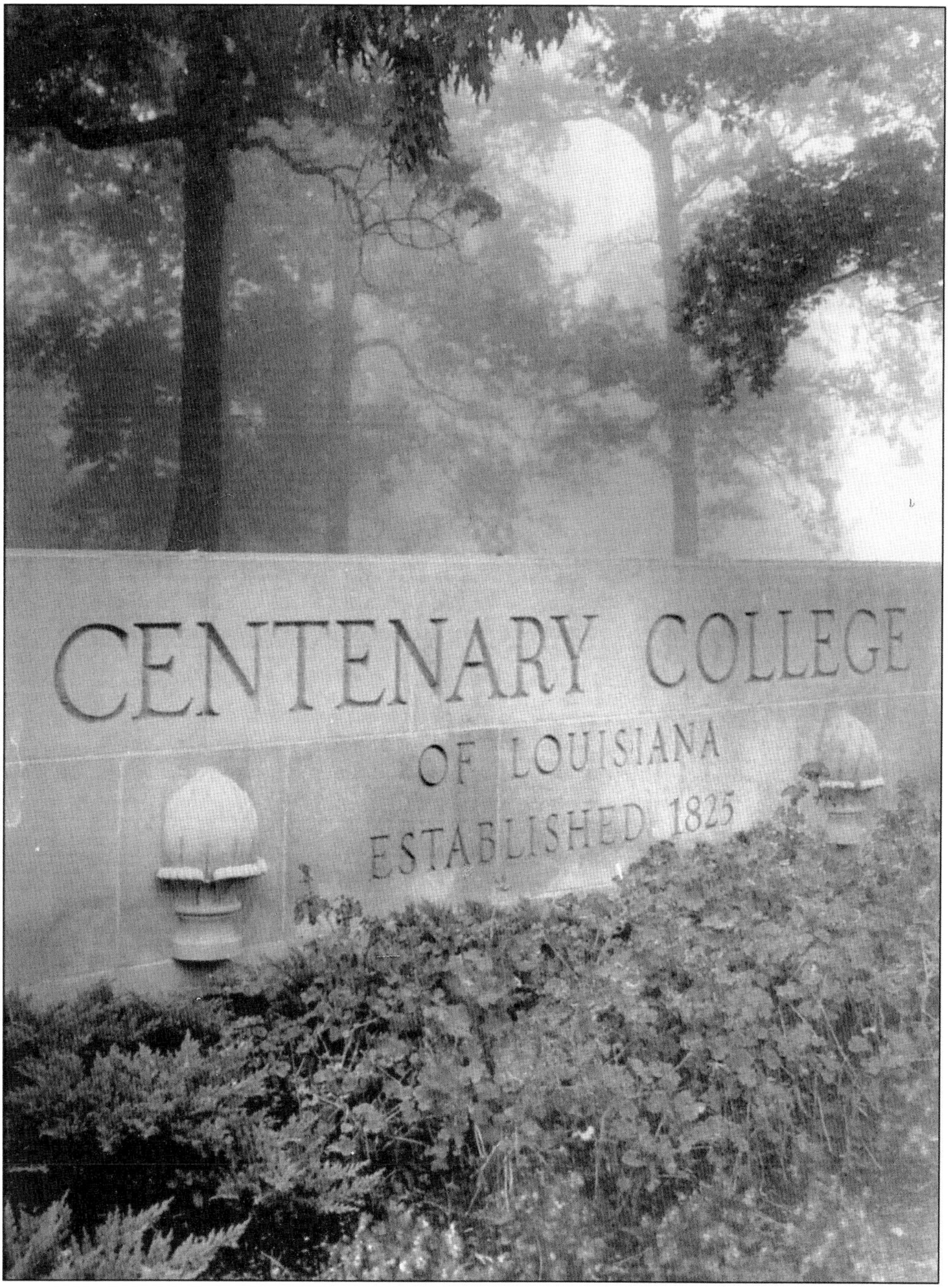

For a century and three-quarters, Centenary College of Louisiana has been a leader in higher education in the South. From its origins in 1825 to the present time, Centenary has produced over 14,000 graduates and has been consistently recognized among the top private liberal arts colleges not only in the South but in the nation. In 2000, over 1,100 students from 25 states and a dozen foreign countries are enrolled at Centenary, matriculating in some 50 major fields of study. Centenary today enjoys a rich past, a vibrant present, and holds promise for a brilliant future.

175 Years

CENTENARY COLLEGE

1825 – 2000

ACKNOWLEDGMENTS

All photographs are either from the archives of Centenary College or the collection of the author, with the exceptions of the following: page 33, courtesy of Roland J. Achee, class of 1944; pages 111, 125, and 127, courtesy of Neil Johnson; both items shown on page 57 are reproduced through the courtesy of Charlton E. Meyer, Jr.

The creators of the vast majority of the photographs reproduced in this volume are unknown. However, photos by the following appear herein: Burch Grabill, William B. Grabill (class of 1934), Neil Johnson (Centenary instructor in photography), Langston McEachern, Lloyd Stilley, Billy Upshaw, Eric J. Brock, and Frank Hampson.

Special thanks go to Centenary's president, Dr. Kenneth Schwab, and to the Centenary Office of Alumni Relations and its director, David Henington (class of 1982), for supporting this project. Special recognition must go also to Dr. Bentley Sloane (class of 1927) and Dr. Ira Lee Morgan (professor of English from 1955 to 1997), who have done much to preserve Centenary's History. They have my undying respect and friendship.

THE AUTHOR

Eric J. Brock is a member of the Centenary College class of 1988. While at Centenary he was recipient of the Fabsteel and Clarence Coon Scholarships. He was also a member of the Conglomerate staff, president of the Sigma Tau Delta Honor Society, and a contributor to the college literary magazine, Pegasus. Today he is a consulting social and architectural historian and historic preservation advocate. He is the writer of a regular column on regional history for Shreveport's *Forum News Magazine* and was an editorial page columnist for the *Shreveport Journal* from 1992 until its closure on January 1, 2000. He is the author of several books, including five others for Arcadia.